JOHN CALVIN,
REFUGEE THEOLOGIAN

"With elegant prose, keen insight, and expansive research, Woo provides the most thorough account to date of the exilic aspects and refugee implications of Calvin's life, leadership, and theology. This book examines intersections between migration and religious violence that prove illuminating for both past and present."

—**G. Sujin Pak**, Boston University School of Theology

"Taking its cue from Heiko Oberman's proposal to understand Calvin's reform as a 'reformation of the refugees,' Ken Woo's introduction goes well beyond to disclose how Calvin's own identity as a refugee molded his program for ministry and reform in Geneva (and even throughout Europe) and can be traced, like the proverbial red thread, throughout his varied and voluminous writings. Calvin was acutely aware that all of God's people are called—even if they never leave their homeland—to live as refugees, strangers, sojourners, and exiles, and to work out their discipleship accordingly. Woo has given us not only a winsome introduction to Calvin but also a timely example of how to read Calvin contextually, not as a disembodied intellect but as one truly shaped by the turmoil and sufferings of his age."

—**John L. Thompson**, Fuller Theological Seminary (emeritus)

"Kenneth Woo's study of Calvin as an exilic reformer is a brilliant reconsideration of Oberman's earlier work. It firmly sets Calvin and his audiences in their historical contexts, and it presents Calvin as a useful resource for today's Christians in exile—whether as refugees or as those experiencing the loss of political, cultural, and social power. Woo is not fawning. Calvin is shown with his strengths and warts, as someone dedicated to his own view of God and politically and rhetorically astute, often to the detriment of the evangelical project and Calvin's own reputation. A wonderful, readable, and astute work!"

—**R. Ward Holder**, Saint Anselm College

"Kenneth Woo's engaging book extends an invitation into the heart of Calvin's theology and the experiences of exile and displacement that shaped his faith and career as a pastor and writer. Through the lens of Calvin's context, Christians today gain crucial perspective for reflecting on their own encounters with spiritual alienation, creating supportive communities in a hostile world, and responding with love to the stranger in their midst."

—**Barbara Pitkin**, Stanford University

"With a historian's rigor, a theologian's insight, and a pastor's contextual awareness, Ken Woo offers the academy and the church a refreshing gift in *John Calvin, Refugee Theologian*. Woo introduces us to Calvin as one whose voice was shaped by exile and attuned to God's comfort for the displaced. In a world of dislocation, this book helps us receive Calvin as a companion in the wilderness—where God still provides manna through Word and sacrament, nourishing the weary with sustaining hope."

—**J. Todd Billings**, Western Theological Seminary, Holland, Michigan

"Dr. Woo presents a fresh and fruitful approach to Calvin's theology by describing his message through Calvin's experience as a refugee. This not only brings Calvin as a person closer to us but also helps us to understand and apply his thoughts. Woo's book is a fine contribution to Calvin research, and it demonstrates the relevance of the reformers' works."

—**Herman Selderhuis**, Theological University Apeldoorn; president, Reformation Research Consortium

JOHN CALVIN,
REFUGEE THEOLOGIAN

Introducing a
REFORMER IN EXILE

KENNETH J. WOO

Baker Academic
a division of Baker Publishing Group
Grand Rapids, Michigan

© 2025 by Kenneth J. Woo

Published by Baker Academic
a division of Baker Publishing Group
Grand Rapids, Michigan
BakerAcademic.com

All rights reserved. No part of this publication may be reproduced, stored in a retrieval system, or transmitted in any form or by any means—for example, electronic, photocopy, recording—without the prior written permission of the publisher. The only exception is brief quotations in printed reviews.

Library of Congress Cataloging-in-Publication Data
Names: Woo, Kenneth J. author
Title: John Calvin, refugee theologian : introducing a reformer in exile / Kenneth J. Woo.
Description: Grand Rapids, Michigan : Baker Academic, a division of Baker Publishing Group, [2025] | Includes bibliographical references and index.
Identifiers: LCCN 2025025357 | ISBN 9781540963055 paperback | ISBN 9781540969682 casebound | ISBN 9781493452088 ebook | ISBN 9781493452095 pdf
Subjects: LCSH: Calvin, Jean, 1509–1564
Classification: LCC BX9418 .W65 2025 | DDC 284/.2092—dc23/eng/20250811
LC record available at https://lccn.loc.gov/2025025357

Scripture quotations are from the work of Calvin under discussion.

Quotations from non-English sources are the author's own translation.

Cover design by John Lucas

Baker Publishing Group publications use paper produced from sustainable forestry practices and postconsumer waste whenever possible.

25   26   27   28   29   30   31   7   6   5   4   3   2   1

For my grandparents:

Woo Nong (1900–1995)
Woo Dere Lai Jane (1917–2004)
Chow Kwock Choi (1924–)
Chow Po Fung (1929–2002)

*—fellow trekkers who cut wide trails in hard places
to make the hopes and journeys of their children, and children's children,
both imaginable and possible. Thank you.*

John Calvin

Public Domain / Gift to the Meeter Center
by James and Florence Tannis.

Map of Geneva in Calvin's Time

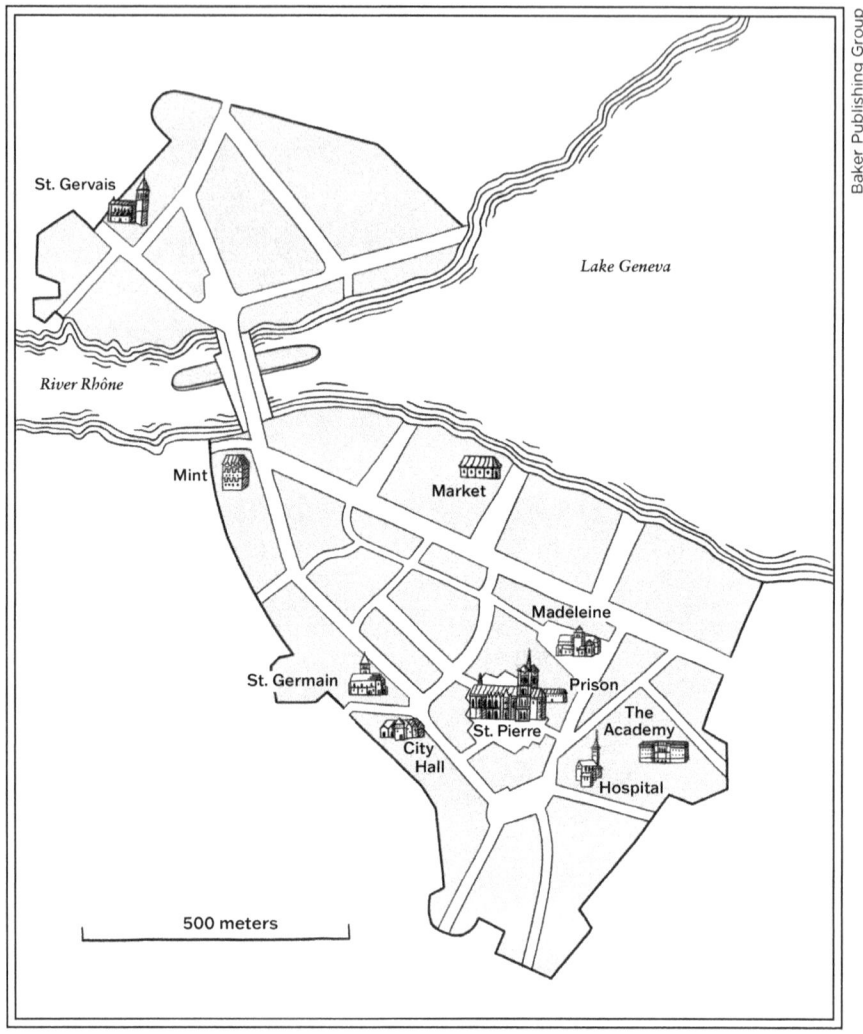

Map of Europe in Calvin's Time

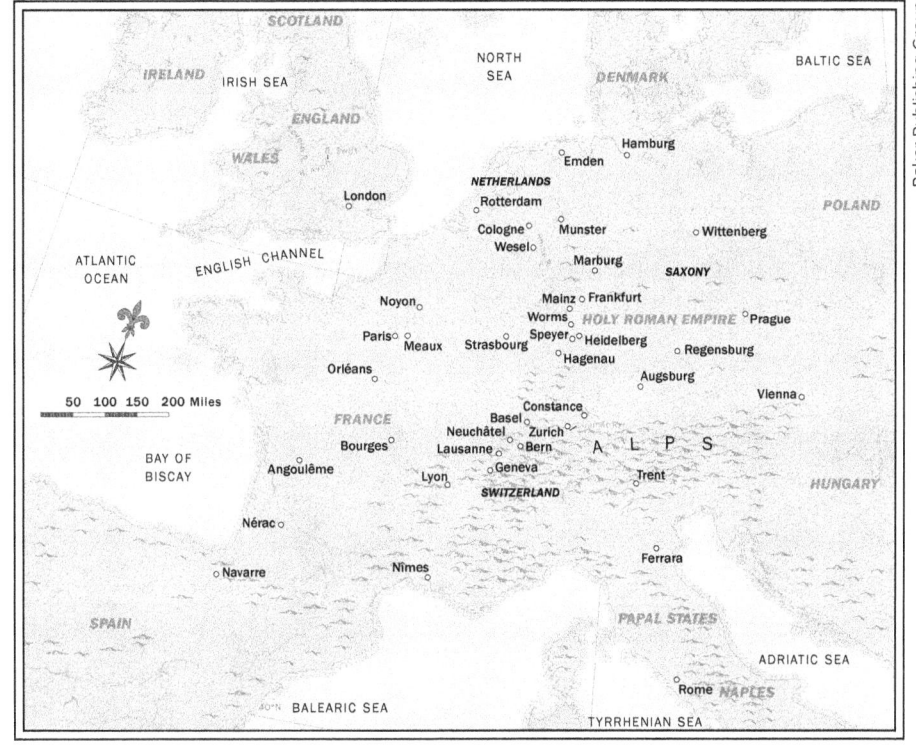

CONTENTS

Acknowledgments xv
Abbreviations xvii
Introduction: Recovering the Refugee Theologian xix

Part 1 The Exilic Contexts of Calvin's Theology

1. From France to Faithfulness: Calvin's Personal History and His Theology of Exile   3
2. Comfort and Confrontation: The Diverse Audiences of Calvin's Works   21

Part 2 Calvin as Teacher

3. Calvin's *Institutes* as Road Map: Theological Coordinates for an Exilic Imagination   47
4. Calvin's Commentaries: The Bible for Exiles   71

Part 3 Calvin as Pastor

5. Schooling God's Children in Exile: Calvin's Writings on Church Organization and Worship   95
6. Stirring the Exilic Imagination: Calvin's Sermons and the Challenge of Faithful Exile   119

Part 4 Calvin as Polemicist

   7. Herding God's Flock in Exile: Calvin's Polemical Works   143

   8. Conformity and Commitment: Calvin's Anti-Nicodemite Writings   165

Conclusion: Reading a Reformer in Exile   179
Appendix: Questions for Continuing the Conversation   189
Index   193

ACKNOWLEDGMENTS

The idea for this book emerged in conversations with faculty colleagues at Pittsburgh Theological Seminary about writing not just for our scholarly guilds but also for students, pastors, and wider audiences in the church and academy. Thanks especially to Jerome Creach, Leanna Fuller, Drew Smith, and Edwin van Driel for encouragement in this regard. True to the seminary's commitment to scholarship in service to the church, the board's gift of a spring 2024 sabbatical helped the manuscript cross the finish line. President Asa Lee and Dean Angela Hancock insisted that it be a true research-and-writing leave; thanks for leaving me alone. The Clifford E. Barbour Library and its librarian staff—especially Mark Russell and Tisha Woo—ensured that the texts I needed were at hand. Holly McKelvey, administrative assistant to the faculty, makes so many tasks easier and less time-consuming for all of us. We will miss Holly in her well-deserved retirement.

Baker Academic has been a delight to work with from start to finish. Bob Hosack received my pitch warmly in 2019, then waited patiently as a global pandemic followed by several years of institutional reaccreditation intervened to delay the project. I could not have asked for a better project editor than Alex DeMarco, who shepherded the manuscript into the best version of itself with timely communication, insightful questions, and expert attention to detail. Dustyn Keepers offered much help with obtaining illustrations for the book. Many thanks to Sam Ha and Karin Maag of the H. Henry Meeter Center at Calvin University for guiding me toward the right ones. Trent Hancock skillfully prepared the helpful index.

Nearly a decade of teaching church history to talented and curious cohorts of future pastors, professors, writers, librarians, and social workers has been the most rewarding part of my job. Taking up Calvin with students in survey courses, Reformation electives, and the historical theology reading group that met in my home for years has led to many stimulating and clarifying conversations as I conceived, reimagined, and eventually settled on an outline for this book. Students have consistently found Calvin's exilic context an inviting starting point for engaging the reformer's theology today.

Friendly critics are valuable, especially those who know when candor is more useful than kindness. Many thanks to friends whose sharp feedback made the manuscript better, especially Kyle Dieleman, Tucker Ferda, Samuel McCann, Jon Balserak, and Randy Blacketer. I received valuable suggestions from Sarah Betzig, Michael Ehrenfried, Josh Ham, Drew Kellogg, Becky Konegan, Barbara Pitkin, and John Thompson, who also taught me that clarity is a virtue and that brevity can be many things other than lucid. Other conversation partners include Tanner Capps, Ward Holder, Scott Manetsch, Don McKim, Roger Owens, Sujin Pak, and Aaron Teter. None of these readers and friends are responsible for any errors or infelicitous expressions that remain.

My wife, Tisha, read every word of the manuscript, including drafts no one else will ever see. I am grateful that she does not hold these against me. My kids are the best reminder that life is not reducible to my pursuits. Hannah, Ryan, and Graeme: Thank you for expertly disregarding most things Dad is up to and making your mother and me unspeakably proud. My parents, Antony and Suzanna, ensured that I knew their parents, to whom this book is dedicated. Strangers and exiles, my grandparents never imagined their courageous choices would enable and inspire my interest in John Calvin, refugee theologian.

ABBREVIATIONS

Bonnet   *Letters of John Calvin*. Edited by Jules Bonnet. Translated by David Constable and Marcus Robert Gilchrist. 4 vols. Philadelphia: Presbyterian Board of Publication, 1858. Translation modified in places for accuracy and clarity.
CCSL   Corpus Christianorum: Series Latina. Edited by B. Dombart and A. Kalb. 233 vols. Brepols, 1953–.
CNTC   *Calvin's New Testament Commentaries*. Edited by David W. Torrance and Thomas F. Torrance. 12 vols. Eerdmans, 1959–72.
CO   *Ioannis Calvini opera quae supersunt omnia*. Edited by G. Baum, E. Cunitz, and E. Reuss. 59 vols. Corpus Reformatorum 29–87. Schwetschke, 1863–1900.
Comm.   Commentary
COR   *Ioannis Calvini opera omnia: Denuo recognita et adnotatione critica instructa notisque illustrata*. Droz, 1992–.
CTS   *Commentaries of John Calvin*. 46 vols. Edinburgh: Calvin Translation Society, 1844–1955. Repr., Eerdmans, 1948–63. Translation modified in places for accuracy and clarity.
Inst.   Calvin, John. *Institutes of the Christian Religion*. Edited by J. T. McNeill. Translated by F. L. Battles. 2 vols. Westminster, 1960. Apart from references to prefatory material, citations will include the book, chapter, and section of the *Institutes* (e.g., *Inst.* IV.1.5). Translation modified in places for accuracy and clarity.
LCC   Library of Christian Classics
Lect.   Lecture(s)
LW   *Luther's Works*. American Edition. Edited by Jaroslav Pelikan, Helmut Lehmann, Christopher Boyd Brown, and Benjamin T. G. Mayes. Concordia, 1955–86; Fortress, 2008–.
NPNF   *The Nicene and Post-Nicene Fathers. First Series*. Edited by Philip Schaff. 14 vols. Christian Literature, 1886–89. Repr., Hendrickson, 1994.
OS   *Ioannis Calvini opera selecta*. Edited by Peter Barth, Wilhelm Niesel, and Dora Scheuner. 5 vols. Chr. Kaiser, 1926–52.
PG   *Patrologiae cursus completus: Series Graeca*. Edited by J.-P. Migne. 162 vols. Vives, 1857–86.

PL	*Patrologiae cursus completus: Series Latina*. Edited by J.-P. Migne. 217 vols. Vives, 1844–64.
SC	*Supplementa Calviniana: Sermons inédits*. Edited by Erwin Mülhaupt et al. Neukirchener Verlag, 1936–.
Serm.	Sermon(s)
Tracts	Calvin, John. *Tracts and Treatises*. Translated by Henry Beveridge. 3 vols. Calvin Translation Society, 1844. Repr., Eerdmans, 1958. Translation modified in places for accuracy and clarity.
WA	Weimarer Ausgabe. *D. Martin Luthers Werke*: Kritische Gesamtausgabe. 127 vols. Böhlau, 1883–2009.

INTRODUCTION

Recovering the Refugee Theologian

> The fast-food of the neo-Calvinist Geneva-burger could not have met the needs of Calvin's contemporaries and fellow-trekkers nor could it have provided the power for Calvin's movement to survive to our own day.
>
> —Heiko A. Oberman[1]

Calvin, Context, and the Problem with Geneva Burgers

Every fall my wife and I drive to Cleveland with our kids. The routine, as these things become, is uncomplicated: lunch, a walk along Lake Erie, then a visit to my grandparents' graves on the city's west side. Occasionally we mix things up, like the time we added a stop to see the house from *A Christmas Story*. One year we skipped lunch. The graveside appointment is the only fixed one. It is no one else's idea of exciting, but our annual pilgrimage to Cleveland holds deep meaning for our family as a link to those who came before us and a reminder of their sacrifices. Like many immigrants, my grandparents were refugees. They left behind possessions and relationships, a familiar language and culture to flee oppression and violence in communist China. Establishing a new life meant long hours in restaurant jobs, time apart from my father and his brother as they were growing up. They embraced American culture, becoming citizens of a place where Asian Americans—even to the fourth and

---

1. Heiko A. Oberman, *John Calvin and the Reformation of the Refugees* (Droz, 2009), 67.

fifth generation—often continue to be viewed as unassimilable, "perpetual foreigners."[2]

My grandparents, the ones we gather annually to remember, sought refuge for us. Our family moved twice during my childhood. First, we left Cleveland, where I was born, for Connecticut. Then we moved to New York City just before I turned five. My parents have lived in the same house ever since. The distance we covered is unimpressive as far as migration stories go. Yet the trip back to Cleveland, even shorter from my current home in western Pennsylvania, is no less profound for me and my children, who never knew their great-grandparents. Even so, that generation's journey of exile to a strange land is woven deeply into our stories in ways we continue to discover and appreciate. My grandfather's frequent preference for the steak and potatoes of his adopted country, as a somewhat trivial example, stands out in my earliest memories. This contextualizes my children's strong interest in Chinese language and culture, which had little bearing on their upbringing. I am struck that what my kids encounter as new is simultaneously a return to their roots, our family history, ground they share with generations they never knew. My guess is that similar moments of recognition occur in many other families struggling to find a sense of belonging, a place to call "home," be it on account of past immigration or amid today's global refugee crises. This, of course, is nothing new. But it is also a story that can turn up in unexpected places.

In January 1545 John Calvin wrote to Martin Luther, the venerable Wittenberg reformer whose pioneering efforts set the course of the Protestant Reformation and, along with it, the entire trajectory of Calvin's life.[3] Like other reformers, Calvin was a prolific correspondent. Yet, out of the thousands of letters he wrote, this is the only surviving one to Luther. Unfortunately, it is entirely one-sided. Calvin, then thirty-five, approaches the sixty-one-year-old Luther delicately—for reasons beyond difference in years. Luther was already cantankerous in his old age from decades of theological conflict and failing health. He also nurtured a special disdain for Swiss reformers dating to disagreements with Ulrich Zwingli in the Reformation's earlier days, speeding "magisterial" Protestantism's split into distinct Lutheran and Reformed branches.[4] In other private correspondence with Philip Melanchthon, Lu-

---

2. Grace Ji-Sun Kim, *Embracing the Other: The Transformative Spirit of Love* (Eerdmans, 2015), 51–53.

3. Calvin to Luther, January 21, 1545 (Bonnet, 1:440–42; CO 12:7–8).

4. Differences over the sacraments culminated in the failed Marburg colloquies in late 1529, which set the Lutheran and Reformed branches of Protestantism on separate courses. These are known as "magisterial" or "mainstream" traditions insofar as they cooperated with civil government to reform church and society in ways rejected by more radical reformers.

ther's trusted confidant, Calvin complains frankly about Luther's pride and ignorance.[5] On this occasion Calvin needed Melanchthon's help to deliver his letter at the right time and remain on Luther's good side.[6]

Calvin sought Luther's endorsement of his published position on Nicodemism, the practice of hiding one's beliefs by pretending to be something different.[7] Calvin describes Protestants, known also as "evangelicals," among "our French people." Despite concluding that the Catholic Church was in error and its worship idolatrous, these particular evangelicals nevertheless "changed nothing about their public profession."[8] In other words, they were playacting as Catholics to avoid persecution, engaging in a form of cryptoreligion. Calvin alleged that such "Nicodemites" took this name from Nicodemus, the Pharisee who initially came to Jesus under the cover of night (John 3).[9] Calvin and other mainstream reformers found it unconscionable that those "privileged to have the light of the gospel" would choose to continue in the darkness of "Popish rituals."[10] Chief among these errant practices was the Catholic Eucharist, the centerpiece of the Mass. For all their theological common ground, magisterial reformers could not agree on the meaning and nature of Christ's presence in the Eucharist,[11] yet all evangelicals abhorred the Catholic teaching of transubstantiation, which held that the Communion elements became Christ's body and blood and were again offered as a sacrifice and worshiped in the sacrament. To evangelicals, in other words, the Catholic Eucharist was a form of idolatry. "True devotion," Calvin had written eight years earlier, "produces true confession."[12] Put another way, faith has to be a visible, internal commitment displayed outwardly. True faith breaks decisively from idolatry, even if that means placing oneself in danger by defying authorities or fleeing, as Calvin had, to find greater religious freedom. We will come back to this dilemma, a persistent issue throughout the Frenchman's career as a reformer, in the chapters that follow.

For now, it suffices to highlight what Calvin's only direct attempt to engage Luther reveals about how lived experience shaped his concerns. The issue

---

5. Calvin to Melanchthon, June 28, 1545 (Bonnet, 1:466–67; CO 12:98–100).
6. Calvin to Melanchthon, January 21, 1545 (Bonnet, 1:434–40; CO 12:9–12).
7. Kenneth J. Woo, "Nicodemism and Libertinism," in *John Calvin in Context*, ed. R. Ward Holder (Cambridge University Press, 2020), 287–91.
8. Calvin to Luther, January 21, 1545 (Bonnet, 1:440; CO 12:7). Sixteenth-century Protestants preferred to be known as "evangelicals," believing that they had recovered the biblical "evangel" (*euangelion*), or gospel, after centuries of neglect in medieval Catholicism.
9. *Answer to the Nicodemites*, 1544 (CO 6:608).
10. Calvin to Melanchthon, January 21, 1545 (Bonnet, 1:435; CO 12:9).
11. For these disputes, see Amy Nelson Burnett, *Debating the Sacraments: Print and Authority in the Early Reformation* (Oxford University Press, 2019).
12. *Two Letters* (COR IV/4:10).

that prompted him to risk Luther's petulance is not predestination or church governance (topics usually associated with Calvin) or an attempt to broker agreement with Lutherans regarding the Lord's Supper, which Calvin earnestly worked toward in other ways. Crypto-religion, or hidden faith, is the topic of the only extant letter between these Reformation headliners who lent their names to theological movements (Lutheranism and Calvinism) that continue to the present day. The letter situates Calvin's theology amid violence and exile, significant practical consequences that could result from one's religious commitments. Nicodemism was no abstract intellectual problem; it was a survival tactic Calvin urged others to abandon. Evangelicals in France remained unpersuaded, according to Calvin, demanding additional opinions on the matter.[13] Managing public opinion is a challenge for leaders in any era. Securing the right endorsement could be critical to success. In the end, Luther never wrote Calvin a reply. He never even saw Calvin's letter. Melanchthon, wary of provoking his friend Luther, sent an apologetic explanation for why he declined to pass along Calvin's request.[14]

We will never know what could have been but for this instance of failed communication between two renowned theologians. Yet the incident illustrates something frequently overlooked about the Reformation. Yes, ideological disagreements divided the church and redrew the map of Europe. The Reformation shattered Western Christianity into pieces, scattered across a myriad of denominations today. But such disagreements also meant an explosion of religious violence that made persecution, migration, and exile a mainstay of life for millions of people. It was not only the French evangelicals Calvin had in mind who faced decisions of whether to resist religious oppression or flee from it, whether to declare one's beliefs or hide them. Depending on who was in power, those adopting various strategies to get along in, or get out of, intolerant situations could be mainstream Protestants, Catholics, or members of Anabaptist and other radical-reform movements. Sometimes a minority group held power over the majority. Such was the case when the Reformed church wielded authority in the early days of the Dutch Republic.

Furthermore, these problems were not limited to Christianity. The Reformation era's dynamics of persecution continued centuries-old patterns of interreligious violence between Christians, Muslims, and Jews. These culminated in the mass expulsions that consolidated Portugal and Spain as Catholic kingdoms at the end of the fifteenth century, the initial phase of what historian Nicholas Terpstra describes as "the first period in European and possibly

13. Calvin to Luther, January 21, 1545 (Bonnet, 1:441; CO 12:8).
14. Melanchthon to Calvin, April 1545 (CO 12:61).

global history when the religious refugee became a mass phenomenon."[15] We tend to remember the Reformation for theological innovation amid doctrinal debates. But what about its role in this broader history—as part of an extended, interreligious, and geographically expansive refugee event?

Heiko Oberman has argued that one cannot fully understand Calvin's theology without setting it within the experience of persecution and displacement that Calvin shared with countless others in his day.[16] Such realities made up the world they inhabited, prompted their questions about where they fit in it, and shaped their conclusions about God and God's will. It is helpful for us to distinguish exile, broadly considered, from refugeeism or migration for any number of other reasons. Each of these categories may be further nuanced by social and psychological factors, making them external or internal, voluntary or compelled. Yet it is important to avoid the anachronism of using modern concepts to describe the past. For our purposes, *exile* denotes simply a state of displacement from one's home. Calvin spoke of both political exile from one's country and spiritual exile from the believer's heavenly home. He also differentiated between voluntary political exile, such as Abram's choice to leave Ur (Gen. 12), and banishment as a form of divine punishment.[17] *Refugees*, more specifically, are those who flee violence, persecution, or other dangers to the safety of another country. Just as in our world today, this definition applied to many in Calvin's context, among whom the desire to escape conflicts over religion was the most common reason for flight. As Calvin himself acknowledged, there were also other reasons one might migrate from one country to another, choosing to spend a season or even a lifetime in exile from one's homeland.[18] The path that he chose, which he also commended to others, was flight for the sake of religious freedom.

Calvin lived most of his adult life as a fugitive in exile, a religious refugee whose commitments estranged him from his native France and its Catholic rulers. To make matters worse, many in his adopted city of Geneva, including those who first welcomed him there, grew frustrated with his attempts to reform the city. Over time, they increasingly came to view Calvin and his fellow pastors (many of whom were also exiled Frenchmen) as foreigners

---

15. Nicholas Terpstra, *Religious Refugees in the Early Modern World: An Alternative History of the Reformation* (Cambridge University Press, 2015), 4.
16. Oberman, *Refugees*, 21–49.
17. Max Engammare, "Une certaine idée de la France chez Jean Calvin l'exilé," *Bulletin de la société de l'histoire du protestantisme français: Études, documents, chronique littéraire* 155 (2009): 22.
18. See chap. 6, below.

whose ministry was meddlesome and unwelcome.[19] Yet being an outsider had advantages. The reformer provided leadership to churches filled with fellow refugees who flooded into the communities Calvin served in Strasbourg and Geneva. These fled oppression in locations as diverse as France, Scotland, Italy, and Poland. Exile constituted common ground for a pastor and the people he served. Over the years, Calvin's ministry turned outward to address a pan-European diaspora of Reformed churches—many in situations similarly disrupted by violence and migration—who looked to Geneva for guidance.

Calvin's letter to Luther reminds us that this complex and volatile setting was never tangential to Calvin's ministry and relationships. It was the contextual reality that contained, connected, and defined them. To read Calvin in his historical context, one must grasp how his situation as pastor to fellow religious refugees shaped his theological outlook. This means recovering Calvin as "refugee theologian." Failure to do this reduces him to "the man who believed that you are either saved or damned, . . . not only the caricature of a man and his message, but the fundamental misunderstanding of his age and his impact."[20] This oversimplified version of Calvin's thought is what Oberman calls "fast-food," a "Geneva-burger" that cannot explain the draw of his theology.[21]

Why This Book?

This book is an invitation to reconsider how Calvin is read and taught. It is especially intended for classroom and church settings. As Oberman has observed, Calvin's ideas continue to capture the imaginations of friends and foes alike five hundred years later. Yet many remain unaware of how the experience of exile left an indelible imprint on the way Calvin interpreted his place in the world and helped others do the same. This book aims to address this neglect by introducing the reformer's theology as shaped by refugee realities within the Reformation era's wider story of persecution, migration, and exile.

But first a word about what this book is not. Plenty has been written about major themes in Calvin's theology, as well as the problems with taking any single doctrine—such as predestination or union with Christ—to be a "central

---

19. Gary W. Jenkins, *Calvin's Tormentors: Understanding the Conflicts That Shaped the Reformer* (Baker Academic, 2018), 77–92; and William G. Naphy, *Calvin and the Consolidation of the Genevan Reformation* (Manchester University Press, 1994).

20. Oberman, *Refugees*, 67.

21. Burgher, or *bourgeois*, was a status denoting citizenship with economic and political privileges in Genevan society.

dogma," or unifying principle, for the whole of the reformer's thought.[22] This is a not a comprehensive deep dive into Calvin's thought nor an attempt to account for the whole under a single concept. In other words, I am not proposing exile as a theme that holds the meaning of Calvin's theology. No such key to unlocking Calvin exists. Like us, Calvin engaged his world equipped with particular knowledge and abilities while also being limited by biases and ignorance, personal capacity, and external circumstances. He was an exceptionally orderly thinker, but he was not always as consistent as he, or his future readers, might like. When I speak of Calvin's "exilic theology" in the pages that follow, I refer more to the context in which his ideas arose and the issues to which they responded than to a conceptual framework he self-consciously imposed on his teaching. The concerns of religious refugees and exiles recur in Calvin's theology simply because these are the realities among which we find him theologizing. This explains the frequency and manner in which, for instance, Calvin looks to King David in exile as an analogy for his own life and an example for others.[23] Experience shaped the questions he asked and the answers he found when he reconstructed David's situation primarily in terms of exile. Yet even this is but one clue among many that help us to place Calvin's theology in its historical context. Rather than giving a comprehensive hermeneutical framework for interpreting Calvin's thought, I paint a portrait of the refugee theologian that I hope will stimulate your imagination as you encounter Calvin's writings.

Similarly, this book is not a detailed history of exile in Calvin's day. Abundant resources reconstruct Calvin's exilic situation on a variety of levels. His alienation from France, difficulties in Geneva, ministry to communities that held increasing numbers of refugees and struggled to welcome them—all this has been taken up by other scholars and featured in excellent biographies.[24] Rather than providing a narrative account of Calvin's life in exile, this book focuses on how Calvin's theology responded to his exilic context. Although I include several accounts of how others reacted to Calvin, we

---

22. For two examples of studies that reject a "central dogma" methodology while also representing contrasting approaches to how far present-day theological concerns should govern historical study of Calvin, see Richard A. Muller, *The Unaccommodated Calvin: Studies in the Foundation of a Theological Tradition* (Oxford University Press, 2000); and Charles B. Partee, *The Theology of John Calvin* (Westminster John Knox, 2008).

23. For Calvin's identification with David and how this influenced his sense of vocation, see Alexandre Ganoczy, *The Young Calvin*, trans. David Foxgrover and Wade Provo (Westminster, 1966), 287–312.

24. See, e.g., Naphy, *Consolidation*; Robert M. Kingdon, *Geneva and the Coming of the Wars of Religion in France, 1555–1563*, rev. ed. (1956; repr., Droz, 2007); Engammare, "Une certaine idée," 15–27; Bruce Gordon, *Calvin* (Yale University Press, 2009); and Herman J. Selderhuis, *John Calvin: A Pilgrim's Life* (IVP Academic, 2009).

will look more closely at Calvin's message, leaving how it was received to other studies. For our purposes, this means primarily examining Calvin's theological and ecclesial writings, commentaries, and sermons—the places he formulated his teaching for others. Oberman has observed that Calvin turned increasingly toward a vision, a "Reformation of the Refugees," that offered believers a spiritual account of home beyond the ability of political regimes to establish or the reach of earthly powers to take away.[25] This does not mean that Calvin, as a magisterial reformer, lacked a nuanced positive account of how church and state expressed God's singular rule over creation.[26] Rather, Calvin's account of spiritual exile and homecoming anchored a pastoral approach to situations that varied greatly. By locating diverse examples of displacement within a shared experience of exile that could unite Reformed churches across geography, language, and culture, Calvin furnished a transnational community with theological categories for imagining its common identity as God's pilgrim people. This book builds on Oberman's argument—that Calvin read scripture as a refugee, with the needs of other refugees in mind—by demonstrating how the reformer did this in his ministry as a pastor and teacher. Read in light of these contextual realities, even doctrines already familiar and commonly associated with Calvin, such as predestination and presbyterian church governance, take on greater importance as expressions of "theology in exile." Again, it is not so much that Calvin set out to write exile theology, to become "The Refugee Theologian." Rather, displacement imposed itself on Calvin, and his theology attempted to make sense of this. Divine election, for example, moves quickly from the abstract to the concrete in sermons that trained listeners to see themselves as God's elect and to see Catholics who burned evangelicals as predestined, like Cain (Gen. 4), to eternal damnation.[27]

At the same time, we must not romanticize Calvin's ministry in exile. The refugee theologian's ministry was complicated in ways not always apparent in Oberman's straightforward account of how Calvin's theology spoke to fellow exiles and refugees. Polarization between Calvin's friends and foes began in his lifetime. Well-distributed biographies appearing after Calvin's death are so divergent in their sympathies and recounting of events that they

---

25. Heiko A. Oberman, "*Europa afflicta*: The Reformation of the Refugees," *Archiv für Reformationsgeschichte* 83 (1992): 91–111; and Oberman, *The Two Reformations: The Journey from the Last Days to the New World* (Yale University Press, 2003), 111–15, 145–50.

26. For a recent assessment of Calvin's views on this subject, see Matthew J. Tuininga, *Calvin's Political Theology and the Public Engagement of the Church: Christ's Two Kingdoms* (Cambridge University Press, 2017).

27. See chap. 6, below.

Introduction   xxvii

might as well be about two different people.[28] Calvin's exilic theology was by no means received warmly by everyone in the Reformed diaspora Calvin sought to reach.[29] Those who opposed Calvin often had good reasons that cannot be dismissed simply as envy or lack of resolve against Rome. Calvin's doctrines of predestination, church authority, and the sacraments were, to detractors among French-speaking Swiss reformers, as much about maintaining control over dispersed churches as they were about comforting the displaced. These critics were not wrong. A more nuanced view of Calvin's theological account of exile defies uncritical characterizations of Calvin as either the nefarious "pope of Geneva" or the valiant "reformer of refugees." Interestingly, Calvin did not even consistently hold exile—especially in contexts away from Geneva—as something to be commended.[30] He could just as easily express impatience with those who chose exile for religious purity when those same people created trouble in their new settings. Even as Calvin attempted to set forth consolation for fellow exiles, his methods and emphases remained far from uniform, and his motives were not always commendable.

The key point is this: In recovering the refugee theologian, this book foregrounds underappreciated aspects of Calvin's teaching that reveal how exile shaped his outlook, and yet there is not just one way to interpret how these contextual concerns show up in Calvin's works or the various ways they could have been understood in his day. The argument threaded through this book is that Calvin articulated his theology to address the needs of exiles around consistent themes of comfort (across multiple literary genres) that simultaneously served to impose conformity on a theological movement made increasingly diverse by its experiences of exile. This rankled and alienated some of the very people Calvin meant to comfort, prefiguring lines along which Calvin's theology has been received as blessing or curse by others ever since. It is precisely in this messy convergence of motives and messaging that remembering the refugee theologian bears its greatest lessons for today.

Calvin had goals that were not realized. His theology, despite his intentions, did not always meet the needs of fellow trekkers. Yet it remains theology forged in the furnace of exile. Oberman was onto something. A fast-food reformer

---

28. See Theodore Beza's highly complimentary *The Life of John Calvin* (1564) versus Jerome Bolsec's hostile account (1577); and Irena Backus, *Life Writing in Reformation Europe: Lives of Reformers by Friends, Disciples and Foes* (Ashgate, 2008), 125–38, 153–67.

29. Michael W. Bruening, *Refusing to Kiss the Slipper: Opposition to Calvinism in the Francophone Reformation* (Oxford University Press, 2021).

30. Mirjam van Veen, "Living in Babylon: Calvin's Correspondence with Believers Living in Exile," in *Calvin, Exile, and Religious Refugees: Papers of the Thirteenth International Congress on Calvin Research*, ed. Arnold Huijgen and Karin Maag (Vandenhoeck & Ruprecht, 2024), 37–54.

cannot explain the power and durability of Calvin's ideas for so many. So this book is an invitation to slow down with Calvin and, perhaps, to think differently about the reformer, the wider Reformed tradition, and why these matters might be of continuing interest to twenty-first-century readers.

Why Read Calvin?

A natural, and fair, question for the modern reader is, Why bother with Calvin at all? Not only are there many other things one could read at a moment awash with information and new media, but Calvin seems particularly out of fashion. Here is someone who appeared to find disturbing satisfaction in the execution of heretics and is perhaps best known for teaching that God assigns some to hell as deliberately as God chooses others for heaven. I am not surprised when my students initially express deep aversion to Calvin. He is one of those historical figures whose reputation precedes him, who is able to elicit strong opinions almost half a millennium after his death, even from those who have never read a single word he wrote. In some ways, scholarship has contributed to this state of affairs. The historiography of Calvin and the Reformed tradition has not been neutral. Even attempts to tell the stories of Calvin's enemies rarely manage to decenter Calvin's perspective, in part because Calvin eventually succeeded in ways his critics did not, and history favors the proverbial winners. Thus it can be a chore to wade through existing opinion in order to arrive at one's own assessment. But one way to ensure that you never get there is not to read Calvin for yourself. A former professor of mine taught church history with the aim of equipping students to read historical texts, to consider the past on its own terms, and only then to settle one's mind about a thinker. This strikes me as a sound strategy, which I commend to readers of this book as the first reason to read Calvin—namely, to form your own opinion by encountering his words and thoughts directly, for yourself. Beyond this, I hope to persuade you that reading Calvin today is valuable because he represents a wider tradition, wrote with unusual clarity, and formulated ideas that are relevant in ways many of us would not intuitively recognize. For example, might Calvin's use of exile as a shared identity to unite Genevans across class, culture, and migration status by emphasizing their common humanity offer insight for navigating our divided moment? What about revisiting Reformed theology as "refugee theology"? These are just two possible points of connection. This book is unapologetically an introduction, an appetizer to cultivate a taste for Calvin's exilic theology before readers set the book aside and dig deeper into Calvin's own works.

Another reason to read Calvin is that *Calvinist* frequently functions as an imprecise synonym for *Reformed*, which more accurately describes a wider tradition of which Calvin and his followers are but a part. Initially denoting elements of Protestantism that were not Lutheran, the term *Reformed* became identified with theological commitments sympathetic to the Zurich Reformation's austere approach to worship and departure from Luther's views on the Lord's Supper. In Calvin's day, theologians such as Heinrich Bullinger, Martin Bucer, and Peter Martyr Vermigli also had international reputations as leaders of the Reformed movement. Even the theology of Zwingli, from whom Calvin assiduously sought to distance himself, continued to influence German- and French-speaking Swiss Reformed churches. In England, it was only later in Calvin's career that Geneva came to hold more influence over Anglican theology than Zurich. *Calvinist*, as a narrower designation for the reformer and his followers, was a pejorative term invented by dismissive Lutherans. Yet it was Calvin's star that rose in historical memory and popular imagination, such that the Reformed tradition as a whole has come to be associated most of all with his name.[31] Some of this has to do with the demand for Calvin's printed sermons and commentaries, especially in English translation. The reformer himself played a role in this, writing for international audiences and being both deliberate and skillful at reaching them with his words. Calvin's clarity in works like his famous *Institutes of the Christian Religion* stands in contrast to the less concise or more emotive styles of reformers such as Bucer or Luther. Here was a mainstream Reformation theologian gifted with uncommon eloquence.

This points to another reason to read Calvin. He is surprisingly approachable for an author from such a different time. Calvin's education was rich in language and literature, and his training as a lawyer taught him to prize persuasive and elegant communication. The "lucid brevity" (*perspicua brevitate*) he adopted for writing commentaries geared toward busy pastors packaged substantial theology in a user-friendly format.[32] Calvin's French continues to influence the language to this day. Whether in his careful approach to gaining Luther's opinion or in how he used his *Institutes* and commentaries in tandem to train pastors, Calvin was meticulous about getting his point across. From the pulpit, he often began a sermon with a succinct statement of its theme. The availability of his works in translation makes it possible for readers to appreciate Calvin's gifts as a communicator. In sum, his notoriety, significance

---

31. For the complex reception of Calvin in historical memory, see Backus, *Life Writing*, 125–227.
32. Calvin to Simon Grynaeus, October 18, 1539 (CO 10b:402).

as a reformer, and elegance with words are but three reasons Calvin is worth reading today.

Reading Calvin also has potential benefits for our current historical moment marked by dizzying transition and significant experiences of displacement. Like other reformers, Calvin lived during a time of sharp tumult, with social and political realignments that would have been unimaginable even when Luther started raising questions in 1517. While the word *Reformation*, denoting an event that permanently ruptured Western Christendom, would not have been used by those living then to describe their moment in history, Calvin and others believed their times were extraordinary and even unprecedented. The reformer thought of himself as a prophet raised up to speak God's truth to a church in need of encouragement and struggling for survival.[33] Calvin's high degree of confidence as interpreter of both scripture and the situations to which he applied biblical teaching could intimidate (or at least annoy) those around him.

What can we learn from how Calvin viewed the import of his ministry? My nation continues to experience the deterioration of civility in public discourse across differences of opinion. For many Americans, the issues dividing us—in areas ranging from public health and law enforcement to college admissions and climate impact—are receiving unprecedented attention. Churches invoke the term *reformation* to describe present times, with new paradigms unsettling the long-standing effects of bias and oppressive practices.[34] Voices purporting to bring a prophetic message unite and galvanize thousands of followers at rallies, with millions more reachable instantaneously through social media platforms.

The fact that such claims have arisen on opposing sides of issues dividing church and society attests to the power of prophetic rhetoric. It also means that many of our most confident personalities will, in fact, end up being somewhat wrong, as Calvin was about many things. France never embraced Protestantism. The tight integration of theology and practices in Geneva was never as complete as Calvin would have liked. In fact, Calvin's system lasted barely into the next generation. Historians have continued to cast light on how Calvin's success as a reformer was as much about who tells the story as it was about the actual changes (or lack thereof) Calvin managed to introduce in forms

---

33. Jon Balserak, *John Calvin as Sixteenth-Century Prophet* (Oxford University Press, 2014); Max Engammare, "Calvin: A Prophet Without a Prophecy," *Church History* 67, no. 4 (1998): 643–61; and Ganoczy, *Young Calvin*, 287–312.

34. See, e.g., the 2017 Big Tent conference sponsored by the Presbyterian Church (U.S.A.) on the theme "Race, Reconciliation, and Reformation." "Big Tent 2017," Presbyterian Historical Society Blog, Presbyterian Church (U.S.A.), July 14, 2017, https://pcusa.org/news-storytelling/blogs/historical-society-blog/big-tent-2017.

that have endured. Reading Calvin in context reminds us that, although the issues were different, the prophetic (in some cases also apocalyptic) urgency of the messaging around us is something we have seen before.

Presenting the Reformation through doctrinal charts differentiating views on scripture, the church, and salvation can be helpful for seminarians preparing for ordination exams. Unfortunately, however, such presentations domesticate the sense of purpose amid momentous change that characterizes the theology done by those trying to change a world that appeared out of control. Studying how and why the original reformers disrupted the status quo, as well as how they established new cultural norms, provides insight for understanding modern claims of reformation. Calvin never intended for his ideas to remain locked up in books, mediated via lectures, and reproduced on tests. His theology met people in the streets as the street names were changing. This book is an invitation to read Calvin with this understanding.

Finally, as an exile theologizing within an age of exiles, Calvin is relevant for times like ours, when the realities of internal and external displacement are felt by millions whose experience cannot be separated from the ravages of war and disease, or from alienation within social systems that make it impossible for some to feel the security associated with notions of "home." As I write this introduction, the United Nations High Commissioner for Refugees recently reported the highest annual global increase of refugees, asylum seekers, internally displaced people, and stateless people ever recorded.[35] The 8.2 million people newly displaced in 2021–22—most from just three countries and for reasons often beyond their control, frequently involving human rights violations—represent an annual increase that is more than double the highest annual increase previously recorded.[36] The sheer scale of this global crisis means that many feel its impact not only as a faraway reality but also as something within their own communities. Christian theologians and scholars of religion have unveiled the dynamics of displacement with much-needed clarity to address the needs of diverse persons and situations, making important conceptual distinctions, for instance, between migrants and refugees or between political and psychological displacement as well as taking up specific case studies of displacement to offer theological responses.[37] Rarely, however,

---

35. United Nations High Commissioner for Refugees, *Global Trends: Forced Displacement in 2022*, June 14, 2023, https://www.unhcr.org/sites/default/files/2023-06/global-trends-report-2022.pdf.

36. Commissioner for Refugees, *Displacement*. The three countries are Afghanistan, Syria, and Ukraine.

37. See, e.g., M. Jan Holton, *Longing for Home: Forced Displacement and Postures of Hospitality* (Yale University Press, 2016); Caroline Redick, "Making a Home for Refugees: Jürgen Moltmann's Trinitarian Theology and Hospitality," *International Journal of Public Theology*

is the theology of the Reformation thought to have something to say about such experiences. Often, in fact, the opinions of such an especially combative era are seen as something to be shed, perhaps with some embarrassment, rather than embraced or examined anew. This book seeks to change that by bringing to light the dynamics of refugeeism and exile that created conditions of displacement that, in turn, produced the theology we associate with the reformers. It is not that Calvin would have used the categories of contemporary pastoral care and exile studies to describe what he felt or was attempting to do. Rather, it is that these fields can help us better understand and learn how a thinker like Calvin might serve as a conversation partner for pastoral care in the present age.

The Approach of This Book

I opened this introduction with my family experience because that experience clarifies both my approach to writing this book and what I hope it can offer readers. Prior to encountering the "Reformation of the Refugees" as a scholarly concept in the work of Oberman and others, my own reading of Calvin already resonated with my family's migration story. Poring over the reformer's *Institutes* and biblical exegesis—first as a church pastor for six years, then in my graduate studies—I was struck time and again by how this careful and confident thinker, to whom scholars attribute the self-assuredness of a "sixteenth-century prophet," frequently betrays a far less assured posture.[38] The way in which Calvin articulated a sense of dislocation rang true with my experience and reminded me of conversations with my children as they negotiated life as Asian Americans. Though my grandparents never read Calvin, they were well acquainted with the feelings of loss that constantly dim the promise of opportunity over a lifetime away from one's homeland. Discovering that preeminent European scholars of the Reformation noticed such themes in Calvin confirmed that my reading was not fanciful.

In the chapters that follow, I offer a historically contextualized portrait of Calvin embedded within a wider exilic community that included many other stories of persecution and displacement throughout the early modern Reformed diaspora. We will proceed in a manner that is selective and concise, previewing topics that one can then engage more extensively as one reads Calvin. Rather than attempting or claiming to offer the last word on John

---

13, no. 1 (2019): 40–54; and Daniel G. Groody, "Crossing the Divide: Foundations of a Theology of Migration and Refugees," *Theological Studies* 70, no. 2 (2009): 638–67.

38. Balserak, *Sixteenth-Century Prophet*.

Calvin, refugee theologian, my more modest objective is simply to introduce this figure as he appears across examples from his writings. First, I explore Calvin's own refugee experience and the different groups he addressed in his writings; then I consider the unique roles—teacher, pastor, and polemicist—that Calvin assumed in his work as a reformer. This helps us appreciate how themes arising from Calvin's refugee experience appear in different facets of his ministry, as well as how he articulated a vision of God's comfort for exiles through multiple genres. These diverse writings include Calvin's magisterial *Institutes* (chap. 3); commentaries and lectures (chap. 4); works on church polity, catechesis, and worship (chap. 5); sermons (chap. 6); and polemical treatises (chaps. 7 and 8). A brief conclusion considers how reading Calvin as refugee theologian invites us to reconsider the Reformed tradition's diverse roots and imagine new opportunities for pastoral theology. Each chapter closes with suggestions for further reading, and additional questions for personal or classroom reflection appear in an appendix at the end of the book.

Appreciating how Calvin's theology, as that of a French émigré, reflects the pressures of the lived realities that produced it avoids the distortion of separating ideas from real people and contexts. Ultimately, this historical approach gets us closer to the real Calvin. In my work, recovering the refugee theologian has revealed a reformer whose theology I have found increasingly inviting and relatable. It has also unearthed a Calvin who is complicated, not always consistent in the ways he thought about subjects and treated people. My goal, therefore, is not to remythologize Calvin or win him new friends as much as to open up facets of his thinking for others to consider for themselves. Along the way, some may indeed find points of connection. Who among us does not treasure a sense of belonging, the freedom of true rest, the gift of a place we can call home? Learning about how Calvin wrestled with a desire for these things has left a mark on our family's annual visits to Cleveland. It has reframed my memories of growing up in New York. And it informs my teaching at Pittsburgh Theological Seminary. Perhaps you will hear similar resonances with your experiences, or with the stories of other members of your community.

Calvinism's long history with political power and social prestige belies its refugee roots, resulting too often in theological imagination that lacks contextual awareness and is subject to oversimplification—what Oberman bemoans as "the fast-food of the neo-Calvinist Geneva-burger." Thus, Calvin's message of hope and comfort in exile, articulated during the Reformation, can be relevant on several levels today.

PART ONE

The Exilic Contexts of Calvin's Theology

ONE

From France to Faithfulness

Calvin's Personal History and His Theology of Exile

> Here is contained almost the sum of that very doctrine which they shout must be punished by prison, exile, proscription, and fire, and be exterminated on land and sea.
>
> —Calvin, Preface to King Francis I (1536)[1]

> In considering the whole course of David's life, it seemed to me that by his own footsteps he showed me the way, and from this I have experienced no small consolation.
>
> —Calvin, Author's Preface, Commentary on the Book of Psalms (1557)[2]

Migration and the Rhetoric of Belonging

The first edition of Calvin's magnum opus, the *Institutes of the Christian Religion*, appeared in 1536. At the time, its author was a relatively unknown man on the move. Having left France the year before, Calvin, now twenty-six, was living in Basel. He had yet to arrive in Geneva, the city with which his name would become forever associated. Yet, despite his youth and relative obscurity, Calvin knew exactly how he wanted to be perceived: as a religious

---

1. *Inst.* 9 (OS 3:9).
2. CTS 8:xliv; CO 31:28.

refugee standing in solidarity with others everywhere suffering for the cause of God's truth. This is evident in his dedication to King Francis I of France, originally penned in 1535. The dedication served as a preface to this and all subsequent editions of the *Institutes* that Calvin produced in his lifetime.

The preface frames the book as a plea for the persecuted and displays how Calvin addressed the powerful of his day. Over many centuries, the Catholic faith had become so closely identified with the French monarchy and its claim to possess divinely appointed authority that to question Catholicism meant risking the appearance of treason against the crown. French Protestants, also called Huguenots or evangelicals, faced persecution that included banishment, violence, and death for the beliefs Calvin defended.[3] Contrary to their enemies' claims, Calvin argues that evangelicals' commitments were neither heretical nor seditious.

As a piece of careful rhetoric, the preface treads lightly at first. Perhaps Francis, whom Calvin knew to harbor sympathy toward religious reform, was unaware of atrocities perpetrated in his name. If so, the king should be distressed upon discovering what people in France endured simply for following the teaching of Christ's apostles. Evangelicals were, in fact, loyal subjects who continued, despite unjust suffering, to pray diligently for the king and his realm. Some, like Calvin, now found themselves "fugitives from home," involuntarily displaced on account of violence.[4] The young author's respectful tone belies the firmness with which he goes on to assert the high stakes of the king's failure to intervene on behalf of persecuted Protestants. Besides tolerating crimes against innocent victims, inaction betrays indifference to God's authority and threatens to expose Francis as a false monarch guilty of "exercising not kingly rule but behaving like a robber."[5] At issue is treason against a higher authority. God would not abide such a usurper—a brigand on the French throne—and would both deliver God's people and "punish those who hate them."[6]

Calvin's dedication to King Francis formally identifies its author with reform movements that had disrupted European societies for nearly two decades since Luther first challenged Rome. It also situates Calvin within a refugee community: the growing number of those displaced on account of

---

3. N. M. Sutherland, *The Huguenot Struggle for Recognition* (Yale University Press, 1980). For early modern Protestants as "evangelicals," see the introduction, above.
4. *Inst.* 30 (OS 3:29).
5. *Inst.* 12 (OS 3:10).
6. *Inst.* 31 (OS 3:30). For the similar impact of exile on the self-perception and rhetoric of the English-speaking refugees in Calvin's Geneva, see Jane E. A. Dawson, "'Satan's Bludy Clawses': How Religious Persecution, Exile and Radicalisation Moulded British Protestant Identities," *Scottish Journal of Theology* 71, no. 3 (2018): 267–86.

the same religious commitments for which French Protestants suffered back home. Calvin thus positions the *Institutes* to speak for this faithful community flung out into a widening diaspora, yet united as unwaveringly loyal subjects of God and France. In so doing, Calvin was aware of his position relative to important francophone audiences, inside and outside France, at both the center and the margins of power.

In that vein, the preface nicely illustrates how, from the moment he left his homeland, Calvin's rhetoric reflected the increasing confidence of an authorial persona he cultivated over time.[7] Modern readers should be sensitive to this carefully crafted public voice. Even before Calvin's fateful arrival in Geneva, an unmistakable "us" against "them" already emerges in his writing. In this case, he notably repudiates identity markers that, until very recently, defined his place in the world as a French Catholic. Also significant is how Calvin's preface distances his brand of evangelicalism from the more extreme sort, such as the radicals whose chaotic takeover of the city of Münster was violently put down just the previous year. While unafraid to speak truth to power, Calvin did not want to be perceived as an insurrectionist.[8] The way he frames the *Institutes* in 1536 foreshadows how Calvin would later identify groups of people across national borders as either within or against his religious movement. A new community was coming into focus from Calvin's vantage point in exile. The lived experience of migration provided categories for inverting the political status of religious refugees as outsiders to society. How so? It produced an alternate theological account of belonging.

This chapter introduces how Calvin's experience of exile shaped his theology in ways that prompted him to reimagine his deepest connections to people and places. In severing old relationships, he found himself narrating what it means to belong to a new society, one defined by heavenly citizenship and a common journey through the present life as spiritual exile. Calvin was not the first to talk about Christianity in terms of exile and homecoming, but this was a distinctively Reformation-era theology of exile. Reflecting the cultural questions and scholarly methods of his early modern European context, Calvin grappled with how the past, including biblical history, gives meaning to the present. Like fellow reformers Ulrich Zwingli and Heinrich

---

7. Olivier Millet, "Calvin's Self-Awareness as Author," trans. Susanna Gebhardt, in *Calvin and His Influence, 1509–2009*, ed. Irena Backus and Philip Benedict (Oxford University Press, 2011), 84–101; and Millet, *Calvin et la dynamique de la parole: Étude de rhétorique réformée* (Slatkine, 1992).

8. For Calvin's preface as an attempt to hide his efforts to undermine the monarchy and evangelize France, see Jon Balserak, *Geneva's Use of Lies, Deceit, and Subterfuge, 1536–1563* (Oxford University Press, 2024), 95–121.

Bullinger, for instance, Calvin saw what God's people encounter in the present day and the stories recorded in scripture as composing a single history.[9] Calvin's use of the past to inform the church's sixteenth-century situation is notable for seizing on exile as a recurring pattern in God's dealings with the church throughout history.[10]

But even before he turned to teaching others, personal experience of exile as a political reality shaped Calvin's self-understanding. Though Calvin's early life rooted him in medieval French Catholicism, his university years brought friendships, new ideas, and mounting political pressures that eventually drove him from the church of his youth, the faith of his family, and the homeland that furnished fertile ground for personal and intellectual growth. As Calvin looked back on these events many years later, his retelling of the story stresses a pivotal conversion from his former life, the theme of exile interpreted through biblical examples like David, and the ever-present hand of God guiding him through the entire journey. The same biblical narratives of exile also gave Calvin a theological pattern through which to understand life for all God's people on earth as progress through exile under God's watchful care. This framework provided Calvin with categories of belonging as he navigated estrangement not only from his French upbringing but also, later, from his first pastorate in Geneva. The comfort he found in belonging to God across geographical borders and despite political citizenship translated into writings that centered on God's faithfulness amid the realities of persecution and migration experienced by a widening audience of exiles and religious refugees throughout Europe.

From Paris to Basel, Geneva to Strasbourg: Exile as a Political Reality for Calvin

> Of even nobler record is the fact that not only do you foster pure religion among yourselves, . . . but you also gather in the tattered fragments, the refugees of the persecuted church driven from other places. . . . Devout worshippers of God, coming to you as exiles from England and other parts, had been given your kind hospitality.
>
> —Calvin, to the city council of Frankfurt (1555)[11]

---

9. Bruce Gordon, "The Changing Face of Protestant History and Identity in the Sixteenth Century," in *Protestant History and Identity in Sixteenth-Century Europe*, ed. Bruce Gordon, 2 vols. (Scolar, 1996), 2:1–22.

10. Gordon, "Protestant History"; also Barbara Pitkin, *Calvin, the Bible, and History: Exegesis and Historical Reflection in the Era of Reform* (Oxford University Press, 2020), 122–40.

11. "Epistle Dedicatory," Comm. Harmony of Matthew, Mark, and Luke (*CNTC* 1:viii; CO 15:711).

About those babblers who mock us, wanting to know if no one can get into paradise without passing through Geneva, I say that it would please God that they had the courage to assemble in the name of Jesus Christ wherever they are.

—Calvin, *Four Sermons Concerning Matters Useful for Our Times* (1552)[12]

John (French: *Jean*) Calvin was born in Noyon, in the French province of Picardy, on July 10, 1509, the second child of Girard and Jeanne. A dutiful son, Calvin benefited from financial stability and spiritual support in his parents' home. Before her death when Calvin was a young child, his mother raised him in the traditional piety of medieval Catholicism. This included visiting shrines and venerating sacred relics, experiences the adult Calvin recollected with savage mockery.[13] Girard arranged for his son's formal schooling—originally to study theology in Paris before changing his mind and directing Calvin to pursue a legal education. The young man's university curriculum at Orléans and Bourges introduced him to the thought patterns and literary forms of Renaissance humanism. So named for its focus on "humane letters" (a term for the writings of ancient Greece and Rome), humanism prized careful linguistic and historical study of texts. Calvin admired the writings of Erasmus and Jacques Lefèvre d'Étaples, scholars who modeled humanistic approaches to interpreting the Bible. This immersion in classical learning and rigorous legal training made a lasting impression. Close attention to texts in their historical contexts, clear argumentation, and eloquent expression—each of these traits would later characterize Calvin's teaching as a reformer.

From Paris to Basel: Calvin's First Exile and the Birth of the Institutes

Calvin cut his authorial teeth on a first book at age twenty-two, a careful study of *De clementia* by the Roman philosopher Seneca (the Younger). To his disappointment, this self-published work was largely ignored by fellow academics. Calvin's scholarly ambition quickly found another outlet as he aligned himself with mentors and peers, such as Melchior Wolman and Nicolas Cop, who desired religious reform within French Catholicism. The budding scholar from Noyon soon found himself on a pathway of estrangement from teachers, friends, and former academic heroes, including Erasmus. While Calvin's friends at school always included those who wanted to reform French

---

12. *Four Sermons* (1552; CO 8:419).
13. *Treatise on Relics* (1543; CO 6:405–52); English: "An Admonition, Showing the Advantages Which Christendom Might Derive from an Inventory of Relics," *Tracts*, 1:289–341.

Catholicism, there is no evidence that Calvin himself was on a path toward reformism. This changed in 1533. When Catholic hard-liners pushed for action against religious dissent, Calvin departed from Paris with friends, keeping a low profile in several locations within France including Noyon, Orléans, and Poitiers. A year later, posters criticizing the Mass appeared throughout France, prompting a government crackdown on those with known sympathies toward reform. In 1535, as religious persecution intensified, Calvin fled to the Swiss city of Basel, commencing what would become a life sentence of exile from his native France.

In Basel, Calvin studied biblical languages along with the writings of reformers such as Luther, Melanchthon, and Zwingli. His inculcation into the evangelical movement went beyond intellectual formation and included forging personal relationships with Swiss Reformation leaders. Among these were French speakers Guillaume Farel and Pierre Viret, as well as Bullinger, Zwingli's successor in Zurich. Out of Basel came the first writings clearly connecting Calvin with the cause of reform. The first edition of the *Institutes* displays Calvin's impressive mastery of classical, patristic, and biblical literature packaged in the clear, logical prose honed through his legal studies. Recall how his preface to King Francis invokes a world in which the faithful are "punished by prison, exile, proscription, and fire . . . exterminated on land and sea" for their beliefs.[14] Calvin did not write as an outsider to that community under siege, but as one of them, a true believer. He was by now fully converted to Protestantism.

How did Calvin make sense of this total shift in his life's direction? A clue exists in his 1557 commentary on the book of Psalms. There Calvin looks back on these earlier events and identifies what he calls a "sudden conversion" (*subita conversio*). Scholars debate what the mature reformer of Geneva meant by this term.[15] On the one hand, Calvin describes a decisive pivot away from an old life. At the same time, this shift took some time. Not a single event, but rather the aforementioned series of developments between 1533 and 1535 link Calvin to "Lutheranism," a label Catholics at the time used broadly for all evangelicals. Scholars have attempted to correlate Calvin's "sudden conversion" to one or more of these events using descriptions from his writings. A key point came in May 1534, when Calvin

14. *Inst.* 9 (OS 3:9).
15. "Author's Preface," Comm. Psalms (CO 31:21). See, e.g., Alexandre Ganoczy, *The Young Calvin*, trans. David Foxgrover and Wade Provo (Westminster, 1966), 241–66; Heiko Oberman, "*Initia Calvini*: The Matrix of Calvin's Reformation," in *Calvinus Sacrae Scripturae Professor: Calvin as Confessor of Holy Scripture*, ed. Wilhelm H. Neuser (Eerdmans, 1994), 113–54; and T. H. L. Parker, *John Calvin: A Biography* (1975; repr., Westminster John Knox, 2006), 199–203.

resigned the chaplaincy of Noyon, a source of financial support from the Catholic Church. Others argue that such a clear ethical break was but the fruition of an earlier change of heart.[16]

Whatever the case, it seemed less of a concern for Calvin to name precisely when he was converted than to describe by whose hand he was led out of darkness. A hint concerning Calvin's early thinking on this appears in his 1539 *Reply* to Cardinal Jacopo Sadoleto, where Calvin describes a layperson's lengthy struggle with his Catholic upbringing.[17] It is not hard to see Calvin's own childhood in this story of a hypothetical convert who came to believe in God without ever hearing doctrine essential for salvation. God was with him even before he knew it.

Perhaps Calvin's 1557 account of fleeing France was never meant to be a precise chronology of events. Rather, it is a theological memoir that highlights doctrinal lessons for what was, by then, the international audience of an established reformer. Seen in this light, it is unsurprising that Calvin expressly connects his personal story to biblical figures such as Paul and, especially, King David in order to magnify the theme of God's faithfulness.

The "suddenness" of Calvin's conversion had long-established roots in God's lifelong care for him. It was thus "sudden" not because of its momentary nature, but as the unmistakable, even surprising, intervention of another's hand.[18] In this case, the same hand guided Calvin's steps from his earliest days in his parents' home into a new reality severed from all that he once held dear. Looking back, he cannot explain his life's course apart from the thought that God was, all along, doing what no one else expected. That is, God became for Calvin the voice of another Father, whose expectations clashed with the authorities he had assiduously obeyed. Faithfulness to this divine Father required embracing new doctrines, a new understanding of the church, and ultimately a new account of home. This is what Calvin means by likening his conversion to being molded into a "teachable frame."[19] We must not separate this comprehensive turning—of heart, mind, and allegiances—from Calvin's refugee experience. His newfound belonging to God demanded falling out with former ideals and associations in a world that suddenly became quite inhospitable. This personal history taught Calvin firsthand lessons about

---

16. See, e.g., Parker, *Calvin*, 199–203; Bruce Gordon, *Calvin* (Yale University Press, 2009), 33–35; Ganoczy, *Young Calvin*, 241–66; and F. P. van Stam, "Calvin's Conversion as His First Step Towards the Ministry," *Reformation & Renaissance Review* 12 (2010): 43–70.

17. *Reply to Sadoleto*, 1539 (CO 5:411–13); see Heiko A. Oberman, *John Calvin and the Reformation of the Refugees* (Droz, 2009), 135–38.

18. Oberman, *Refugees*, 140–41.

19. "Author's Preface," Comm. Psalms (CTS 8:xl; *CO* 31:21); and Oberman, "*Initia Calvini*," 152.

providence and predestination—namely, that God governs the world for the sake of the elect. Both doctrines would become central to Calvin's attempts to comfort others throughout his ministry.

Calvin's Second Exile: From Geneva to Strasbourg (and Back)

Embracing the theology of the reformers set Calvin on a path out of France, though neither Geneva nor pastoral ministry were obvious destinations. Introverted by nature, he preferred the company of books and imagined serving an evangelical readership through scholarly research and writing.

A layover in Geneva while en route to Strasbourg famously became an extended stay in 1536. Farel prevailed upon Calvin to remain in Geneva, threatening to call down God's curse if Calvin refused. The city had just abolished the Mass and officially adopted evangelical preaching. Farel needed assistance leading the church through these changes. Initially serving as a lecturer in scripture, Calvin was soon appointed as a pastor by city authorities, taking up a position as assistant to Farel and Viret. He was now properly a reformer, but the newly installed minister's tenure in Geneva had a rocky start, including a lengthy period of public opposition.[20] External pressure from the city of Bern—at the time Geneva's ally and military protector—created a delicate political situation. Geneva was never fully disentangled from its benefactor's preferences for how it ordered its affairs. Tensions mounted quickly within the city as well. Ministers zealously imposed new doctrine and practices. Prominent families balked at pastoral oversight by newcomers, who eventually replaced all the native Genevans in the city's ministerial ranks. The pastors hailed from elite social classes, and their wealthy and educated backgrounds further alienated them from many people. To make matters worse, a large number of pastors were French refugees like Calvin. Those who defied these immigrant ministers framed their defiance in terms of resistance to foreign influence over cherished local traditions and privileges.

Not surprisingly, Calvin and Farel found themselves entrenched in conflicts over worship and church discipline, resulting in their expulsion from Geneva in May 1538. For Calvin, this experience set the exilic contours of his life into even sharper relief. Now twice exiled, and stinging from a failed first pastorate, Calvin found refuge in Strasbourg, the German-speaking city whose reform was led by men such as Martin Bucer, Wolfgang Capito, and Matthew Zell. As one biographer put it, "This new exile, with its implication

---

20. See chap. 2, below.

of personal failure, was even more disheartening than Calvin's flight from France."[21] Any initial discouragement, however, quickly gave way to a sense of belonging, purpose, and joy. The young Calvin's Strasbourg sojourn afforded him much-needed space to grow personally as well as pastorally. In August of 1540, Calvin wed Idelette de Bure, the Flemish widow of an Anabaptist pastor who had two children from her first marriage. Bucer, who introduced the pair, became a father figure to Calvin, who never forgot his mentor's kindness for taking him in amid the embarrassment of leaving Geneva.[22]

In Strasbourg the refugee theologian honed his craft as a pastor and teacher. He lectured in the city's academy while serving as minister of its newly established congregation for French refugees. He learned much from Bucer's approach to ministry, set forth in Bucer's pastoral manual, *On the True Care of Souls* (1538). The immigrant church also had its own mechanism for discipline, a "consistory" comprising pastors and elders, as well as a diaconate devoted solely to the refugee community's poor. These institutions later served as models for Calvin's church in Geneva.

Daily ministry as an exile among exiles in Strasbourg left an impression on Calvin, who wasted no time setting what he learned about pastoral work into writing. He published his first revision of the *Institutes* (1539), expanding considerably the sections on church office and the visible church to reflect his Strasbourg experience. That same year, Calvin produced his commentary on Romans, crafted in the style of "lucid brevity" for the sake of busy pastors (like him).[23] His Strasbourg years were a bona fide oasis in the wilderness of Calvin's exilic ministry, teaching him how a twice-exiled person could yet find belonging and encouragement in the spiritual community of God's people.

The Frenchman purchased citizenship in Strasbourg in 1539, signaling his intent to stay put. Bucer, however, had other plans. He arranged for Calvin's recall to the setting of his greatest failure. Returning to Geneva was an assignment, Calvin confided to Farel, less appealing than anything else he could imagine.[24] Again acknowledging God's providence over his steps, Calvin reluctantly packed his bags. He resumed his Genevan ministry in September 1541. This move ended his many migrations across political borders. His experience of alienation in exile, however, was just beginning.

Stepping into the pulpit in Geneva for the first time in three years, Calvin picked up his preaching exactly where he had left off—in fact, with the very

---

21. William J. Bouwsma, *John Calvin: A Sixteenth-Century Portrait* (Oxford University Press, 1988), 20.
22. Calvin to Bucer, October 15, 1541 (Bonnet, 1:294; CO 11:296).
23. See chap. 3, below.
24. Calvin to Farel, August 1541 (Bonnet, 1:280–81; CO 11:99–199).

next verse.²⁵ Being thirty-two years old, he could not have known that this second tour in Geneva would occupy the remainder of his life. Even so, he was determined to achieve a different outcome with this tenure. In addition to redrafting the city's constitution, he set to work solidifying structural changes in the church with a new set of *Ecclesiastical Ordinances*. Besides defining church offices—pastor, elder, deacon, and teacher—in line with Calvin's experience in Strasbourg, the *Ordinances* establish new bodies for ministerial training and oversight (the Company of Pastors and *congrégation*) and church discipline (the Consistory).²⁶ The *Ordinances* also sketch plans for the Genevan Academy, which would not come into being until 1559. A holistic program for transforming church and society through biblical teaching thus emerged under the supervision of the city's pastors.²⁷

Not everyone was on board. Even some of Calvin's early supporters grew impatient with policies they identified with his reforms.²⁸ Estrangement from large segments of Genevan society only compounded Calvin's sense of displacement within his adopted city. Church discipline reemerged as a source of conflict. Could the Consistory, comprising church and government officials, impose excommunication apart from other magistrates?

Changes to worship also, predictably, provoked hot dissent. Street riots ensued after pastors, seeking to wean parents from superstition regarding saints' names, ignored their wishes and substituted biblical names for children at the moment of baptism. Bans on taverns, dancing, and theatergoing likewise proved unpopular. So was the practice of pastors publicly shaming citizens who flouted such restrictions. For Calvin and his colleagues, the excesses of "libertinism" demanded such strong measures. The resulting tension with vocal and powerful opponents left ministers to carry out their work amid intense factionalism and struggles with public relations.²⁹

Beyond the city's walls, Geneva's regional connections ensured that none of this occurred in isolation. Local feuds with figures such as Jerome Bolsec, who challenged Calvin on predestination, and Sebastian Castellio, who promoted greater toleration of diverse views, put Calvin at odds with fellow Swiss reformers. In both France and French-speaking Switzerland (Romandy; French:

---

25. Calvin to an unknown recipient, January 1542 (CO 11:366).
26. Scott M. Manetsch, *Calvin's Company of Pastors: Pastoral Care and the Emerging Reformed Church, 1536–1609* (Oxford University Press, 2013); and Erik de Boer, *The Genevan School of the Prophets: The Congrégations of the Company of Pastors and Their Influence in 16th Century Europe* (Droz, 2012).
27. See chap. 5, below.
28. Gary W. Jenkins, *Calvin's Tormentors: Understanding the Conflicts That Shaped the Reformer* (Baker Academic, 2018), 77–107.
29. See below, chaps. 2, 5, 6, and 8.

Suisse romande), Geneva's Protestant detractors noted how its totalitarian streak bore striking resemblance to the Catholic hegemony it purported to hate.[30] Calvin would look back on these struggles and liken them to King David's hardships in exile and betrayal by friends.[31]

Personality also played a role in these conflicts. Upon first arriving in Geneva, Calvin had embraced Farel's rigid, bellicose posture in promoting reformist ideals, which was already beginning to divide French evangelicals. Further polarizing was Calvin's confidence in his own abilities and his general sensitivity to criticism. Likability was never his strength. Yet Calvin believed God had called him to Geneva with orders to purify the church. Over against resistance, he taught Genevans from the pulpit and lectern, established means of catechizing their children, and visited the sick and dying.[32] Calvin put Geneva on the map as a city of refuge for exiles fleeing persecution and as a major publishing center, with his theological writings and printed commentaries.[33]

As much as Geneva demanded his time, France claimed Calvin's heart.[34] French affairs, especially the mistreatment of evangelicals, appear constantly in Calvin's writings and teaching. His engagement with France took different forms over time, from letters filled with advice to the powerful and the friendless alike to unrelenting critiques of so-called Nicodemites, who hid their evangelical faith, to a clandestine campaign to influence French religion and politics with money and ministers from Geneva.[35] Political missteps by Calvin's enemies secured his standing by 1555, when elections in Geneva turned his way and his opponents were implicated in public disturbances.[36] This new position of strength made it possible for Calvin to shift energy toward international affairs, such as sending a steady stream of missionary

---

30. Michael W. Bruening, *Refusing to Kiss the Slipper: Opposition to Calvinism in the Francophone Reformation* (Oxford University Press, 2021), 250–51, 299.

31. See Ganoczy, *Young Calvin*, 287–312; "Author's Preface," Comm. Psalms (CTS 8:xliv, xlviii; CO 31:27, 33).

32. See below, chaps. 5 and 6.

33. On the former, see chap. 2, below. On the latter, see Jean-François Gilmont, *John Calvin and the Printed Book*, trans. Karin Maag (Truman State University Press, 2005).

34. Max Engammare, "Une certaine idée de la France chez Jean Calvin l'exilé," *Bulletin de la société de l'histoire du protestantisme français: Études, documents, chronique littéraire* 155 (2009): 15–27.

35. Charmarie Jenkins Blaisdell, "Calvin's Letters to Women: The Courting of Ladies in High Places," *Sixteenth Century Journal* 13 (1982): 67–84; Jon Balserak, "Geneva's Use of Lies, Deceit, and Simulation in Their Efforts to Reform France, 1536–1563," *Harvard Theological Review* 112 (2019): 76–100; Balserak, *Subterfuge*; and Robert M. Kingdon, *Geneva and the Coming of the Wars of Religion in France, 1555–1563*, rev. ed. (1956; repr., Droz, 2007).

36. William G. Naphy, *Calvin and the Consolidation of the Genevan Reformation* (Manchester University Press, 1994), 167–99.

pastors into France for Reformed churches and even preparing these church leaders for the outbreak of religious war.[37]

All the while, Calvin maintained extensive correspondence with, and on behalf of, refugee communities across Europe. Exile, conceived both politically and theologically, became a recurring theme of Calvin's multifaceted ministry. Yet, as the preceding account has shown, Calvin's embrace of exile as a theological concept cannot be divorced from his journey into political exile as a religious refugee. These experiences profoundly influenced what he found in scripture and how he shared these lessons with others.

Redefining Boundaries: Exile as Theological Identity

> In baptism our Pharaoh is drowned, our old man is crucified, our members are mortified. We are buried with Christ and removed from the captivity of the devil and the power of death—but removed only into the desert, a land arid and poor, unless the Lord rain manna from heaven, and cause water to gush forth from the rock. For our soul, like that land without water, is in want of all things, until he, by the grace of his Spirit, rains upon it.
> —Calvin, *Psychopannychia* (1534/42)[38]

> If heaven is our homeland, what else is earth but our place of exile?
> —Calvin, *Institutes* III.9.4 (1559)[39]

With exile playing such a significant role in Calvin's biography, it is not surprising that both geographical displacement and its emotional effects featured prominently in Calvin's self-awareness and how he retold his story. Exile always involved more than political status. It was a theological identity that made sense of literal experiences of migration while stretching past these to encompass the entire present life for the faithful. The durability and versatility of Calvin's thinking on this topic come across in three works spanning the early and mature periods of his career. First, the conceptual arc of the Christian life's movement from wilderness to promised land appears in Calvin's theology as early as the *Psychopannychia*, which was written in 1534, before Calvin departed from France, though it was not published until 1542.[40] One

---

37. Jon Balserak, *John Calvin as Sixteenth-Century Prophet* (Oxford University Press, 2014), 127–78.
38. Calvin, *Psychopannychia*, 1542; in *Tracts*, 3:467 (translation modified for clarity) (CO 5:214).
39. *Inst.* III.9.4 (OS 4:174).
40. Calvin, *Psychopannychia*, 414–90 (CO 5:165–232). See Sam Ha, "The Exile Motifs in Calvin's Early View on the Doctrine of Covenant," in *Calvin, Exile, and Religious Refugees:*

can imagine how working through ideas that would become fixtures of his exilic theology may have strengthened his resolve to leave France. Next, we once again consider how Calvin frames the 1536 *Institutes* in terms of exile and how he returns two decades later to similar themes in the preface to his 1557 commentary on the book of Psalms, which casts his whole life as an exilic journey.

Like countless others, Calvin found stories in scripture that made sense of his own. The trove of Old Testament exilic narratives—from Abraham's call out of Ur, to Israel's exodus and wilderness wandering, to the nation's captivity in Babylon—remain paradigmatic for Jewish identity as God's people. These same stories have provided Christian theology with rich imagery of exile and return, beginning with the New Testament's appropriation of such examples as models for Christian faith. Hebrews 11 and 1 Peter 2, for example, apply Old Testament figures and the language of "strangers and exiles" to Christian churches in the Roman Empire.[41] In his commentaries on these passages, Calvin likewise commends Abraham's faith in exile (Heb. 11:10) as a model for the Christian's heavenly hope, so that "wherever they may go on earth [Christians] are only guests in this world."[42] Similarly, Calvin takes Paul's christological reading of Israel's history in 1 Corinthians 10 as a metaphor for the Christian life in the *Psychopannychia*. Pauline allegory, centering on Christ as "the rock" accompanying God's people out of Egypt, teaches that baptism, signified by Israel's Red Sea crossing, commences a wilderness journey. Ongoing sustenance, "manna from heaven," is needed until the soul passes into death, "a land flowing with milk and honey."[43]

Nourishment is always essential, but Calvin emphasizes the journey itself in the *Psychopannychia*. Against those who denied the soul's immortality or conscious state after separation from the body, Calvin stresses the soul's passage from life into death as one continuous movement—from exile to a homecoming characterized alternatively as "rest," "peace," and "reward" in "the invisible place," also known as "Abraham's bosom."[44] From there the journey proceeds seamlessly toward reunion with the body at the final resurrection. The present life is not the main theme of the *Psychopannychia*.

Papers of the Thirteenth International Congress on Calvin Research, ed. Arnold Huijgen and Karin Maag (Vandenhoeck & Ruprecht, 2024), 157–59.

41. For Calvin's prevalent turn to political exile as a theme for narrating the hardships and hopes of Old Testament patriarchs, but singular use of the phrase "strangers and exiles" (*peregrini et inquilini*), see Ha, "Exile Motifs," 160–61.

42. Comm. Heb. 11:10 (*CNTC* 12:168; *CO* 55:153); and Comm. 1 Pet. 2:11 (*CNTC* 12:267–68; *CO* 55:242).

43. Calvin, *Psychopannychia*, 467 (*CO* 5:214).

44. Calvin, *Psychopannychia*, 467–68 (*CO* 5:214–15).

However, Calvin's narrative of the soul's journey functions as an extended gloss on our earthly days. This is a time of expectation and progress, a pilgrimage toward death, when the soul will be clothed with a heavenly dwelling to cover the nakedness of mortality (2 Cor. 5:1–10).[45] Previewing a key theme in Calvin's later teaching and preaching, Abraham in exile emerges here as an example of such anticipation.[46] Calvin relates political exile to spiritual exile in his reflections on Abraham's appearance in Hebrews 11:

> The Apostle is speaking of Abraham and his posterity who dwelled in a foreign land among strangers; not only exiles, but certainly sojourners, scarcely sheltering their bodies by living in poor huts, in obedience to the command of God given to Abraham, that he should leave his land and his kindred. God had promised them what he had not yet exhibited. Therefore they trusted the promises afar off, and died in the firm belief that the promises of God would one day be fulfilled. In accordance with this belief, they confessed that they had no fixed abode on the earth, and that beyond the earth there was a country for which they longed, viz., heaven.[47]

Scripture presented the young humanist from Picardy with a story of how profound separation from land and kindred, into parts unknown, could open one's eyes to the greater promise of a more lasting home. Whether or not this insight helped launch Calvin toward his future life as reformer of Geneva, he would return to the theme frequently.

In his preface to King Francis, written as he departed from France at the outset of his career, Calvin identifies a new community to replace the one he was leaving behind. Belonging was less about political loyalty than fealty to God. Exile from one's homeland became the mark of an insider alongside other forms of marginalization, including religious persecution. Calvin would have constant regard for French evangelicals over the next thirty years in exile, turning Geneva into a base for influencing religious reform in France.[48] This early address to the French king locates Calvin's international aspirations and strategic approach to political power as aspects of his ministry from the start. Through the years, whether in formal publications or personal correspondence, Calvin displayed uncanny awareness of his need to bridge cultural differences and, frequently, seek influence to advance his goals. In retrospect, the "silent margins" of Calvin's preface hold places for characters whose presence, while implied in 1536, emerge more clearly only as his ministry continued in exile.

45. Calvin, *Psychopannychia*, 442, 463–66 (CO 5:195, 211–13).
46. Calvin, *Psychopannychia*, 463–66, 473 (CO 5:211–13, 218–19).
47. Calvin, *Psychopannychia*, 473 (CO 5:218).
48. See chap. 2, below.

Who were these other characters? Fellow migrants, whether present with Calvin in Basel or scattered throughout Europe, composed a significant segment of this new community. In 1536, Calvin placed himself among "fugitives from home" for the cause of true religion. This refugee category would shape his complex relationship to Geneva. As leader of a church of exiles from many nations, Calvin distinguished native Genevans from foreigners while articulating a shared theological identity that included both.[49] The impact of migration required an account of belonging to God and to one another that could overcome national, linguistic, and cultural barriers. Besides cultivating unity, identity construction also involved drawing fresh boundaries. Outside the faithful community were cowardly Nicodemites, whose faceless presence is nevertheless implied here when Calvin praises evangelicals and religious refugees for suffering in opposing idolatry. Similarly, Calvin's preface suggests that the French evangelical movement was not alone in the world. Though often not cited by name, references to the positions of Lutherans and other Swiss Reformed theologians appear in this first edition and certainly influenced Calvin's positions.[50] Even though he would find elements of their beliefs problematic, especially on the sacraments, Calvin generally embraced such fellow Protestants as allies in a common cause.

The reformer invokes this broader international context when recounting, twenty years later, his motives for first publishing the *Institutes*. The uncharacteristically autobiographical preface to his 1557 commentary on the Psalms discloses his desire, in 1536, that "foreign nations might be touched with at least some compassion toward" persecuted French evangelicals.[51] Perhaps Calvin revised his recollection of events to suit his international prestige and ambitions in 1557, claiming now that his ministry always had other nations in view. Whatever the case, the fact that he characterizes the 1536 *Institutes* as an intervention for the persecuted reminds us that all theology is embedded in lived realities that shape a theologian's concerns and how they are expressed. For readers of the *Institutes*, so often treated as a source for Calvin's ideas with little reference to situations out of which they emerged, this invites us to ask better questions about how context formed Calvin's theology.

In 1557 the reformer narrates the path his life has taken by describing his vocation as a journey into exile. The Psalms preface depicts four exilic movements—two conceptual, two literal—that frame the forty-eight-year-old

---

49. See chap. 6, below.
50. Ford Lewis Battles, "Introduction," *Institutes of the Christian Religion: 1536 Edition*, by John Calvin, trans. Ford Lewis Battles (1975; rev. ed., Eerdmans and Meeter Center, 1986), xxxvi–liii.
51. "Author's Preface," Comm. Psalms (CTS 8:xlii; CO 31:23).

reformer's entire career. The first conceptual exile is a departure from the faith and culture of his family, which he dismissively refers to as a deep "abyss of mire" out of which God lifted him against all odds.[52] Calvin criticizes his secure and privileged childhood as malformation in "the superstitions of Popery," marked additionally by his father's unseemly striving after wealth. He shrugs off this "obscure and humble condition" by contrasting it to his eventual high calling as "preacher and minister of the gospel."[53] Here Calvin's narrative of advancement beyond the religious and relational ties of his upbringing makes its first connection to the life of David, who similarly rose from "the sheepfold . . . to the rank of supreme authority."[54] Then follows Calvin's account of two literal migrations: his removal from France and his expulsion from Geneva. These early hardships anticipate the final movement Calvin narrates in this preface: the second conceptual exile, into a life of continual conflict with enemies near and far. Among these are unnamed thinkers who disputed with Calvin about divine providence and predestination, colleagues who betrayed him, and Lutherans who slandered him worse than Catholics would. These experiences cast Calvin's calling into exile as consignment to multiple levels of estrangement—from people as well as places. In Calvin's hands, exile paradoxically involves both faithfulness to God and conflict with others, at once framing Calvin's ministry as suffering and true to David's example.

Olivier Millet has noted Calvin's use of the "sacrificial reformer" trope in this 1557 preface.[55] Just as striking is its association here with David. Calvin cites David's hardships as his key for interpreting the Psalms.[56] As we will show in later chapters, this is far from the only place Calvin finds lessons for contemporary believers in David's exilic circumstances. It is, however, where Calvin most clearly claims these for himself. David knew betrayal and conflict, so much so that following in David's "footsteps" was not, for Calvin, to "wander into an unknown region."[57] In his comments on individual psalms, Calvin lifts up David's faith through various seasons of removal from Jerusalem as a model for Christians in all places. Migration and estrangement—already styled as the lot of a fugitive reformer in his 1536 address to the king—remain central to how the Psalms validated Calvin's calling through their depictions of David's life. The way of faithfulness was unmistakably the path of exile.

52. "Author's Preface," Comm. Psalms (CTS 8:xl–xli; CO 31:21).
53. "Author's Preface," Comm. Psalms (CTS 8:xl–xli; CO 31:21).
54. "Author's Preface," Comm. Psalms (CTS 8:xl–xli; CO 31:21).
55. Millet, "Calvin's Self-Awareness," 94–95.
56. Ganoczy, *Young Calvin*, 287–312.
57. "Author's Preface," Comm. Psalms (CTS 8:xliv, xlviii; CO 31:27, 33).

Conclusion

Calvin's journey away from a community defined geographically, politically, and religiously by the French Catholicism of his youth demanded the reimagining of what it meant to belong to God and others. The Bible helped Calvin interpret his personal experience as fugitive and foreigner in theological terms, with ongoing implications of political displacement. This process involved identifying some as insiders while excluding others. Evangelicals were in, Catholics banished. The king, as it were, had a choice before him in 1536. Exile, reconceived as a spiritual reality for the sixteenth century, could unify a religious movement struggling with new forms of diversity. In so doing, exile transformed the trappings of political disenfranchisement into emblems of God's favor and belonging to God's people. The church that Calvin found in political exile was a community perpetually displaced, waiting in hope to arrive at a better, more lasting city. The next chapter identifies how Calvin's use of exile as a theological concept brings specific audiences into focus. Frequently a means of comfort, yet always with a divisive edge, exile grounded believers in a spiritual community that, despite being scattered across political borders, knew its way home in an era of constant migration.

For Further Reading

In Calvin's Words

1534/42 *Psychopannychia*. In *Tracts*, 3:414–90.

1536 "Prefatory Address to King Francis I of France." In *Inst*. 9–31.

1543 *An Admonition, Showing the Advantages Which Christendom Might Derive from an Inventory of Relics*. In *Tracts*, 1:289–341.

1557 "The Author's Preface." In *Commentary on the Book of Psalms*, CTS 8:xxxv–xlix.

For Digging Deeper

Bouwsma, William J. *John Calvin: A Sixteenth-Century Portrait*. Oxford University Press, 1988.

Gordon, Bruce. *Calvin*. Yale University Press, 2009.

Huijgen, Arnold, and Karin Maag, eds. *Calvin, Exile, and Religious Refugees: Papers of the Thirteenth International Congress on Calvin Research*. Vandenhoeck & Ruprecht, 2024.

Millet, Olivier. "Calvin's Self-Awareness as Author." In *Calvin and His Influence, 1509–2009*, translated by Susanna Gebhardt, edited by Irena Backus and Philip Benedict, 84–101. Oxford University Press, 2011.

Oberman, Heiko A. *John Calvin and the Reformation of the Refugees*. Droz, 2009.

Terpstra, Nicholas. *Religious Refugees in the Early Modern World: An Alternative History of the Reformation*. Cambridge University Press, 2015.

TWO

Comfort and Confrontation

The Diverse Audiences of Calvin's Works

There has never been in ordinary life a circle of friends so heartily bound to each other as we have been in our ministry.
  —Calvin, dedication to Farel and Viret, Commentary on Titus (1549)[1]

The more the wicked strive to exterminate the memory of [God's] name from the earth, the more efficacy will he bestow on our blood to cause that memory to flourish more and more.
  —Calvin, to the faithful in France (June 1559)[2]

We will make it our business by all the means in our power to rouse the King of Navarre to claim the regency of the kingdom that had been wrested out of his hands.
  —Calvin, to François Hotman and Jean Sturm (June 4, 1560)[3]

Addressing a Community in Need of Consolation

When Calvin wrote Guillaume Farel in 1541 to express misgivings about returning to Geneva, he knew his friend would understand. It was Farel, after all, who recruited Calvin to Geneva only to be expelled from the city with him under the same cloud of controversy in 1538. Shared defeat also meant

---

1. *CNTC* 10:347; *CO* 13:477.
2. Bonnet, 4:52; *CO* 17:572.
3. Bonnet, 4:109; *CO* 18:98.

double exile for two native Frenchmen already estranged from their homeland. Farel, who left France in 1525, was deeply ensconced among the "fugitives from home" with whom Calvin identified himself in his preface to the 1536 *Institutes*.[4] Beyond the shared language and memories of a place left behind, their common status as exiles also shaped the friends' identity in relation to others. Farel harbored resentment toward reformist French Catholics, including the intellectuals gathered around Bishop Guillaume Briçonnet in the city of Meaux, and he accused them of Nicodemism.[5] Calvin adopted Farel's brand of reform, with its harsh polemics around religious purity. It meant hatred of this "Meaux Circle" in France and bitter animosity toward Genevans who had rejected the pair. In both cases, refugee status and uncompromising ideals separated Farel and Calvin from their adversaries.

How else did Calvin's experience of exile shape his associations and influence his theology? His cobelligerency alongside Farel reminds us that Calvin did not establish community in exile from scratch but found relationships and factions that existed before his arrival. This chapter examines Calvin's community with particular attention to his audiences. In preaching, publications, and thousands of letters, he sought to comfort believers struggling with diverse situations, including persecution and migration. For the faithful, scripture offered a way of interpreting hardship as evidence of their identity as God's people and, consequently, assurance of God's favor and care. Consolation framed the reformer's message to others across several layers of relationships, extending outward from those closest to him: (1) his inner circle of friends; (2) his complex situation amid refugee realities in Geneva; (3) his efforts as a fugitive to influence France; and (4) his interactions with the growing diaspora of Reformed churches that relied on his teaching. Such comfort in belonging also involved knowing that your enemies did not belong. Thus, we must also consider how Calvin identified the faithful in exile by carefully distinguishing them from other groups, as insiders versus those without God's favor. These outsiders included Rome and even fellow French evangelicals who disagreed with him.

Calvin's Inner Circle

From family to old friends, work acquaintances to "followers" on social media, you and I navigate life in connection with others who influence what

---

4. *Inst*. 30 (OS 3:29).
5. Frans Pieter van Stam, "The Group of Meaux as First Target of Farel and Calvin's Anti-Nicodemism," *Bibliotheque d'humanisme et renaissance: Travaux et documents* 68, no. 2 (2006): 253–76; and Jonathan A. Reid, *King's Sister—Queen of Dissent*, 2 vols. (Brill, 2009), 553–60.

we know, how we act, and how people perceive us. Calvin was no different. At the center of these relationships were decades-long friendships with Farel and Pierre Viret.[6] The three were known to admirers and detractors alike as a "most holy trio" (*sanctissimus ternio*); this moniker, depending on who used it, was a term of respect or disdain.[7] From his earliest days in exile, Calvin looked to these men for mutual encouragement. They, in turn, became proponents of their younger colleague's theological vision. Despite bumps along the way, such as fallout over the sixty-nine-year-old Farel's marriage to a teenager in 1558, these colleagues were a consistent reminder to Calvin that, through the ups and downs of establishing a theological program in exile, he was not alone. Whatever others thought of them, they were always in it together.

Theirs was an intimacy wrought in the trenches of theological conflict. Calvin dedicated his commentary on Titus (1550) by warmly acknowledging Farel and Viret as "dearly beloved colleagues and brothers," calling their friendship a "holy bond."[8] An extraordinary "circle of friends," the three had served the Genevan church together in the 1530s, where they were "of one mind." This unified ministry extended to new contexts. Farel found his way to Neuchâtel, and Viret to Lausanne, while Calvin remained in Geneva. Tellingly, resistance to shared enemies sits at the heart of Calvin's description of solidarity with Viret and Farel. They were brothers-in-arms, connecting Calvin's work in Geneva to a wider reform movement struggling to establish itself in Romandy. Though they were geographically dispersed, their mission as "God's children" remained clear and focused: to protect "Christ's fold," whether from the external threat of Rome or from "unclean dogs" who sabotaged the faith from within.[9] Sometimes they had to defend themselves against similar charges. In the 1530s, antagonists such as Pierre Caroli (d. ca. 1545) accused Calvin and Farel of denying the Trinity. Decades later the tables turned when the friends battled antitrinitarian theology emerging among Italian refugees in Geneva. These experiences fostered closeness. Calvin's letters to Farel and Viret could be emotional and candid in ways few others saw. Following the death of his wife, Idelette, for instance, Calvin confides that he is "overwhelmed with grief" over the "exceedingly painful" departure of

---

6. Michael W. Bruening, "Triumvirs, Patriarchs, or Friends? Evaluating the Relationship between Calvin, Viret, and Farel," *Reformation & Renaissance Review* 10 (2008): 125–36; Heiko A. Oberman, "Calvin and Farel: The Dynamics of Legitimation in Early Calvinism," *Reformation & Renaissance Review* 1 (1999): 7–40; and Jean-François Gilmont, *Insupportable mais fascinant: Jean Calvin, ses amis, ses ennemis et les autres* (Brepols, 2012), 15–30.

7. Bucer to Calvin, August 1549 (*CO* 13:356).

8. Preface to Comm. Titus (1550; *CNTC* 10:347–48; *CO* 13:477–78).

9. Preface to Comm. Titus (1550; *CNTC* 10:347–48; *CO* 13:477–78).

"the best companion of my life."[10] Similarly, Calvin had written earlier with "great anxiety" about the premature birth of the couple's child Jacques and their subsequent "grave and bitter wound in the death of [their] infant son."[11]

Martin Bucer's declaring the three a "most holy trio" is one example of how contemporaries recognized the common vision uniting these kindred spirits. After Calvin's death, Theodore Beza praised the "elite tripod" whose distinctive gifts converged in reforming the church.[12] Others were less impressed. Disputes reverberating throughout the Swiss Reformed world included Calvin's well-publicized clashes with Jerome Bolsec and Sebastian Castellio over divine election and religious toleration, respectively. Among those who sided with Calvin's enemies were many who similarly endured flight from France for their beliefs. Thus Calvin's exilic theology did not speak for all refugees. In truth, he came into an already-established French evangelical diaspora. As Farel and Viret deferred to Calvin's theological acumen and promoted his theology, this exacerbated existing factionalism in the community despite its shared language and, for many, roots in France.[13] Controversial topics such as predestination, church discipline, and how to handle theological diversity took distinctive shape in Calvin's thought.[14] Though reliably supported by Farel and Viret, Calvin's opinions on these issues simultaneously constituted points of fissure with opponents who more than disagreed: they loathed Calvin and his circle. Viret lamented how "hatred of Calvin" (*odium Calvini*) rubbed off on him.[15] Readers today must remember that Calvin's theological vision for a community of spiritual exiles was never uncontested. Heavy-handed tactics by Calvin and Farel, such as calling for universal subscription to a confession of faith in Geneva, forever associated them with authoritarianism, even though they never got their wish.[16] Bucer's "holy trio" was for some more like "three patriarchs" of a new Romanism, with Calvin sitting atop as its pope. How dare he presume

---

10. Calvin to Farel, April 11, 1549 (Bonnet, 2:218; CO 13:228); and Calvin to Viret, April 7, 1549 (Bonnet, 2:216; CO 13:230–31).

11. Calvin to Viret, July 1542 (Bonnet, 1:335; CO 11:420); Calvin to Viret, August 19, 1542 (Bonnet, 1:344; CO 11:430).

12. Theodore Beza, *Les vrais portraits des hommes illustres: Avec les 30 portraits supplémentaire de l'édition de 1673* (Paris, 1581; repr., Slatkine, 1986), 127, quoted in Bruening, "Triumvirs," 131.

13. Michael W. Bruening, *Refusing to Kiss the Slipper: Opposition to Calvinism in the Francophone Reformation* (Oxford University Press, 2021), 54–55; and Oberman, "Calvin and Farel," 10–20.

14. See chap. 3, below.

15. Bruening, "Triumvirs," 132.

16. Robert M. Kingdon, "Confessionalism in Calvin's Geneva," *Archiv für Reformationsgeschichte* 96 (2005): 109–16.

to speak for francophone evangelical Christianity with the same arrogance as the Catholicism from which they had all recently departed?[17]

In the end, it is impossible to understand Calvin as refugee theologian apart from friendships with men who empowered his ministry, shared the load, and even taught him a few things. Calvin's first anti-Nicodemite publication targeted Gérard Roussel for becoming a bishop in the French Catholic Church.[18] Roussel was part of the Meaux Circle of reform-minded Catholics whom Farel loved to deride as compromisers. Calvin's sharpness toward so-called Nicodemites was something he could easily have learned from his older colleague. Like Farel, who officiated Calvin's wedding, Viret was someone around whom Calvin could truly let down his guard.[19] He called Viret his "dearest friend," even seeking him out to vacation together.[20] A native Swiss, Viret fled persecutions in Paris after his university studies. He was known for warmth and a sense of humor, popular with others in ways Calvin never managed to become. Though frequently credited as a solo act, the Calvin we remember through his writings cannot be separated from the support of these friends.[21]

This cooperation extended to their care of refugees. In December 1553, Calvin wrote to Farel about distributing a substantial gift to support poor exiles in Geneva, Lausanne, and Neuchâtel.[22] Ruthless persecution of evangelicals during the reign of England's Queen Mary (1553–58) prompted further coordination between the "holy trio" in their ministry to exiles. Calvin routinely supplied letters of reference for English and Scottish refugees moving between cities, enlisting Viret and Farel to help secure accommodations for exiles.[23] Calvin knew firsthand the benefit of a warm welcome. After receiving the boot from Geneva in 1538, he and Farel wrote Heinrich Bullinger with their side of the story.[24] The letter asserts their shared call from God and persecution by God's enemies, first in France, now in Geneva. Most of all, it seeks Bullinger's sympathy for two maligned exiles. The trio could also give as good as they got. Upon returning to Geneva, Calvin wrote his friends belittling a fellow pastor, Henri de La Mare, who had sided with those who expelled

---

17. Bruening, *Refusing to Kiss the Slipper*, 300–303.
18. *Two Letters* (1537; COR IV/4:1–119). The second letter addresses Roussel, the first Calvin's former friend Nicolas Duchemin (COR IV/4:xx–xxv).
19. Calvin to Farel, February 28, 1538 (Bonnet, 4:110).
20. Calvin to Viret, March 27, 1547 (Bonnet, 2:108; CO 12:505–6); Calvin to Viret, December 26, 1547 (Bonnet, 2:152; CO 12:639); Calvin to Viret, July 23, 1550 (Bonnet, 2:275; CO 13:603–4).
21. Bruening, "Triumvirs," 132–35.
22. Calvin to Farel, December 30, 1553 (Bonnet, 2:448; CO 14:723–24).
23. See, e.g., Calvin to Viret, November 20, 1553 (Bonnet, 2:439–40; CO 14:667); and Calvin to Viret, March 1, 1554 (Bonnet, 3:28–29).
24. Calvin and Farel to Bullinger, June 1538 (Bonnet, 4:392–400; CO 10:203–9).

Calvin and Farel.[25] Such skirmishes shed light on why Calvin characterized his pastoral calling as a struggle in exile, marked by constant conflict in an inhospitable world, conflict that stemmed from one's loyalty and belonging to God. It was a vision of reform that Calvin's best friends shared. For better or worse, their priorities were his, and Calvin's foes were theirs as well. The refugee theologian was never without his trusted inner circle.

A Refugee Ministry in Geneva

Calvin was pastor and teacher in Geneva where, for nearly three decades, he served fellow refugees in a relationship both strengthened and complicated by his own status as a foreigner. Chief among Calvin's pastoral duties was regular preaching to the congregation gathered at St. Pierre, the city's main cathedral. Calvin also preached in St. Gervais and La Madeleine, the other two parishes established by the 1541 *Ecclesiastical Ordinances* as official sites of worship.[26] As is the case with most preachers, his sermons favor some themes. Political exile appears frequently as a matter of current events. But it was also much more than that. For a disparate community comprising native Genevans and religious refugees from all over Europe, Calvin did not simply acknowledge exile. He presented a theological account of exile that offered a sense of belonging around shared markers such as common humanity and identity as the family of God. Anti-foreign sentiment strained relations between neighbors, resulting in particular resentment toward Calvin himself, whose immigrant status diminished his authority with some. Preaching became a means of addressing cultural divisions. In sermons on the Psalms, Calvin comforts those who fled home and country for an uncertain situation in Geneva, where they received less than the welcome they expected. Take heart, the reformer counsels, even in exile they remain "nonetheless in the house of God."[27] Calvin's efforts to forge a unified community across factions also addressed those who received refugees. In a 1558 sermon on Galatians 6:9–11, Calvin invokes the same household imagery in a strong appeal to receive even the "unfamiliar," "friendless," and "most foreign" as one's kin and fellow bearers of God's image. Shared faith requires welcoming outsiders as "brothers" whom God has "gathered together . . . as children . . . in one house."[28]

---

25. William G. Naphy, *Calvin and the Consolidation of the Genevan Reformation* (Manchester University Press, 1994), 59–60.

26. Elsie Anne McKee, *The Pastoral Ministry and Worship in Calvin's Geneva* (Droz, 2016), 460–502.

27. *Four Sermons* (CO 8:439).

28. Serm. Gal. 6:9–11, May 1, 1558 (CO 51:106–7).

Both newcomers and those already in Geneva—more and more of whom were immigrants—must learn to embrace this spiritual family. Still, divisions persisted and vexed Calvin's decades-long ministry.

Like many cities during the Reformation, Geneva underwent transformations that would have been unimaginable just a generation before. Calvin's ministry coincided with dramatic changes, many of which had nothing to do with him.[29] Geneva's embrace of Protestantism, abolishing the Roman Mass just months prior to Calvin's arrival in 1536, set into motion a trajectory that included the city's emergence as a popular destination for thousands migrating for religious reasons. We must remember that Calvin did not start this trend but was, in fact, one among a flow of immigrants arriving from France since the 1520s. Also unrelated to Calvin was the city's political and physical precariousness. It was dependent on the military support of Swiss neighbors, especially Bern, and within close striking distance of France and the Duchy of Savoy, from which Geneva had asserted independence by 1535. Maintaining a measure of autonomy from powerful neighbors with a vested interest in Geneva's politics and resources was no small feat for local magistrates. On top of this, city officials had to negotiate the internal balance of power with leaders of a newly reformed church brimming with their own aspirations for Geneva. Another development that predated Calvin was the city's decision in 1531 to raze its suburbs as a defensive measure against military threats.[30] This sensible move, to protect residents behind city walls and to clear sight lines for military defense, had unintended consequences. Bringing thousands of refugees into close proximity with Genevans ripened tempers. Simultaneously, established citizens loyal to Savoy and the old church departed for friendlier parts, amplifying perception of foreigners' numbers and impact. To accommodate population growth, city planners simply added stories to existing buildings, stacking more people on Geneva's already-crowded footprint. Even a populace that had supported independence from Savoy and the Roman Church could not anticipate the tensions a swell of émigrés brought to cramped quarters. Such was the table set by 1536 for the novice pastor from Noyon.

Upon Calvin's arrival, Geneva's internal divisions and conflicts quickly escalated into a maelstrom around his own rising prominence. Bernese influence produced a rupture between officials and ministers over the limits of ecclesiastical authority. Calvin and Farel balked when the magistrates imposed

---

29. See the fine essays in Jon Balserak, ed., *A Companion to the Reformation in Geneva* (Brill, 2021).

30. E. William Monter, *Calvin's Geneva* (Robert E. Krieger, 1975), 2–3.

Bern's liturgy, and they refused to administer Easter Communion. Caught up in the city's delicate dance with Bern's patronage, the pair were sent packing in 1538. A key figure in Calvin's 1541 recall to Geneva was Ami Perrin, who was once numbered among the "Guillermin" faction named for its support of (Guillaume) Farel. Perrin became leader of the self-proclaimed *Enfants de Genève*, a patriot group of social elites that traced its roots to the city's earlier struggle for independence from Savoy.[31] He was Calvin's chief antagonist when the latter's reforms clashed with Geneva's old ruling class. Calvin, for his part, dismissed the Perrinist *Enfants* as "Libertines" who wanted only to justify immoral behavior. The conflict drew in prominent members of society at all levels of government, making elections particularly fraught. People could not look away when the head of a native family, instrumental to Geneva's independence, squared off against the rigid leader of its predominantly immigrant clergy, himself a refugee. The symbolic struggle against a new kind of foreign oppression was not lost on citizens. The Consistory, comprising pastors and lay officials, gave civil leaders a voice alongside ministers in church discipline. Calvin's exercise of discipline included once refusing Communion to a prominent (but unrepentant) citizen "over my dead body," which did little to quell complaints about pastoral overreach.[32]

Outsiders kept coming, owing to both Calvin's fame and circumstances beyond his control. Anti-Protestant developments, such as Emperor Charles V's "Edict of Blood" (1550), French King Henry II's Edict of Châteaubriant (1551), and the accession of Mary Tudor to the English throne (1553) made the early 1550s particularly deadly for evangelicals. Waves of persecution in the Netherlands, France, and England forced thousands out of these places in search of freedom and safety. By 1557 Geneva's population had doubled over a decade, owing in large part to this international community of refugees, many drawn by Calvin's teaching. This dizzying multiplication of cultural diversity added pressure to already limited resources, optimizing conditions for misunderstanding within the city's tight confines. Refugees poured in from Poland, Italy, England, and the Low Countries in sufficient numbers to establish their own communities within Genevan society. They worshiped in their mother tongues and devised systems for supporting their own poor and infirm.[33] Besides welcoming refugees in large numbers, Geneva under Calvin's

---

31. Gary W. Jenkins, *Calvin's Tormentors: Understanding the Conflicts That Shaped the Reformer* (Baker Academic, 2018), 77–92.

32. Naphy, *Consolidation*, 184–86; also Christian Grosse, *L'excommunication de Philibert Berthelier: Histoire d'un conflit d'identité aux premiers temps de la Réforme genevoise, 1547–1555* (Société d'histoire et d'archéologie de Genève, 1995).

33. Monter, *Calvin's Geneva*, 165–87.

leadership helped relocate thousands who could not be accommodated, further cementing its reputation as a sanctuary city.

The largest, most influential, and arguably most complicated migrant community was the French. Their experience in Geneva anticipated patterns that would characterize the later diaspora of Reformed exiles, including those displaced from central Europe during the Thirty Years' War (1618–48) after Calvin's lifetime.[34] The Calvinist theology that spoke to these later experiences of persecution, migration, and exile originated in Calvin's ministry among the displaced from France.[35] Genevans spoke Savoyard, a local dialect of French, which made for easier daily interaction with French émigrés. Refugees entered Genevan life as both naturalized citizens, who could vote, and registered aliens—in the process rewiring the city's circuits of political and cultural influence. Many who came were wealthy merchants and tradespeople, whose resources and skills made for easy access to citizenship, whether granted or purchased. Among these were Robert Estienne, erstwhile printer to the French monarchy, and Jean Crespin, the attorney who took up publishing and chronicled the heroic stories of French Protestant martyrs. Both were instrumental in producing Calvin's works, connecting Geneva to the European book trade, contributing to the city's rapid ascent as a publishing center, and supporting the pastors' efforts to influence French affairs.[36] Scores of less prominent refugees also found their way to Geneva. As in other cities of asylum, Geneva's poor migrants were a source of anxiety and resentment, competing with citizens and *natifs* (nonvoting, and often impoverished, locals) for work and shared resources. A fund dedicated to poor relief among French refugees, the *Bourse Française*, helped soften the blow.[37]

Linguistic similarity did little to ensure cultural affinity. Often the opposite was true, as the ability to communicate simply escalated tensions. Again, a flashpoint was the rocky relationship between prominent families, such as the Perrins and Favres, and their immigrant pastors. Philibert Berthelier's offer to "belch or fart" instead, when censured for interrupting Calvin's preaching with a coughing fit, exemplifies this spirit of resistance.[38] Like other refugees whose lofty ideals led them into exile, Geneva's pastors adopted a stricter, more dogmatic religious outlook than their hosts. Upon returning from

---

34. Ole Peter Grell, *Brethren in Christ: A Calvinist Network in Reformation Europe* (Cambridge University Press, 2011).

35. Ole Peter Grell, "The Creation of a Calvinist Identity in the Reformation Period," in *Religion as an Agent of Change*, ed. Per Ingesman (Brill, 2016), 149–65.

36. Andrew Pettegree, *The French Book and the European Book World* (Brill, 2007), 89–106.

37. Jeannine E. Olson, *Calvin and Social Welfare: Deacons and the Bourse Française* (Susquehanna University Press, 1989).

38. Jenkins, *Calvin's Tormenters*, 77.

Strasbourg, Calvin led a purge of unqualified ministers, further homogenizing a "Company of Pastors" that would include no native Genevans until the seventeenth century.[39] Bans on dancing, card playing, and the cherished tradition of giving children names of saints at baptism stirred intense opposition. For the first two decades of Calvin's ministry, conflict with the *Enfants* destabilized his standing in Geneva. The ministers took their case to the court of public opinion, especially making use of sermons. Meanwhile, partisans for and against Calvin vied for control of the government. Relief came in 1555, when voters elected Calvin's supporters as all four city syndics, the chief administrators responsible for Geneva's operations. That same year a series of public disruptions resulted in Perrin's flight to Bern in May, sealing his faction's defeat.[40]

The refugee theologian, at once celebrated and reviled, encountered uneven reception not only among native Genevans but also among fellow newcomers. Many came for Calvin's teaching, which vigorously repeated reasons for rejecting Romanism and even for leaving their homeland. Critics accused Calvin of courting immigration for political support, a claim he explicitly refuted.[41] Still, some refugees clearly followed Calvin's promise of pure religion to Geneva only to be sorely disappointed by what they found there. The reformer's sermons frequently rebuke disillusioned migrants, who were not above stirring the pot in their own ways. Genevan Protestantism, ostensibly united in Reformed doctrine, varied in practical matters that caused strife between neighbors. Unlike their native hosts, refugees chose to leave family, community, and livelihood for their faith, often at great financial and relational cost. The religious fervor that drove such decisions could boil over into moral complaints against Genevans, such as when French exiles tried to enforce old edicts against public swearing long regarded with indifference in Geneva.[42] Judgmental immigrants did not mix well with the less observant in daily life, provoking annoyance that was easy to redirect toward Geneva's foreign-born pastors. Calvin's prominence as Zealot-in-Chief was a perception he did little to soften. Still, others applauded his rigor and probably wished for more of it in his church. Diverse local reception meant negative publicity exerted constant pressure on Calvin's ministry—viewed by some as

39. Naphy, *Consolidation*, 53–79.
40. Naphy, *Consolidation*, 167–232.
41. Eugénie Droz, "Calvin et les Nicodemites," in *Chemins de l'hérésie: Textes et documents*, 4 vols. (Slatkine, 1970–76), 1:155–57; Calvin, *Four Sermons* (CO 8:419–24); and Calvin to the church at Poitiers, February 20, 1555 (Bonnet, 3:147; CO 15:443).
42. See, e.g., the case involving Humbert Troillet, rebuked for blaspheming while working in a field; *Registres du Consistoire de Genève au temps de Calvin*, 18 vols., ed. Isabella M. Watt et al. (Droz, 1996–2024), 12:224, 231–34.

a reminder of how foreigners were changing Geneva, by others as the embodiment of disappointed hopes in exile.

Calvin attempted to unite disparate religious cultures in Geneva with an inviting, if uncompromising, theology of the present life as spiritual exile. His preaching stressed the church's identity as family of God and sojourners in the present life. This meant that exile was not the concern of émigrés alone. Often viewed as a dividing category, exile was recast as a shared experience. Immigrant and native alike were pilgrims en route to a heavenly home. Each belonged to God and also to one another. Welcoming outsiders was just the beginning for Genevans, whom Calvin called to self-identify as exiles regardless of whether they had migrated to Geneva or had lived there from birth. Applying the language of displacement to all opened new possibilities for imagining solidarity around religious reform. This shared identity further shaped the church's ministry priorities. Calvin persistently argued for mobilizing the diaconate and directing the city's resources toward poor refugees.[43] Highlighting the plight of the friendless, Calvin stressed generosity as the ethical demand of spiritual solidarity when he crafted and defended policies regarding refugee assimilation and poor relief.[44]

Calvin's Lifelong Preoccupation with Reforming France

Scholars have long recognized Geneva's role in training and clandestinely sending refugee pastors back into France to serve the French Reformed Church.[45] Despite the unsettled state of Genevan affairs, Calvin always maintained active efforts to influence French religion and politics from the time of his arrival in Geneva.[46] France was geographically close and never far from Calvin's mind.[47] His writings abound with references to French developments, with many letters and even entire publications written for audiences in France. This was not nostalgia for a romanticized past. Calvin, after all, looked back on his

---

43. *Inst.* IV.4.5–9; Elsie A. McKee, *John Calvin on the Diaconate and Liturgical Almsgiving* (Droz, 1984), 109–13; and Olson, *Social Welfare*, 29–36.

44. Esther Chung-Kim, *Economics of Faith: Poor Relief in Early Modern Geneva*, Oxford Studies in Historical Theology (Oxford University Press), 151–60.

45. Robert M. Kingdon, *Geneva and the Coming of the Wars of Religion in France, 1555–1563*, rev. ed. (1956; repr., Droz, 2007).

46. Jon Balserak, "Geneva's Use of Lies, Deceit, and Simulation in Their Efforts to Reform France, 1536–1563," *Harvard Theological Review* 112 (2019): 76–100; and Jon Balserak, *Geneva's Use of Lies, Deceit, and Subterfuge, 1536–1563* (Oxford University Press, 2024).

47. Max Engammare, "Une certaine idée de la France chez Jean Calvin l'exilé," *Bulletin de la société de l'histoire du protestantisme français: Études, documents, chronique littéraire* 155 (2009): 15–27.

French upbringing as a period of darkness in idolatry that required rescue, not return.[48] A letter to French Protestants in 1559 predicts waves of persecution after the Treaty of Cateau-Cambrésis, a peace accord with Spain that freed the French monarchy to focus domestically on eradicating Huguenot "heretics." Calvin urges evangelicals not to fear death, which for "pilgrims in this world" amounts to entering their "enduring inheritance." God will ensure that the harder "the wicked strive" to erase God's name "from the earth," the more the blood of Protestant martyrs will make God's name known.[49] This was bold assurance coming from a refugee reformer safely ensconced in Geneva.

Calvin's fixation on reforming his homeland was as strategic as it was persistent. Concern to provide an educated ministry for French Reformed churches informed the founding of the Genevan Academy, which didn't launch until 1559 despite being planned since 1541.[50] From the rhetoric of writings calling on believers to defect from French Catholicism, to organizing Geneva as a training center for ministers and source of funds for churches in France, Calvin's efforts also involved the Company of Pastors' subterfuge to cover the extent of these activities.[51] Calvin and his associates hid the use of the *Bourse Française* to fund clandestine work in France, not only from outsiders but even from Geneva's magistrates. Meddling in military and political affairs could provoke unwanted conflict with France. For all his efforts, however, a Protestant France never materialized. Still, one cannot speak of Calvin as refugee theologian apart from his preoccupation with French affairs and how this shaped his ministry in exile. This is especially apparent in the reformer's militant posture toward French political and religious authorities, his multifaceted publishing agenda, and other activities that similarly sowed seeds of evangelical resistance to French Catholicism.

Calvin, like other mainstream reformers, held that kings and princes express God's authority and therefore must be obeyed as a matter of loyalty to God. Also like other reformers, Calvin criticized Rome's misappropriation of secular authority to the papacy. Pope and prince alike answer to a higher authority.[52] For all its niceties, Calvin's preface to Francis pleads the case of persecuted evangelicals before the French monarchy while assigning the final

---

48. See chap. 1, above.

49. Calvin to the faithful in France, June 1559 (Bonnet, 4:49–54; CO 17:570–74).

50. Karin Maag, *Seminary or University? The Genevan Academy and Reformed Higher Education, 1560–1620* (Ashgate, 1995), 8–34.

51. Balserak, *Subterfuge*, 122–65.

52. The actual relationship between church and state was not, for Calvin, as cut-and-dried as positing a distinct but related "two kingdoms" of Christ. For instance, the Consistory was, for Calvin, clearly a religious institution in which the civil magistrate played an active role. See William Naphy, "Church and State in Calvin's Geneva," in *Calvin and the Church: Papers*

verdict to the "mighty hand of the Lord."[53] Calvin's revisions to the *Institutes* consistently affirm the same basic position—that magistrates demand honor as God's surrogates while always remaining accountable to divine law.[54] This makes additions that appeared in 1559 all the more fascinating. In the closing paragraphs of the 1559 *Institutes*, Calvin inserts the example of Daniel's resistance to King Darius's "impious edict" (Dan. 6). Daniel, Calvin writes, was justified insofar as Darius, "in lifting up his horns against God," had "abrogated his power."[55] Resistance was one thing, arguably implied in Calvin's insistence on pure worship in defiance of local laws. But what did it mean for a king to abrogate his power? Did Calvin believe this was happening in his day? On the record, he was ever careful to forbid rebellion, even in the case of unjust persecution. While he did offer theological rationale for lesser magistrates to marshal armed resistance as a restraint on higher authorities, this was not an option for individual citizens.[56] Daniel, after all, led no armed rebellion. Calvin's narrowly defined pathway for resistance involved two legitimately installed magistrates. Would the rules change under a "king" in name only, no longer legitimate in God's view? Calvin left this unanswered. He never called publicly for violent rebellion. Yet decrying French Catholicism as idolatry was a form of treason, given the church's official relation to the crown. Far from passive in seeking change, Calvin made no secret of his wish for a Protestant France, and he was happy to accelerate this outcome if he could.

From exile, Calvin was an outsider to French politics. His platform as a theologian rested on persuasion. Plenty of people rejected his opinion. For those who took it to heart, Calvin's theology presented French evangelicals with an irresolvable dilemma. His anti-Nicodemite polemic, for example, brooks no compromise between the faithful and the old church, which was integral to the monarchy in a nation that maintained a centuries-old identity rooted in "one faith, one law, one king."[57] For thousands, this meant the hard decision to leave France, a path Calvin encourages in both publications and private letters.[58] Calvin's *Four Sermons* (1552) is an especially forceful

---

Presented at the 13th *Colloquium of the Calvin Studies Society, May 24–26, 2001*, ed. David Foxgrover (Calvin Studies Society, 2002), 20.

53. *Inst.* 31 (OS 3:30); see chap. 1, above.

54. *Inst.* IV.20.1–32 (OS 5:471–502).

55. *Inst.* IV.20.32 (OS 5:502).

56. *Inst.* IV.20.31 (OS 5:501); for the ambiguity of Calvin's stated position, see Carlos Eire, *War Against the Idols: The Reformation of Worship from Erasmus to Calvin* (Cambridge University Press, 1986), 289.

57. Raymond A. Mentzer, "French Christianity in the Early 1500s," in *John Calvin in Context*, ed. R. Ward Holder (Cambridge University Press, 2020), 17–23.

58. See, e.g., Calvin to Falais, October 14, 1543 (Bonnet, 1:395–98; CO 11:628–31); and Calvin to an Italian lady, 1553 (Bonnet, 2:450–51; CO 14a:739–42).

appeal to French evangelicals to choose exile over idolatry.[59] Many went to Geneva. Others, while sympathetic to the argument for flight, chose to stay put. Organizers of the French Reformed Church considered themselves Calvin's disciples; Geneva's *Ecclesiastical Ordinances* served as the model for their polity.[60] Geneva's Company of Pastors thus played a significant role in Protestantism's organization within France's borders, where the Reformed Church convened under the noses of Catholic authorities, exacerbating tensions that led to violent clashes. Religious wars erupted in 1562, with powerful factions in the royal court lining up variously for and against Protestantism.[61] Theological rhetoric stoked hatred between French Protestants and Catholics as preachers on both sides portrayed the enemy as worse than infidels. They were subhuman, requiring cruel punishment or, better yet, extermination in God's name.[62] French authorities were understandably wary of Geneva's influence and propaganda. Directives like the Edict of Châteaubriant banned Genevan books and attempted to sever links to the city. Calvin's theology, even without calling for violence, cannot be held blameless for such consequences in French society. One simply cannot imagine the French Wars of Religion (1562–98) apart from Calvinism's unyielding demands for religious purity and resistance to Catholicism as vile idolatry.

Calvin's publishing included works produced for the Huguenot minority. These differ from Latin writings that turned Geneva into a printing center for an international audience. Some French works were translations from Latin, such as the 1560 *Institutes*, though Calvin's French publishing was never merely a translation project.[63] Until the final edition, the French *Institutes* remained largely independent of its Latin counterpart, organized specifically to suit the needs of evangelicals in Calvin's homeland.[64] Similarly,

---

59. Rodolphe Peter, "Genève dans la prédication de Calvin," in *Calvinus ecclesiae genevensis custos*, ed. Wilhelm H. Neuser (Peter Lang, 1982), 24–26; Droz, "Nicodemites," 156–65; and see chap. 8, below.

60. R. J. Knecht, *The Rise and Fall of Renaissance France: 1483–1610*, Blackwell Classic Histories of Europe (Blackwell, 2001), 243–44.

61. Mack P. Holt, *The French Wars of Religion, 1562–1629*, 2nd ed. (Cambridge University Press, 2005).

62. Natalie Zemon Davis, "The Rites of Violence," in *Society and Culture in Early Modern France: Eight Essays* (Stanford University Press, 1975), 152–87; and Barbara Diefendorf, *Beneath the Cross: Catholics and Huguenots in Sixteenth-Century Paris* (Oxford University Press, 1991), 49–63, 145–58.

63. Jean-François Gilmont, *John Calvin and the Printed Book*, trans. Karin Maag (Truman State University Press, 2005), 303–6. Calvin preferred to produce his own French translations but rarely translated his own work into Latin, delegating this task to others, most frequently Nicolas des Gallars.

64. J. W. Marmelstein, *Étude comparative des textes latins et français de l'institution de la religion Chrétienne par Jean Calvin* (Wolters, 1923), 35–50.

nearly all of Calvin's anti-Nicodemite writings appeared first in French.⁶⁵ This both launched an exodus of the faithful from France in search of pure worship and fleshed out a strong martyrdom ideal within French Protestantism. Calvin and Viret persistently called on the Reformed to choose death before compromise.⁶⁶ In 1544 Calvin cited 1 Peter 4:12 ("Do not be surprised at the fiery ordeal that is taking place") and asserted his willingness to die resisting idolatry, should God require it.⁶⁷

Calvin's sermons constituted another major publishing initiative targeting France. Calvin had little time to revise his sermons and did not like the idea of publishing words meant for a specific local context.⁶⁸ Yet he relented to the requests of French refugees, who hired stenographers to record his preaching. To one in particular, Denis Raguenier, we owe thanks for producing the bulk of Calvin's surviving sermon manuscripts. Except for the self-edited *Four Sermons* (1552), Calvin had almost no role in publishing his sermons.⁶⁹ Instead, he supported an arrangement in which Geneva's printers directed proceeds from the sale of these volumes to the French refugee community. In this way, Calvin's publications benefited refugees in Geneva while simultaneously extending, through printed works, the reach of the city's pulpits. Destined first for French communities in need of preaching, Calvin's sermons also found a large following among English readers.⁷⁰ This enterprise ensured that Calvin's teaching on exile could cultivate the spiritual imaginations of millions around themes of suffering, nurture, pilgrimage, and homecoming.

Finally, the production of French vernacular Bibles and the massive undertaking of producing the *Genevan Psalter*, a congregational songbook of metrically arranged psalms set to music, required the combined efforts of all the city's printers. Even so, they scarcely kept up with demand among Huguenots. French publishers had to be enlisted to pick up the slack, often at great risk to their own safety.⁷¹ Ensuring that these works reached intended audiences "behind enemy

---

65. See chap. 8, below.
66. Nikki Shepardson, *Burning Zeal: The Rhetoric of Martyrdom and the Protestant Community in Reformation France, 1520–1570* (Lehigh University Press, 2007); and Brad S. Gregory, *Salvation at Stake: Christian Martyrdom in Early Modern Europe* (Harvard University Press, 1999), 154–55.
67. *Answer to the Nicodemites*, 1544 (CO 6:607).
68. Gilmont, *Printed Book*, 74–81.
69. For *Four Sermons*, see T. H. L. Parker, *Calvin's Preaching* (T&T Clark, 1992), 60–61; and Kenneth J. Woo, *Nicodemism and the English Calvin, 1544–1584* (Brill, 2019), 1–68. Revised and published in 1552, these sermons were likely delivered in 1549. Erwin Mülhaupt, "Einleitung," in *SC* VII:xxxviii–xxxix.
70. I. M. Green, *Print and Protestantism in Early Modern England* (Oxford University Press, 2000), 168–238.
71. Pettegree, *French Book*, 96–97.

lines," as it were, required coordinated efforts between Geneva's Company of Pastors, the *Bourse Française*, and brave booksellers. Laurent de Normandie, for example, paid anonymous smugglers to transport books—containing the more than one hundred thousand words Calvin wrote annually—to countless French Reformed believers who hungered for these resources.[72]

Returning briefly to a matter introduced earlier, a lingering question for readers is whether Calvin's intentions for France went beyond fanning the flames of religious and political discontent. Did he seek war as an outcome of his theological program in exile? Calvin's relationship with the growing, and increasingly impatient, Huguenot movement was complicated. As an outsider, Calvin was nevertheless deeply connected to France through his teaching, correspondence, and diplomatic efforts. Letters to people across all strata of French society cultivated strategic relationships and provided spiritual counsel eagerly sought by many, while leaving others unconvinced about Calvin's hard line against Catholicism.[73] Many letters sent into France were signed with a pseudonym to hide Calvin's identity but, even more, to protect recipients. Though he was never personally at risk after his own flight, Calvin always maintained interest in the plight of the persecuted. On several occasions he wrote to prisoners awaiting execution with consolation and encouragement to hold fast to ideals they shared with others.[74] The presence of French nobility among Geneva's émigrés opened additional pathways of influence, such as sending Beza to court the friends of these men and women as allies to the evangelical cause.

These activities, alongside fundraising and turning Geneva into a sending ground for French Reformed pastors, were not in themselves inconsistent with Calvin's eschewal of war. Yet his increasingly violent rhetoric against idolaters and his deception about Geneva's role in French affairs point to greater involvement in pursuing regime change than his stated positions suggest. Calvin's preface to his lectures on Daniel, addressed to French evangelicals in 1560, applies strikingly violent language to the notion of exterminating idolatry in France at all costs.[75] While Calvin and Beza disavowed the failed Amboise Conspiracy of 1560, which sought a Protestant military takeover of the throne after the death of King Henry II, they did not oppose this in

---

72. Olson, *Social Welfare*, 50–69, 168–69; and Pettegree, *French Book*, 91–92, 95.

73. Knecht, *Renaissance France*, 275–77; and Charmarie Jenkins Blaisdell, "Calvin's Letters to Women: The Courting of Ladies in High Places," *Sixteenth Century Journal* 13 (1982): 67–84.

74. Calvin to five men imprisoned at Lyons, June 10, 1552 (Bonnet, 2:350–53; CO 14:331–34); and Calvin to women imprisoned at Paris, September 16, 1557 (Bonnet, 3:363–66; CO 16:632–34).

75. Balserak, *Subterfuge*, 221–28; and Jon Balserak, *John Calvin as Sixteenth-Century Prophet* (Oxford University Press, 2014), 102–78.

principle. Calvin viewed the accession of fifteen-year-old Francis II and his regents from the staunchly Catholic Guise family as a grave threat, prompting him to redouble efforts to see a Reformed "Prince of the Blood" (descendent of the royal line) mount a challenge for the French throne. In letters exchanged with Beza, Bullinger, François Hotman, and Jean Sturm (among others), Calvin did not hide his belief that the monarchy was stolen from the Protestant Antoine of Navarre.[76] Jon Balserak has shown how Geneva's secretive program to resource French Protestantism's war against idolatry by providing books, pastors, and direct assistance to Reformed churches pivoted seamlessly toward supporting militarized regime change. Letters exchanged in 1559 and 1560 implicate the Genevans in another plot, the Maligny affair, to supply funds and weapons for Antoine's claim to the throne and suggest Calvin's attempts to conceal this.[77] Similarly, Calvin's sermons on 2 Samuel, delivered in 1562 as war broke out in France, signaled openness to resistance by private citizens. Perhaps his restrained position on violence could not fully contain his hope for France's reformation.[78]

If not, who could blame him? That the change Calvin longed for his whole adult life seemed within reach must have been exhilarating, especially if one imagined this to be God's will. While the precise ways Calvin's motives come out in his theology remain elusive, the growth of French Protestantism surely influenced his teaching in exile. Calvin cultivated a theological imagination around exilic themes to unite those outside France with siblings in faith struggling to establish pure religion in the kingdom he fled years earlier. Readers will find notes of comfort, conviction, and militance as Calvin interpreted violence as both present experience and ongoing possibility, even accelerating such developments with his teaching.

The International Horizons of Calvin's Community

Calvin's interest in reforming the church always extended beyond Geneva, France, and Romandy. Geneva's influence in the English Reformation grew as Calvin's star rose and Zurich's diminished for English reformers.[79] There were missteps, such as Calvin's attempt to insert himself into English affairs upon the Protestant Elizabeth I's sudden accession after years of harsh persecution

---

76. Calvin to Hotman and Sturm, June 4, 1560 (Bonnet, 4:109; CO 18:98).
77. Balserak, *Subterfuge*, 169–97.
78. N. M. Sutherland, *The Huguenot Struggle for Recognition* (Yale University Press, 1980), 88–91; and Balserak, "Lies," 86.
79. Andrew Pettegree, "La réception du Calvinisme en Angleterre," in *Calvin et ses contemporains: Actes du colloque de Paris 1995*, ed. Olivier Millet (Droz, 1998), 261–82.

under her Catholic sister, Mary (1553–58). Elizabeth ignored Calvin's letters and rejected the gift of his commentary on Isaiah.[80] Her ears still rang with the misogynistic writings of John Knox, the future Scottish reformer whose *First Trumpet Blast Against the Monstrous Regiment of Women* (1558) was a brutal rhetorical broadside against female rulers. Intended for Mary, the screed appeared just in time for Elizabeth's coronation. Knox wrote from exile in Geneva, and the queen blamed his hosts. The damage was beyond Calvin's power to repair. Despite this rocky start, Calvin's profound influence on Elizabeth's kingdom extended far beyond her long reign (1558–1603). No other Continental reformer's works were translated into English more in the sixteenth century than Calvin's, which made "Calvinism" the default theology of factions that, despite shared doctrine, bitterly disagreed about the forms and practices of English Protestantism.[81] Beyond England, the wider growth of international Calvinism followed a similarly indirect course. Heiko Oberman's proposal of a "Reformation of the Refugees" describes Calvin's attempt to establish a common theology across borders. In truth, a distinctive Reformed confessional identity uniting believers scattered across Europe came into being apart from Calvin's direct influence, after his death, and often without self-conscious relation to his legacy.[82] Beginning in the late 1560s, shared experiences of persecution and migration reinforced confessional ties between Reformed believers already connected through commercial and relational networks.[83] Italian Reformed families who fled Lucca in the 1560s, for example, intermarried with Protestants abroad and found their members among the waves of refugees fleeing France and the Netherlands in the 1570s and 1580s. The bonds of persecution and exile already strengthened their sense of shared identity even while they interpreted these events through their faith. Calvin never saw his theology take shape in these new contexts but was always open to its spread far and wide.

One way to broaden this reach was through theological consensus with others. Calvin's partnership with German-speaking reformers in Zurich, Strasbourg, and Basel involved forming close friendships with leaders such as Bucer in

---

80. Calvin to William Cecil, January 29, 1559 (Bonnet, 4:15–17); and Calvin to Cecil, May 1559 (Bonnet, 4:46–48).

81. Pettegree, "Réception," 270; Francis M. Higman, "Calvin's Works in Translation," in *Calvinism in Europe, 1540–1620*, ed. Andrew Pettegree et al. (Cambridge University Press, 1994), 87–88; Patrick Collinson, "England and International Calvinism, 1558–1640," in *International Calvinism, 1541–1715*, ed. Menna Prestwich (Clarendon, 1985), 197–223; Jane E. A. Dawson, "Knox, Goodman, and the 'Example of Geneva,'" in *The Reception of Continental Reformation in Britain*, ed. Polly Ha and Patrick Collinson (Oxford University Press, 2011), 107–35; and Peter Lake, "Calvinism and the English Church 1570–1635," *Past & Present* 114, no. 1 (1987): 35–47.

82. Grell, "Calvinist Identity," 149–65.

83. Grell, *Brethren in Christ*.

Strasbourg and Bullinger in Zurich. With the Zurichers, Calvin labored intensely to produce the Zurich Consensus (1549), which stated their common understanding of the Lord's Supper. Such ecumenism was also a matter of survival. A united front would better position Swiss Reformed churches against increasing criticism—from Rome, yes, but also from Lutheran and Anabaptist opponents.[84]

It is no exaggeration that Calvin brought international stature to Geneva's printing industry during the Reformation era. His writings turned the city into a publishing powerhouse, with printers in England and the Dutch Republic contributing to the steady output of Calvin's works in the decades following his death.[85] Like Luther before him, Calvin chose his publishers carefully, curating his image for international audiences. This meant using Geneva's printshops sparingly at first, mainly for French polemical tracts, while outsourcing his major Latin manuscripts—meant for wide, international distribution—to the gifted tradesmen in Strasbourg. This changed in the 1550s, when he judged Genevan printing standards to be sufficiently up to snuff for all his works.[86] Calvin's publishing for international audiences centered on the *Institutes* and biblical commentaries, the core curriculum of his teaching for students and pastors charged with teaching others.[87] One did not have to enroll in the Genevan Academy to learn from Calvin. His publications also included polemical works against heretics and works on topics ranging from predestination to sacraments. All this occupied much of Calvin's time and energy. His letters express anxieties about meeting deadlines for major multinational markets, such as the Frankfurt Book Fair, where Geneva's publishers sold many volumes twice a year.[88]

The prefaces to Calvin's major publications display his interest in foreign affairs and specific concern for the plight of exiles.[89] Dedications to English rulers encourage them to make progress for the evangelical cause. These include a number addressed to the teenage King Edward VI and his guardians.[90] Several prefaces highlight the needs of refugees as an international

---

84. R. Ward Holder, "The Pain of Agreement: Calvin and the Consensus Tigurinus," *Reformation & Renaissance Review* 18 (2016): 85–94.

85. Andrew Pettegree, "The Printed Word," in *John Calvin in Context*, ed. R. Ward Holder (Cambridge University Press, 2020), 211.

86. Pettegree, *French Book*, 95.

87. See chap. 3, below.

88. Gilmont, *Printed Book*, 220–22.

89. These include Calvin's commentary on Galatians, Ephesians, Philippians, and Colossians, dedicated to the Lutheran Duke of Württemberg (1548; CO 12:658); commentary on Hebrews, dedicated to King Sigismund Augustus of Poland (1549; CO 13:281–86); and lectures on the Minor Prophets, dedicated to King Gustavus Vasa of Sweden (1559; CO 17:445–48).

90. Commentaries on 1 and 2 Timothy (1548; CO 13:16–18); and James, 1 and 2 Peter, 1 John, and Jude (1551; CO 14:30–37); and the first edition of his Isaiah commentary (1551; CO 13:669–74).

issue, such as the dedications of his commentary on the Synoptic Gospels (1555) and lectures on Jeremiah and Lamentations (1563).[91] Dedicated, respectively, to leaders of Frankfurt and the Palatinate, Calvin commends their kindness to refugees in their midst. Closer to home, Calvin's preface to his commentary on John (1553) praises Geneva's magistrates for turning the city into a prominent asylum for refugees coming from all over Europe.[92] Such expressed concern for the conditions of exiles did not mean uncritically affirming refugees or praising their behavior. Calvin had little sympathy for exiles who acted entitled upon arrival, even if they followed his advice to get there.[93]

Calvin's letters shed light on his various international interests. Jules Bonnet's 1854 French edition, subsequently translated into English by David Constable and Marcus Robert Gilchrist, makes many of them accessible to English-language readers.[94] His pastoral letters often echo the teaching of his sermons, which we will examine in chapter 6, and present exile as comfort to God's elect, sometimes by way of excluding their enemies. In one example, the ministers of the church of Montbéliard in France had been banished on account of their Reformed faith. Calvin praises their commitment to pure religion, having chosen "exile over damnable dissimulation." To be cast out of their former charge was to find Christ, who was himself exiled when Montbéliard restored Catholicism.[95] Calvin similarly encourages others to embrace political exile for the sake of pure religion. Refusing to "defile yourself with superstition" invites hardship. But this was the way of "our father Abraham" in exile. "There is no spot on earth," Calvin writes to a friend considering flight to Geneva, "where you can be beyond the reach of trial, as indeed it is not reasonable to expect our faith to be exempt from anxieties."[96] Writing another Frenchman contemplating exile, Calvin tries to temper unrealistic expectations. Things could become even more difficult, but "you will have the pure doctrine of the Word, you will call upon His name in the fellowship of faithful men, you will enjoy the true use of the sacraments; . . . let us be

---

91. CO 15:710–12; 20:72–79.

92. CO 47:iv–vi.

93. Mirjam van Veen, "Living in Babylon: Calvin's Correspondence with Believers Living in Exile," in *Calvin, Exile, and Religious Refugees: Papers of the Thirteenth International Congress on Calvin Research*, ed. Arnold Huijgen and Karin Maag (Vandenhoeck & Ruprecht, 2024), 37–54.

94. For the limitations of Bonnet's translations, see Douglas Kelly, "The Transmission and Translation of the Collected Letters of John Calvin," *Scottish Journal of Theology* 30, no. 5 (1977): 432, 434.

95. Calvin to the Ministers of the Church of Montbéliard, January 16, 1549 (Bonnet, 2:208–9; CO 9:50).

96. Calvin to Budé, June 19, 1547 (Bonnet, 2:121; CO 12:543).

content with this invaluable blessing."⁹⁷ To the persecuted, Calvin counsels taking care while not neglecting nurture through corporate worship: "We must not allow the fear of persecutions to hinder us from seeking the food of life, and continuing under the guidance of our good Shepherd."⁹⁸ This is a matter of pressing forward during "the time of our pilgrimage." Similarly, Calvin movingly reminds women awaiting execution in a French prison that a homecoming lies before them, as it did for martyrs past, who "feared not to quit this perishable life to obtain a better one, full of glory and everlasting."⁹⁹ Exile as a distinctive identity plays a role in Calvin's letters to France, where he narrates persecution as a mark of "pilgrims in this world" who await an "enduring inheritance . . . when it pleases God to summon us away."¹⁰⁰

Calvin's theology of exile thus addressed a community without political borders. Its fruit never materialized as a single multinational church, instead finding expression in other ways. Diverse communities across the globe—from Scotland, to Hungary, to Indonesia—would embrace Calvin's theology amid shared experiences of persecution, migration, and refuge.¹⁰¹ Such resonance between Calvin's thought and later histories of displacement was possible because themes others would find relevant were central to his teaching from the beginning. The refugee theologian of Geneva addressed violence and political exile with comfort that never minimized these struggles in the present life but instead centered and elevated them as marks of belonging to God. This theological identity could relativize powerlessness and marginalization by setting these against an alternate account of home and belonging beyond the reach of rulers and idolators to disrupt or destroy. Spiritual exile redefined community across geopolitical boundaries, uniting Reformed Christianity beyond Calvin's lifetime—despite its increasingly diverse locations and expressions—with categories for theological kinship. In an early modern world very much in transit, there was great comfort in knowing where, and to whom, one belonged.

A Community's Contested Boundaries

But not everyone wanted to belong. For many, Calvin's vision of unity and consolation in exile was little more than an attempt to control followers, a

---

97. Calvin to unnamed Frenchman, October 18, 1548 (Bonnet, 2:181–82; CO 13:63–64).
98. Calvin to Christians at Poitou, September 3, 1554 (Bonnet, 3:69–71; CO 15:223–24).
99. Calvin to the women detained in prison at Paris, September 1557 (Bonnet, 3:366; CO 16:634).
100. Calvin to the brethren of France, June 1559 (Bonnet, 4:49–54; CO 17:570–74).
101. Philip Benedict, *Christ's Churches Purely Reformed: A Social History of Calvinism* (Yale University Press, 2002); Grell, *Brethren in Christ*; and Charles H. Parker, *Global Calvinism: Conversion and Commerce in the Dutch Empire, 1600–1800* (Yale University Press, 2022).

project that invited opposition both locally and abroad. His vision for unifying the church as spiritual exiles was specific and unyielding. In Geneva, the welcoming themes of comfort and nurture centered on practices of public worship overseen by a ministry carefully defined in the city's *Ecclesiastical Ordinances*.[102] Faithfulness in exile had a doctrinal and ecclesial flavor that did not agree with everyone. Calvin had little patience with dissent, decrying critics as "Libertines" (or worse). Even refugees were not spared his rebuke. From the pulpit, Calvin states his preference that ungrateful exiles "[break] their necks than ever set foot in this church, where they conduct themselves so badly."[103] The very markers of God's comforting presence in exile could become symbols of exclusion against those who refused to go along with Calvin's program.

Beyond Geneva, one can hardly blame those whom Calvin maligned as nonbelievers for being skeptical of his views. He derided Rome and secular rulers loyal to the papacy, to name just one example, as "false church," "anti-Christ," "the pope's executioners"—or simply "dragons" and "dogs" who preyed upon God's people in exile.[104] Yet Calvin also found himself at odds with other Protestants, not just Lutherans and Anabaptists but also fellow French-speaking Reformed evangelicals. The focal points of division were doctrines central to Calvin's account of the church's identity and nurture in exile. His teachings on predestination, ecclesiology, and sacraments were anything but comforting to evangelicals who opposed the way of Geneva. It was one thing to debate Lutherans, like Joachim Westphal (d. 1574), on the sacraments, where confessional divisions had already emerged and hope for any agreement was dim.[105] More concerning were the Reformed voices in Geneva's vicinity and throughout francophone Switzerland. This was another matter, especially dissent arising within Calvin's movement that turned others against Calvin and his lieutenants, Viret and Farel.[106] Such disputes over the priorities, boundaries, and identity of Reformed Christianity sharpened the polemical edge of Calvin's theology, which could also turn inward against those already in his community who lacked commitment to his doctrine. By attending to this context, we learn how Calvin used exile and related themes in his teaching on predestination, the church, and sacraments not only as a means of offering comfort in an age of displacement but also to insist on his own particular views about the church's identity and aspirations for its behavior. Later chapters will take up how the same theology of belonging in exile could both unite and divide people.

102. See chap. 5, below.
103. *Four Sermons* (CO 8:422).
104. *Inst.* IV.2.1–12 (OS 5.30–42); and Serm. Gen. 4:10–12, October 30, 1559 (*SC* XI/1:283–84).
105. See chap. 7, below.
106. Bruening, *Refusing to Kiss the Slipper*.

Conclusion

This chapter has surveyed the audiences Calvin addressed as refugee theologian. Along the way, I have gestured at how Calvin responded to challenges but have focused on the contexts shaping his message. We turn now to the message itself—particularly, to how Calvin the teacher, pastor, and polemicist addressed the various audiences identified in this chapter. Shaped by his own experience as a refugee, his theology found in exile a helpful concept for identifying, encouraging, and defending God's people amid realities wrought by religious violence. The same vision sharpened boundaries around a community scattered across political borders that looked for guidance to Calvin's Geneva.

For Further Reading

In Calvin's Words

1528–64 *Letters of John Calvin*. In Bonnet, vols. 1–4.

For Digging Deeper

Balserak, Jon. *Geneva's Use of Lies, Deceit, and Subterfuge, 1536–1563: Telling the Old, Old Story in Reformation France*. Oxford University Press, 2024.

Holt, Mack P. *The French Wars of Religion, 1562–1629*. 2nd ed. Cambridge University Press, 2005.

Jenkins, Gary W. *Calvin's Tormentors: Understanding the Conflicts That Shaped the Reformer*. Baker Academic, 2018.

Naphy, William G. *Calvin and the Consolidation of the Genevan Reformation*. Manchester University Press, 1994.

Olson, Jeannine E. *Calvin and Social Welfare: Deacons and the Bourse Française*. Susquehanna University Press, 1989.

PART TWO

Calvin as Teacher

THREE

Calvin's *Institutes* as Road Map

Theological Coordinates for an Exilic Imagination

> If you had insulted me personally, I would easily forgive this in light of your learning and credentials. But when I see that my ministry, which I have no doubt has been established and confirmed by God's call, is stabbed through my side, it would be treachery—not patience—if I were quiet and pretended not to mind. In [the church of Geneva] I discharged first the office of teacher, then pastor.
>
> —Calvin, *Reply to Sadoleto* (1539)[1]

> If we should think that through death we are recalled from exile to dwell in the fatherland, in the heavenly fatherland, would we get no comfort from this fact?
>
> —Calvin, *Institutes* (1559)[2]

Teacher to Refugees

The year was 1539, and Calvin had strong words for Cardinal Jacopo Sadoleto. He accused the Catholic leader of denigrating Calvin's "legitimate calling" as pastor and teacher in Geneva. Unlike fellow reformers Martin Bucer and Ulrich Zwingli, Calvin was never ordained to the Catholic priesthood. A further

---

1. John C. Olin, ed., *A Reformation Debate: Sadoleto's Letter to the Genevans and Calvin's Reply* (Harper & Row, 1966), 50; CO 5:386.
2. *Inst.* III.9.4–5 (OS 4:174–75).

irony is that he wrote from Strasbourg, having left Geneva under a cloud the year before. Ministry setbacks aside, Calvin remained undaunted about his calling from God, summarizing it this way in his will: "John Calvin, minister of the Word of God in the church of Geneva: . . . I have attempted according to the measure of grace I have been given, to teach [God's] Word purely, in both sermons and writings, and to expound Holy Scripture faithfully."[3] Above all, Calvin wanted to be remembered for teaching the Bible.

In Geneva, teachers and pastors held distinct church offices. Both were "ministers of the Word."[4] Their duties centered on interpreting scripture, but in different modes: "There is this difference between [pastors and teachers]: teachers are not put in charge of discipline, or administering the sacraments, or warning or exhortations, but only of scriptural interpretation—to keep doctrine whole and pure among believers. But the pastoral office includes all these functions."[5] Pastors preached sermons, led worship, and, with elders, oversaw daily congregational life. Teachers, or "doctors," focused on a narrower audience that included pastors and others charged with giving instruction. Doctors of the church ensured "that the purity of the gospel be not corrupted either by ignorance or by evil opinions."[6] They did this through scholarly writings and academic presentations. Beginning in 1560, the Genevan Academy was a key center for such scholarship.[7] The Academy aimed to produce both a learned citizenry and a well-trained ministry. Its lower school (the *schola privata*) grounded students in Latin, Greek, and religious subjects; its upper school (the *schola publica*) focused on preparing pastors, especially for churches in France. In his official capacity as a teacher, Calvin delivered lectures and wrote books, including biblical commentaries, for pastors, fellow academics, and students training for ministry. Audiences included communities in exile, like the French refugees Calvin served in Strasbourg, and persecuted evangelicals gathered clandestinely for worship.

Calvin's teaching circulated beyond Geneva in publications for international audiences. This meant that he could not possibly know, much less address in detail, every reader's situation. He did, however, repeat certain themes. Among these was how spiritual exile connected to political exile for believers. On one level, Calvin couldn't help doing that. It was his own story.

---

3. Bonnet, 4:365–66 (CO 20:299).

4. John Calvin, *Draft Ecclesiastical Ordinances*, in John Calvin, *Calvin: Theological Treatises*, trans. J. K. S. Reid, LCC (Westminster John Knox, 1954), 58–63 (CO 10a:15–22); and *Inst.* IV.3.4–6 (OS 5:45–49).

5. *Inst.* IV.3.4 (OS 5:46).

6. Calvin, *Ecclesiastical Ordinances*, 62 (CO 10a:21).

7. Karin Maag, *Seminary or University? The Genevan Academy and Reformed Higher Education, 1560–1620* (Ashgate, 1995).

This meant that Calvin's ministry was ever attuned to refugee realities. Also, he was as strategic in his pedagogy as he was clear about his calling. This chapter and the next introduce Calvin as teacher. His scholarly publications, especially the *Institutes* and biblical commentaries, worked in tandem to present a comprehensive vision of the church in exile.

Calvin's specialized ministry as a teacher involved writing biblical commentaries and books such as the *Institutes*. Like any skilled educator, he thought carefully about how to accommodate students. Calvin set out to train specialists in scripture, but he also sought to spare busy pastors and theological students "great annoyance and boredom."[8] How so? He eventually settled on what we might today call a "mixed modality" approach to teaching.

The *Institutes* became Calvin's most famous work. But that volume was never intended to stand alone. Nor did Calvin think of it as his main academic project. That distinction belongs to commentaries on (nearly) every book of the Bible. Like his sermons, which we will examine in chapter 6, Calvin's commentaries move verse by verse through entire books. He felt that this approach, known as *lectio continua* (continuous reading), best "lay open the mind of the [biblical] writer."[9] Calvin's humanist studies in classical literature and rhetoric trained him to prize clarity and eloquence. He told his friend Simon Grynaeus that preachers often have little time to prepare sermons. A commentator should practice "lucid brevity" (*perspicua brevita*s).[10] By this, Calvin meant concise clarity uncluttered with needless information. He refused to interrupt a commentary's flow by pausing for lengthy, though important, discussions of theological topics (*loci*) and disputed questions. There was a better place to collect those.

For Calvin, this was the *Institutes*. Like others of his era, Calvin believed that scripture contains theology that can be set forth thematically. This doctrinal framework, in turn, was necessary for interpreting the Bible correctly.[11] Though the *Institutes* was originally a catechetical work for lay Christians, Calvin repurposed it in 1539 as a textbook for teachers and preachers in training, stating, "It has been my purpose to prepare and instruct candidates in sacred theology for the reading of the divine Word, in order that they may be

---

8. "John Calvin to the Reader, 1559," in *Inst.* 5 (*OS* 3:6).

9. Calvin to Simon Grynaeus, October 18, 1539 (*CO* 10b:403); this letter appears as the preface to Calvin's commentary on Romans.

10. Calvin to Grynaeus (*CO* 10b:402); see also T. H. L. Parker, *Calvin's New Testament Commentaries*, 2nd ed. (T&T Clark, 1993), 85–93.

11. Elsie Anne McKee, "Exegesis, Theology, and Development in Calvin's *Institutio*: A Methodological Suggestion," in *Probing the Reformed Tradition: Historical Studies in Honor of Edward A. Dowey, Jr.*, ed. Elsie Anne McKee and Brian G Armstrong (Westminster John Knox, 1989), 154–56.

able both to have easy access to it and to advance in it without stumbling."[12] The author desires to present "the sum of religion in all its parts," to guide readers toward what they "ought especially to seek in Scripture."[13] Here is the theology Calvin only gestures at in his commentaries to avoid spoiling his lucid brevity with "long and wordy" digressions.[14] Beginning in 1539, two complementary genres, exegetical works and the *Institutes*, worked together to help students grasp the full teaching of scripture. This dual-modality approach also reflects Calvin's multifaceted teaching ministry. Lectures and exegetical presentations to colleagues and students in Geneva served as incubators for Calvin's commentaries, which were the bedrock of a teaching program that also featured the *Institutes*.[15] For centuries, scholars paid little attention to Calvin's exegetical writings, assuming that works like the *Institutes* represent his comprehensive thinking on theological topics. This was accepted despite Calvin's own clear statements about how the *Institutes* and commentaries work in tandem. Reading them side by side, as Calvin intended, reveals a rich, unified vision of the church as exilic community. Aside from avoiding boredom and annoyance, Calvin's multimodal pedagogy illustrates how exile—as political and spiritual reality—permeated his reading of scripture. This shaped how Calvin, as teacher, sought to stimulate the imaginations of others.

The present chapter begins our two-part examination of Calvin's "core curriculum" as a teacher in Geneva (and beyond) by considering the *Institutes*. Chapter 4 takes a closer look at the reformer's commentaries. In both modes of teaching, Calvin turned naturally toward themes like pilgrimage and nurture when applying theology to lived realities. This should not surprise us. From Abraham's wandering to Israel's captivity to Christ's sojourn in Egypt, exile is prominent in scripture and was ubiquitous in early modern Europe. It is also a theme that Christians adopted long before Calvin. Just as he did not create a community in exile from scratch, neither did his theology and exegesis emerge ex nihilo. Calvin's ideas reflect conversations stretching back to the origins of Christianity and, before that, to the long history of Jewish biblical interpretation. Calvin addressed his moment by receiving, reframing, and, in some cases, rejecting traditional exegesis and doctrine. Divine providence, predestination, and the notion of the church as a pilgrim people are

---

12. "John Calvin to the Reader, 1559," in *Inst.* 4 (*OS* 3:6). The text quoted first appeared in 1539.
13. "John Calvin to the Reader, 1559," in *Inst.* 4 (*OS* 3:6).
14. Calvin to Grynaeus, October 18, 1539 (CO 10b:403, 405).
15. Erik de Boer, *The Genevan School of the Prophets: The Congrégations of the Company of Pastors and Their Influence in 16th Century Europe* (Droz, 2012), 147–214; and Richard A. Muller, *The Unaccommodated Calvin: Studies in the Foundation of a Theological Tradition* (Oxford University Press, 2000), 27–31.

not ideas original to Calvin. Yet he formulated them for his historical situation in distinctive ways.[16] Together, Calvin's *Institutes* and exegetical works offer a coherent vision of God's accompaniment and nurture. The books plot a theological map to guide spiritual pilgrims through exile.

The *Institutes* as an Exilic Text?

There is no shortage of studies that analyze the structure, themes, and publication history of the *Institutes*.[17] Calvin likely followed Philip Melanchthon's *Loci communes* (1521) and Paul's Letter to the Romans to arrive at the *Institutes*'s topics and arrangement.[18] Alas, Calvin did not write a book expressly about refugees or exile. But he returns to these themes often. Pilgrim theology (*theologia viatorum*; lit., "theology of the pilgrims") is a concept that Calvin would have known from a theological tradition shaped especially by Augustine's depiction, in *City of God* (426 CE), of the Christian as a sojourner passing through this world.[19] In this sense, *pilgrim theology* denotes the mode of theology that pertains to believers' sojourn, as pilgrims, prior to arriving at their heavenly home. Calvin's use of exilic language both assumed this provisional and limited nature of all theology "on the way" (*in via*) and described specific expressions of such spiritual exile in his day. His was pilgrim theology fashioned into a road map specifically for sixteenth-century travelers. It arose from personal experience and spoke to concerns of his day. These included widespread persecution and exile. As we have already noted, Calvin's preface, which accompanies every edition of the *Institutes*, invokes his identity as a fugitive advocating for others who suffered "prison, exile . . . and fire" in France.[20] The *Institutes* might thus be called an "exilic text" on two levels: (1) its theological *content* directed to spiritual exiles; and (2) its

16. See below, chaps. 4 and 6.
17. See, e.g., J. W. Marmelstein, *Étude comparative des textes latins et français de l'institution de la religion Chrétienne par Jean Calvin* (Wolters, 1923); Ford Lewis Battles, *Analysis of the "Institutes of the Christian Religion" of John Calvin* (Baker, 1980); Wilhelm H. Neuser, "The Development of the *Institutes* 1536 to 1539," in *John Calvin's "Institutes," His Opus Magnum: Proceedings of the Second South African Congress for Calvin Research, July 31–August 3, 1984* (Potchefstroom University for Christian Higher Education, 1986), 33–54; Muller, *Unaccommodated Calvin*; and Michelle C. Sanchez, *Calvin and the Resignification of the World: Creation, Incarnation, and the Problem of Political Theology* (Cambridge University Press, 2019).
18. Muller, *Unaccommodated Calvin*, 118–39; and Bruce Gordon, *Calvin* (Yale University Press, 2009), 109.
19. A century after Calvin, John Bunyan's allegorical *Pilgrim's Progress* (1678) would also famously build on this theme.
20. "Prefatory Address to King Francis I of France," in *Inst.* 9 (*OS* 3:9); see chap. 1, above.

original *context* of political exile, with the author positioning himself as a religious refugee and his theology as that of the persecuted.

Acknowledging exile on these planes does not alter the organizational logic that reflects Melanchthon and Paul. Nor does it mean that "exile" controlled Calvin's theology. Rather, it simply invites readers to remember that Calvin presented his ideas with a deep awareness of exile as inescapable spiritual and political realities. Calvin depicted the present life, with its myriad struggles, as a time of spiritual exile. Salvation, on this account, is a kind of homecoming predicated on Christ's return from exile. Although Calvin was neither the first nor the last Christian theologian to draw on biblical imagery of exile and pilgrimage to frame reality, it is still worth noting its implications for specific ideas. For example, the famous dialectic that opens the 1559 *Institutes*—that knowledge of God and of ourselves is reciprocal and mutually informing—describes an experience in spiritual exile.[21] Knowing God simultaneously reveals our limits and neediness, which "not only arouses us to seek God, but also . . . leads us by the hand to find him."[22] Exile, as our present circumstance, is where we encounter God.

This alerts us to another dimension of how exile functions in the *Institutes*: as a narrative background for doctrine. Calvin had already drawn on scripture to depict life as a journey from wilderness to promised land in the *Psychopannychia* (1534).[23] The *Institutes* extend this storyline with sections on the future life and Christ's ascension first appearing, respectively, in the editions of 1539 and 1559.[24] Nurture also appears as a related theme in both works, as well as in biblical commentaries that compare the Lord's Supper to manna in the desert.[25] It is easy to overlook how this story of humanity's return from exile adds "narrative coherence" to doctrines that Calvin arranges logically in the *Institutes*. Three areas that Calvin relates directly to spiritual and political exile are providence, predestination, and the church (ecclesiology). These are topics modern readers most readily associate with Calvin, though rarely in connection with exile. But what if, as Heiko Oberman suggests, Calvin is memorable on these subjects precisely because he adapted his teaching to spiritual pilgrims whose lives intersected with violence, migration,

---

21. *Inst.* I.1.1–3 (*OS* 3:31–34).
22. *Inst.* I.1.1 (*OS* 3:32).
23. See chap. 1, above.
24. *Inst.* II.16.14; III.9–10 (*OS* 3:501–3; 4:170–81).
25. See chap. 1, above; and Comm. 1 Cor. 10:1 (1546; *CNTC* 9:200–202; *CO* 49:451–52). For others on this theme, see Wolfgang Musculus, *In ambas apostoli Pauli ad Corinthios epistolas, commentarii* (Basel, 1566), 309; and Jacques Lefèvre d'Étaples, *Epistolae divi Pauli Apostoli: Cum commentariis praeclarissimi viri Jacobi Fabri Stapulensis* (Paris, 1517), Lib. II, Fol. XCV-v.

and exile?[26] To explore this connection, it is helpful first to sketch how the *Institutes* describes the present life in terms of exile and homecoming. Then we will return to how this conceptual framework inflects Calvin's portrayal of providence, predestination, and the church.

The Present Life as Spiritual Exile

According to Calvin, people were created to know and worship God, with creation serving as a sure guide to such knowledge.[27] The reformer follows others in depicting Adam's banishment from Eden (Gen. 3) as a paradigm for fallen humanity's exile from God and conflict with creation.[28] Redemption in Christ involves knowing and responding to God properly as Creator and Redeemer.[29] This is the path back from exile. For God's elect, a category we define below, homecoming is guaranteed. This life is a sojourn, death a blessing.

Pilgrimage and nurture, death as homecoming, the church's spiritual context as wilderness—all these themes punctuate Calvin's portrayal of the future life in the *Institutes*. Most of this material, from III.9–10, first appeared in 1539. By 1559 it became the last part of a longer section (III.6–10) sometimes published separately under the title *On the Christian Life*.[30] The constant tension of honoring God's daily generosity while holding the present life in contempt grips the entire meditation. "There is no middle ground," Calvin insists. "Either the world must become worthless to us or hold us bound by intemperate love of it."[31] Even our best experiences pale before what awaits in the future life: "If heaven is our homeland, what else is earth but our place of exile?" Death is but a doorway through which "we are recalled from exile to

---

26. Heiko A. Oberman, *John Calvin and the Reformation of the Refugees* (Droz, 2009), 67. See the introduction, above.

27. Edward A. Dowey, *The Knowledge of God in Calvin's Theology*, 3rd ed. (Eerdmans, 1994); and Susan E. Schreiner, *Theater of His Glory: Nature and the Natural Order in the Thought of John Calvin* (Baker, 1995). Calvin calls such worship "true piety" because it consists in reverence and love toward God as Creator and source of all good (*Inst.* I.2.1–2; I.3.3; OS 3:34–37, 39–40).

28. *Inst.* II.6.1 (OS 3:320–21). See also Augustine, *Literal Meaning of Genesis*, XI.39.54 (Latin: *De Genesi ad litteram*, in PL 34:451); Hugh of Saint-Cher, *Opera omnia in universum Vetus, & Novum Testamentum*, 8 vols. (Venice, 1703), I:6v; Denis the Carthusian, *Enarrationes piae ac eruditae, in quinque Mosaicae legis libros . . .* (Cologne, 1534), xxxiiii (v); and Peter Martyr Vermigli, *In primum librum Mosis, qui vulgo genesis dicitur commentarii doctissimi* (Zurich, 1569), 18v.

29. *Inst.* I.2.1–3 (OS 3:34–40).

30. See the excellent new translation: John Calvin, *On the Christian Life: A New Translation*, trans. Raymond A. Blacketer (Crossway, 2024).

31. *Inst.* III.9.2 (OS 4:172).

dwell in the fatherland, the heavenly fatherland."[32] "A sepulcher" is the world, the "body a prison."[33] Was Calvin an early modern Gnostic, who elevated the spiritual while denigrating material creation as evil? Despite appearances at first blush, Calvin was not reviving ancient heresy. He affirmed that creation is intrinsically good. It is God's workmanship; thus it is "never to be hated, except in so far as it holds us subject to sin."[34]

The *Institutes* situates all human history in a comprehensive account of the present life as spiritual exile marked by the consequences of sin. These include "barrenness," "poverty," "fire," "wars," "robbery," and, yes, political exile.[35] In view of such suffering, God's people learn from sources like Paul (2 Cor. 5) to "eagerly hasten to death not because they want to be unclothed but because they long to be more fully clothed."[36] Calvin persistently points his readers toward the future life by affirming their disappointment in present realities and reassuring them of God's presence in the wilderness. As we will see in a moment, the pilgrim's hope for homecoming surfaces prominently in Calvin's teaching on providence, predestination, and ecclesiology.

Christ's Exile and Our Homecoming

Calvin relates exile to Christology by depicting the work of Christ as exile that ensures humanity's future homecoming. Though his Lutheran critics would disagree, Calvin is not known for particularly innovative Christology.[37] That said, scholars have noted distinctive aspects of Calvin's teaching on Christ's incarnation and participation in Christ.[38] In each of these cases, Calvin improvises on established themes rather than departing from the theological tradition in any serious way. Similarly, Calvin's view of exile as central to Christ's work as Redeemer can be gleaned directly from the Gospel narratives. Episodes in Christ's earthly ministry, such as his family's Egyptian sojourn to escape Herod's murder of the innocents (Matt. 2) and the adult Jesus's flight from his foes (Matt. 12:14–15), invite Calvin to identify exile with God's mode of salvation. God

---

32. *Inst.* III.9.5 (OS 4:175).
33. *Inst.* III.9.4 (OS 4:174).
34. *Inst.* III.9.4 (OS 4:174).
35. *Inst.* III.9.1 (OS 4:171).
36. *Inst.* III.9.4 (OS 4:174).

37. For Lutheran critiques of Calvin's Christology for denying the communication of divine attributes to Christ's human nature, see Irene Dingel, "Calvin in the Context of Lutheran Consolidation," *Reformation & Renaissance Review* 12 (2010): 155–87.

38. Edwin Chr. van Driel, "'Too Lowly to Reach God Without a Mediator': John Calvin's Supralapsarian Eschatological Narrative," *Modern Theology* 33 (2017): 275–92; and J. Todd Billings, *Calvin, Participation, and the Gift: The Activity of Believers in Union with Christ* (Oxford University Press, 2007).

reveals power in weakness, siding with exiles by becoming one of them.[39] Calvin observes from John 1 that Christ came only "for a time, as a guest" among us.[40]

Calvin again invokes exile to describe the significance of Christ's ascension. Bodily absence, he notes with Augustine, commences Christ's presence with believers through the Holy Spirit.[41] People underappreciate Calvin's emphasis on the ascension, which makes it easy also to miss the doctrine's connection to exile in his theology. The ascension unwraps the gift of Christ's "more immediate power," which accompanies "believers still on their earthly pilgrimage." This benefit exists only because Christ's exile has ended while ours has not: "It is more useful to us—a presence that had been confined in a humble abode of flesh as long as he sojourned on earth."[42] Christ leads the way, having completed his sojourn and returned from exile. Now he accompanies believers on their journey after him. This spiritual accompaniment is also important for what it lacks. Christ's body has ascended. Human flesh (Christ himself) sits at God's right hand, assuring today's exiles of their future inheritance: "We do not await heaven with a bare hope, but in our Head already possess it."[43] Thus Christ's bodily absence sustains our hope.

Finally, Calvin relates pilgrimage to Christ's office as king, the king who leads the church toward its heavenly home, recalling it from exile: "We may patiently pass through this life with its misery, hunger, cold, contempt, reproaches, and other troubles—content with this one thing: that our King will never leave us destitute, but will provide for our needs until, our warfare ended, we are called to triumph."[44]

Conflating pilgrimage and warfare was nothing new for Christian theology, which had applied the New Testament's use of both images to justify militarized pilgrimage in the Crusades. This is not Calvin's concern. For him, present trials are symptoms of exile as a time of spiritual "warfare."[45] Theological tradition characterizes the church in the present age as "militant" (*ecclesia militans*), at war with the devil, the flesh, and the world. Christ the King accompanies this community through exile and guarantees their homecoming.

---

39. Comm. Matt. 2:13–18 (1555; *CNTC* 1:99–103; *CO* 45:97–100); and Comm. Matt. 12:14 (*CNTC* 2:34; *CO* 45:329–30).
40. Comm. John 1:14 (1553; *CNTC* 4:21; *CO* 47:14–15).
41. *Inst*. II.16.14 (*OS* 3:502).
42. *Inst*. II.16.14 (*OS* 3:501).
43. *Inst*. II.16.16 (*OS* 3:504).
44. *Inst*. II.15.4 (*OS* 3:476).
45. Comm. 1 Pet. 4:16 (*CNTC* 12:309–10; *CO* 55:280). For the striking application of warfare language to the task of reforming the church in Calvin's preface to the 1538 Latin edition of Geneva's *Catechism* amid conflicts with Caroli, see John L. Thompson, "Confessions, Conscience, and Coercion in the Early Calvin," in *Calvin and The Early Reformation*, ed. Brian C. Brewer and David M. Whitford (Brill, 2020), 168–76.

For Calvin, providence, predestination, and ecclesiology are essential to this story. Such teaching oriented the theological imaginations of spiritual pilgrims struggling to make sense of a Europe in which Christian martyrdom and involuntary migration were anything but imaginary.

Divine Providence and the Promise of Order

A tumultuous student career and young adulthood attuned Calvin to the comfort of God's providence, the doctrine that God not only creates but also actively governs creation.[46] Providence frames Calvin's later retelling of these formative years of moving from city to city, eventually fleeing his homeland under threat.[47] None of this was random. God was its cause. Nothing, for Calvin, happens outside of God's will. Augustine had articulated the same idea a millennium earlier: "Nothing happens but by the will of the Omnipotent, He either permitting it to be done, or Himself doing it."[48] Did Calvin's insistence on God's power and purposefulness in some way also assuage personal anxiety about chaos and uncertainty?[49] Whatever the case, Calvin found biblical teaching about God's sovereignty reassuring. In training lectures for pastors, Calvin boldly asserts that preachers "reduce the world to order" by speaking God's truth to power, error, and uncertainty.[50] Providence offers assurance in the form of an ordered cosmos. Like others before him, Calvin found providence in scripture, where vivid images drive home the point that God's rule over creation extends to the smallest creatures (Matt. 10:29) and has ultimate power over human salvation (Rom. 9).[51]

Calvin's teaching on providence met resistance and ridicule. Criticism from Sebastian Castellio prompted Calvin to write *Concerning the Secret Providence of God* (1558).[52] This frequently overlooked treatise, which addresses divisions arising in francophone evangelical circles around Calvin's teaching on predestination, sets forth arguments that appear in the *Institutes* a year later (I:16–18). In *Secret Providence*, Calvin assumes an aggressive tone, charging Castellio

---

46. For the nuances and background of Calvin's understanding of providence, see Schreiner, *Theater of His Glory*, 7–37.

47. Calvin, "Author's Preface" to Comm. Psalms (CTS 4:xxxv–xlix; CO 31:13–36).

48. Augustine, *Enchiridion* 94–95, in *NPNF* 3:267; and Richard A. Muller, *Post-Reformation Reformed Dogmatics: The Rise and Development of Reformed Orthodoxy, ca. 1520 to ca. 1725*, 2nd rev. ed., 4 vols. (Baker Academic, 2003), 3:436–43.

49. William J. Bouwsma, *John Calvin: A Sixteenth-Century Portrait* (Oxford University Press, 1988), 32–65.

50. Lect. Jer. 1:9–10 (CTS 17:42–48; CO 37:480).

51. *Inst.* I.16.1, 5 (OS 3:188); and III.23.4 (OS 4:397).

52. CO 9:269–318 (English: John Calvin, *The Secret Providence of God*, ed. Paul Helm, trans. Keith Goad [Crossway, 2010]).

with "barking," "babbling," reasoning from "a darkened mind," and "shamelessly polluting [scripture] with [his] snout."[53] Pastoral care is not his agenda, except indirectly through silencing this teacher of errors. By contrast, Calvin reserves a warmer presentation of the same doctrine of providence for readers of the *Institutes* in 1559.

The *Institutes* locates human existence firmly within God's purposes. This has wide implications for the present life as spiritual exile. The very opposite of chance or chaos is God, the "Governor" and "Preserver" of the universe, whose plans never fail. Calvin decries the "blind," impersonal fate taught by Stoic philosophy.[54] Fortune, as such, does not exist. Contrary to appearances (and the "natural science" of Calvin's day), even the sun is not strictly necessary for life. It is an "instrument God uses because he so wills"—free anytime to "abandon it, and act through himself."[55] Indeed, "not one drop of rain falls without God's sure command."[56] Providence is not God's "mere foreknowledge" of events, as if the Creator is but a passive spectator to creation. God is an active governor. Nothing less than God's "ceaseless activity" determines everything that comes to pass: "As keeper of the keys, he governs all events."[57] This means that the circumstances of life in exile are never a surprise to God but, rather, are God's design.

What makes such total power anything but wholly terrifying? Only God's character, since providence reflects God's "fatherly favor toward us."[58] For some critics of Calvin, God's sovereignty is too restrictive or authoritarian, even if wielded by a loving father. But what is the alternative? Leaning on Augustine, Calvin warns that providence stands between creation and chaos: "Nothing is more absurd than that anything should happen without God's ordaining it, because it would then happen without any cause."[59] Unapologetically, then, "God's will is the highest and first cause of all things because nothing happens except from his command or permission."[60] Such permission, however, is never "bare," never blanket or perfunctory assent to our desires.[61] Calvin criticizes those who distinguish between God's "doing" and "permitting" or contrast God's "effective" will to God's "permissive" will.[62]

---

53. Calvin, *Secret Providence*, 117 et passim.
54. *Inst*. I.16.1–2 (*OS* 3:187–90).
55. *Inst*. I.16.2 (*OS* 3:189–90).
56. *Inst*. I.16.5 (*OS* 3:195).
57. *Inst*. I.16.3–4 (*OS* 3:190–94).
58. *Inst*. I.16.2; I.17.1 (*OS* 3:188–90, 202–3).
59. *Inst*. I.16.8 (*OS* 3:199).
60. *Inst*. I.16.8 (*OS* 3:199). See note 48, above.
61. *Inst*. I.18.1 (*OS* 3:219–21).
62. *Inst*. I.18.1 (*OS* 3:219–21); also *Inst*. III.23.8 (*OS* 4:402–3); Augustine, *Enchiridion* 95–96, in *NPNF* 3:267; and Muller, *Post-Reformation*, 3:441–42. For how Calvin applies scholastic distinctions between God's secret will and God's revealed will to the question of whether God

Sometimes events seem contrary to God's will. In such cases, Calvin concedes, it can be helpful to use the language of God's "permitting" something. But to speak this way is never to imply that such permission is passive or contrary to God's purposes.[63] We may not know God's intentions, but providence assures us that God has the first and final say in all that comes to pass. For Calvin, this preserves the meaningfulness of our existence. No detail of life is left to chance or to the flippant decisions of sinners. To the refugee theologian, confidence that God is no hapless, unwilling bystander to creation makes all the difference for believers living in exile.

Turning to the hard realities of life, how could Christians reconcile these with the goodness and favor of an omnipotent God? Put differently, what about the dark side of providence? Evil and its apparent triumph in a world beset with suffering, often at the hands of others, was no theoretical question for sixteenth-century Europeans. Calvin's sermons and letters do not shy away from these problems, referring to "fires," "massacres," and other forms of "execution" imposed on evangelicals in France and elsewhere.[64] These concrete expressions of spiritual exile also include the literal losses and displacements of political exile necessitated by violence and hate. But how were such painful realities expressions of God's fatherly care?

Calvin was ruthlessly consistent in applying providence to the question of evil. Yet he was also concerned to comfort believers facing persecution and trials. On the one hand, evil is not always as it appears to us. Reflecting on the story of Job's suffering, Calvin notes how God constrained Satan's desire at every turn.[65] The same holds true for other biblical examples of evil against God's people, from Ahab's imposition of idolatry in Israel (1 Kings 16–22), to Absalom's violence against his father, David (2 Sam. 15–18), and Judah's oppression by its Babylonian captors. None of this sits outside God's providence. Not even the crucifixion poses an exception. Calvin distinguishes between the evil intent of Christ's tormentors and the good purposes of God. While the former leaves humans accountable for sin, their evil desires and actions could not disrupt God's plan. In fact, human sin is frequently how God carries out God's desires.[66] God's will prevails over our wills and the apparent triumph of evil. For early modern refugees, this was assurance that

---

"permits" things we perceive as evil, see Paul Helm, "Editor's Introduction," in Calvin, *Secret Providence*, 13–31.

63. *Inst*. I.18.1 (OS 3:219–21).

64. Calvin to the Faithful in France, November 1559 (Bonnet, 4:81; CO 17:682); Calvin to Bullinger, July 2, 1563 (Bonnet, 4:321; CO 20:54); and Serm. Gen. 4:10–12, October 31, 1559 (SC XI/1:283–84).

65. *Inst*. I.18.1 (OS 3:219–21).

66. *Inst*. I.18.1 (OS 3:219–21).

their situations—even at the most complex and disheartening—were never random, haphazard, or outside God's providence.

Perhaps unsurprisingly, such an uncompromising view of divine sovereignty had detractors. Castellio accused Calvin of making God the author of sin. Calvin responds by doubling down and insisting that, yes, even the fall of Adam, humanity's original sin, was no mere instance of God's permission. It was God's will.[67] Consistency, for Calvin, requires that nothing in God's universe, not even evil, lies outside God's will as its final cause. Yet humans are still culpable for sin, a view Calvin shared with Augustine, who taught that people retain "free choice" within an overall account of divine sovereignty.[68] Calvin goes further to insist that, while Adam's sin was his own, God nevertheless ordained it. Employing medieval distinctions between "proximate" and "ultimate" causes, Calvin concludes that suffering and death have their "proximate cause" in human decisions to disobey God. Yet these things cannot "ultimately" be attributed simply to the choices of creatures.[69] God's will stands before and behind our choices. To say less would subject God to others, to randomness outside God's control. For Calvin, such a view of God contradicts scripture and gives daylight to the more terrifying idea that suffering is haphazard and meaningless.

But what more can believers know about their suffering? Calvin offers this comfort. Yes, providence begins in the hidden counsel of God, which we, as creatures, cannot see let alone expect to understand. But God's self-revelation shows that God is good. Thus, everything God wills must be good because of who God is. In this case, God's power is not limited by anything outside of God. But neither is it lawless. There is no division in God; therefore, God's power cannot be separated from God's goodness and righteousness. Calvin unapologetically says that God's will is the ultimate cause of all things. Even so, God's will does not exist apart from God's righteousness but is the very expression of it. Therefore, whatever God ordains is righteous: "[God's] will is, and rightly ought to be, the cause of all things that are. For if it has any cause, something must precede it, to which it is, as it were, bound; this is unlawful to imagine. For God's will is so much the highest rule of righteousness that whatever he wills, by the very fact that he wills it, must be considered righteous."[70]

---

67. *Inst.* III.23.7–11 (OS 4:401–5).
68. Augustine, *De libero arbitrio* 3.16.46.155–60; English: Augustine, *On the Free Choice of the Will, On Grace and Free Choice, and Other Writings*, trans. and ed. Peter King (Cambridge University Press, 2010), 105–6.
69. *Inst.* III.23.7–11 (CO 2:704–7); also *Concerning Eternal Predestination*, 1552 (CO 8:313–18).
70. *Inst.* III.23.2 (OS 4:395–96).

Even the fall of humanity into sin—the outworking of which is experienced daily in suffering and evil, sickness and death—is ultimately good simply because God ordained it. In the absence of answers about why God would do this, Calvin's doctrine of providence falls back upon biblical examples of God's character and concern for individuals.[71] The payoff? Spiritual pilgrims have reasons to rejoice with gratitude in prosperity and trust God in adversity. Faith sees God's good purposes behind both, even if our eyes cannot. Although inaccessible to us, God's purposes, ever at work, are infallibly good. This was meant to comfort an international diaspora of persecuted and displaced Reformed communities.

Predestination: A Gentler Face to That "Dreadful" Decree

Calvin's understanding of providence is distinct yet inseparable from his doctrine of predestination, which is perhaps the teaching for which he is best known. For many, *Calvinism* is synonymous not only with the Reformed tradition but also with the doctrine of predestination more narrowly. Even in the sixteenth century, ardent admirers like the English Presbyterian John Field already called it the "foundation" of Calvin's theology.[72] Today, popular references to the Canons of Dort (1619) as the "Five Points of Calvinism," often summarized by the acronym "T-U-L-I-P," continue what is, in fact, a reductionistic approach to Calvin.[73] This was how I encountered Calvin as an undergraduate, and it continues to represent the extent of what many seminarians come (and some are content to leave) knowing about "that predestination guy." This is unfortunate. While the doctrine was important to Calvin, it was never the main point of his theology. Alas, admirers and critics alike often miss how predestination functions alongside other doctrines as part of Calvin's teaching on God's comfort for spiritual exiles.

Initially bundling providence and predestination together, Calvin separates the doctrines in the 1559 *Institutes*, placing them, respectively, at the ends of book I and book III. Predestination, God's election of some humans for salvation, is for Calvin more than simply a subset of providence, though he frequently treats them in the same place. In *Secret Providence*, for example, Calvin addresses both subjects in relation to disputes over his

---

71. *Inst.* I.17.6–11 (OS 3:209–16).
72. John Field, *Thirteene Sermons of Maister John Calvine, Entreating of the Free Election of God in Jacob, and of Reprobation in Esau* (London, 1579), B1v.
73. Edwin H. Palmer, *Five Points of Calvinism* (Baker, 1996); and John Piper, *Five Points* (Christian Focus, 2013).

doctrine of reprobation. Still, he never simply conflates the two. In fact, Calvin so stresses the salvific trajectory of all God's work in creation that predestination is, for him, in some ways prior to providence in the logical ordering of God's decrees.[74] God, in other words, governs all creation (providence) with special concern for the salvation of his elect (predestination). Predestination thus imbues the scope of providence with further reassurance. Even God's most perplexing acts have purposes relating to God's ultimate concern for human flourishing.

Calvin's exposition of predestination in the 1559 *Institutes* (III.21–24) was a word of comfort to exiles and refugees in several ways. These include detailing God's promises for the future and clarifying God's present accompaniment of the church. On the first point, Calvin, like many mainstream reformers, continued the Augustinian teaching about God's free election of some to salvation from the sinful whole of humanity. He further held to a doctrine of "double predestination," in contrast to contemporaries like Melanchthon or Bullinger, who either rejected this teaching or were less consistent.[75] For Calvin, not only has God chosen in eternity to save some individuals, but God has also just as deliberately rejected those not elected to salvation.[76] Predestination thus involves two active, coordinating decrees of God: election and reprobation. Calvin acknowledges that the idea that God decrees reprobation is hard to swallow: "The decree is dreadful indeed, I confess."[77] For this reason, Calvin's contemporaries derided this teaching for diminishing moral responsibility, denying God's gracious disposition toward all humanity, and, frankly, turning God into a monster.[78] On the other hand, the same doctrine could serve as a boon to spiritual exiles, especially those who suffered further displacement as political exiles in Calvin's day. God's electing decree renders the world's judgment of them provisional, even contrary to God's assessment. People experiencing rejection now can draw comfort from the fact that God has, in fact, chosen them for God's household—a more secure form of belonging, one that will not change with circumstances. For Calvin, John's Gospel furnishes support for this assurance: The Father entrusts the elect to

---

74. François Wendel, *Calvin: Sources et évolution de sa pensée religieuse* (Presses Universitaires de France, 1950), 202–3; and Richard A. Muller, *Christ and the Decree: Christology and Predestination in Reformed Theology from Calvin to Perkins* (Baker Academic, 2008), 23.

75. Richard A. Muller, *Predestination in Early Modern Reformed Theology* (Reformation Heritage Books, 2024), 9–26.

76. Kenneth J. Woo, "Election in John Calvin," in *The T&T Clark Handbook of Election*, ed. Edwin Chr. van Driel (Bloomsbury, 2023), 209–25.

77. *Inst*. III.23.7 (OS 4:418–19).

78. "Articles Against Calvin's Teaching on Predestination," in Calvin, *Secret Providence*, 37–56.

Christ (6:37–39; 10:27–30; 17:6, 12), who will ensure that they attain eternal life.[79] Election answers anxiety about the future: "Christ has freed us from this anxiety, for these promises apply to the future: . . . 'No one shall snatch them out of my hand.' . . . We shall ever remain safe because we have been made his once for all."[80] Similarly, reprobation explains the blind "madness" behind the church's persecutors.[81] Calvin cautions against speculation about reprobation and advises preachers to avoid it.[82]

For Calvin, God's good future defines the present, even in ways not apparent to us. The reformer speaks of election intensifying, rather than mitigating, hardship for Christ's people in a world that rejects him: "If we are branded with disgrace and ignominy, we but have a fuller place in the Kingdom."[83] In God's economy, suffering is inversely proportional to the reward awaiting the elect. It is a form of parental discipline to wean their hope off of "the vanity of the present":

> That [believers] might not promise themselves a deep and secure peace [in this life, God] permits [*permittit*] them often to be troubled and plagued either with wars or tumults, or robberies, or other injuries. That they may not pant with too great eagerness after fleeting and transient riches, or repose in those which they possess, he sometimes by exile, sometimes by barrenness of earth, sometimes by fire, sometimes by other means, reduces them to poverty, or at least confines them to a moderate station. That they might not too complacently take delight in the goods of marriage, he either causes them to be troubled by the depravity of their wives or humbles them by evil offspring, or afflicts them with bereavement.[84]

Notice the language of permission here, which Calvin applies to the apparent dissonance that bad things happen to God's children. In the end, he explains that God "causes" such things. "In the very harshness of tribulations," Calvin reasons, "we must recognize the kindness and generosity of our Father toward us, since he does not even then cease to promote our salvation."[85] Consequently, political exile for the sake of finding pure religion (the lot Calvin shared with many in his audience) heightens anticipation of a more lasting home: "If we are cast out of our own house, then we will be the more intimately received into God's family."[86]

79. *Inst.* III.24.6 (*OS* 4:417).
80. *Inst.* III.24.6 (*OS* 4:417).
81. Serm. Gen. 4:10–12, October 30, 1559 (*SC* XI/1:283–84); see chap. 4, below.
82. Paul Jacobs, *Prädestination und Verantwortlichkeit bei Calvin* (Kreis Moers, 1937), 158–59.
83. *Inst.* III.8.7 (*OS* 4:167).
84. *Inst.* III.9.1 (*OS* 4:171).
85. *Inst.* III.8.6 (*OS* 4:165–66).
86. *Inst.* III.8.7 (*OS* 4:166).

The *Institutes* thus orients readers' imaginations toward a future that promises God's final vindication of the elect. This casts suffering in a different light. Together with providence, election assures Calvin's readers of Christ's accompaniment in exile.[87] Because all things serve God's plan to bring the elect to salvation, believers need not doubt that their circumstances, however trying, manifest God's goodwill toward them. Even political exile is, for the elect, always more than evidence of humanity's spiritual estrangement from God. It deepens longing for a more lasting home. Calvin graphically likens even the pleasures of this life to "prison" and a "corpse"—"worthless" compared to the future life that awaits God's elect.[88] Death, a present danger in an age of martyrdom, is ultimately also "recall from exile."[89]

Yet, for reasons known only to God, this exilic life takes diverse forms. While welcome, death should not be sought. Contempt for this life must be tempered with faith in God's good purposes for the exilic journey and gratitude for God's provision along the way.[90] Variety in clothing, food, and drink are "not only to provide for necessity but also for delight and good cheer."[91] God is a generous father toward the elect, who hope in future vindication with confidence that God works ceaselessly for their good in the meantime. This could be hard to see for the many people in Calvin's audience who were suffering at the hands of human power.

Manna in the Wilderness: Church, Sacraments, and the Gift of Assurance

It is precisely the unseen aspects of predestination and providence that demand faith. In 1559 Calvin broke from a tradition that presented predestination as a subset of providence concerned with salvation by relocating predestination between chapters treating prayer (III.20) and final resurrection (III.25).[92] We should not make too much of this change, which Calvin does not bother to explain.[93] It does, however, carry implications for pedagogy. By bookending predestination between two topics that focus on a person's subjective exercise of faith and its forward-looking cousin, hope, Calvin highlights the doctrine's

---

87. *Inst.* II.16.14 (OS 3:501–2).
88. *Inst.* III.9–10 (OS 4:170–81).
89. *Inst.* III.9.5 (OS 4:175–76).
90. *Inst.* III.10.1–6.
91. *Inst.* III.10.2 (OS 4:178).
92. See, e.g., Thomas Aquinas, *Summa Theologiae* I.23.1.
93. Richard A. Muller, "The Placement of Predestination in Reformed Theology: Issue or Non-Issue?" *Calvin Theological Journal* 40 (2005): 184–210.

experiential nature.[94] This was crucial for exiles and refugees requiring assurance of God's favor beyond the abstract. Faith invited them to see the challenges of their political situation and current suffering as tokens of their elect status. These were chastisements of a loving father to bring forth the fruit of faith, hope, and love in God's children. Luther explicitly spoke of suffering as a mark of the church.[95] Calvin implies the same when he teaches believers to expect conflict with the world, the devil, and their own abiding sinfulness: "To suffer persecution for righteousness' sake is a singular comfort."[96] Belonging to God begets new enemies. Present-day persecution and trials make salvation visible by confirming one's status as a child of God.

Did Calvin teach "salvation by suffering"? Not at all. The elect attain salvation not through their affliction but from Christ, who obtained for them the benefits of redemption. "How do we receive those benefits which the Father has bestowed on his only begotten Son—not for Christ's own private use, but that he might enrich poor and needy men?"[97] This question, which opens book III of the 1559 *Institutes*, has but one answer for Calvin. A metaphysical gap must be bridged: "As long as Christ remains outside of us, and we are separated from him, all that he has suffered and done for the salvation of the human race remains useless and of no value for us."[98] Prompting some to dub him a "theologian of the Holy Spirit," the reformer resolves the dilemma with reference to the Spirit: "The Holy Spirit is the bond by which Christ effectually unites us to himself."[99] These succinct declarations frame the remainder of the *Institutes*. Book III expounds upon the Spirit's invisible work of forging this union with Christ. Book IV unfolds Calvin's ecclesiology and describes the visible church as the external means by which the Spirit does this, especially through preaching and sacraments.[100] These practices are like homing beacons supplying coordinates for an exilic imagination, pointing the faithful beyond exile to their surer belonging with God in Christ. Calvin's sermons frequently stress how Christ, presented in preaching and sacraments, is the "true mirror" in which believers "view [their] election" and thus gain

---

94. Michelle C. Sanchez, "Reading Tradition as Pedagogy in Calvin and Augustine: The Case of Election," *Scottish Journal of Theology* 72 (2019): 37–44.

95. Martin Luther, "On the Councils and the Church, 1539," in *LW* 41:164–65; and "Von den Konziliis und Kirchen, 1539," in *WA* 50:641–42.

96. *Inst.* III.8.7 (OS 4:166–67).

97. *Inst.* III.1.1 (OS 4:1–2).

98. *Inst.* III.1.2 (OS 4:2–3).

99. *Inst.* III.1.3 (OS 4:3–5); and B. B. Warfield, *Calvin as a Theologian and Calvinism Today* (Evangelical Press, 1969), 6.

100. For Calvin's ecclesiology, see Tadataka Maruyama, *Calvin's Ecclesiology: A Study in the History of Doctrine* (Eerdmans, 2022).

assurance.[101] Through the church's ministry, the elect can experience union with Christ as a present-day reality, even while they await that reunion when faith, in the end, becomes sight.

We have just described what, for Calvin, is the faith of Abraham. The *Institutes* single him out as the best example of faith in exile: "We ought to esteem Abraham as one equal to a hundred thousand if we consider his faith, which is set before us as the best model of believing."[102] Joining others before him, Calvin praises Abraham's willingness to answer God's call into the unknown. He wandered in exile and died without possessing the land promised: "Throughout life he was so tossed and troubled that if anyone wished to paint a picture of a calamitous life, he could find no model more appropriate than Abraham's."[103] Calvin makes similar comments in the *Psychopannychia*: "[Abraham and his companions] trusted the promises afar off, and died in the firm belief that the promises of God would one day be fulfilled. In accordance with this belief they confessed that they had no fixed abode on the earth, and that beyond the earth there was a country for which they longed."[104] Biblical stories of Abraham and other exiles, to which we return in the next chapter, texture Calvin's teaching on providence, predestination, and ecclesiology in both the *Institutes* and his biblical commentaries, which work together to shape readers' theological imaginations.

The *Institutes* prescribes a spirituality centered on the church's ministry as the place where spiritual exiles gather regularly to receive a foretaste of home. Such theology resonated with the Reformed diaspora's felt need for permanence: "Reading the Scriptures as an exiled refugee in light of his own experience, [Calvin] addressed his listeners and readers not as citizens of Geneva or any other European city, but rather as uprooted wayfarers who had signed up for the hazardous trek to the eternal city."[105] For Protestants like Calvin, God speaks to believers directly through scripture. He joined other reformers in rejecting the institutional church as indispensable intermediary between God and humanity through its priesthood. At the same time, Calvin maintained a high view of the church's ministry. With Cyprian (d. 258), he calls the church "mother": "There is no other way to enter into life unless this mother conceive us in her womb, give us birth, nourish us at her breast, and lastly, unless she keep us under her care and guidance

---

101. Serm. 2 Tim. 1:9–10, May 5, 1555 (CO 54:54).
102. *Inst.* II.10.11 (OS 3:411–12).
103. *Inst.* II.10.11 (OS 3:411–12); and David C. Steinmetz, "Calvin and Abraham: The Interpretation of Romans 4 in the Sixteenth Century," *Church History* 57 (1988): 443–555.
104. Calvin, *Psychopannychia*, 473 (CO 5:218–19).
105. Oberman, *Refugees*, 187.

until, putting off mortal flesh, we become like the angels."[106] For Calvin, the church's mothering function is inseparable from its role as steward of the gospel.[107]

Calvin's view of scripture is closely related. Scripture, for Calvin, preserves what God first revealed by the prophets and apostles.[108] Through the Bible the church has access to the gospel: the message of salvation through Jesus Christ. Building upon the imagery of spiritual exile, one might say that God speaks to the elect to guide them home: "[In scripture] God, to instruct the church, not merely uses mute teachers but also opens his own hallowed lips. Not only does he teach the elect to look upon a god, but also shows himself as the God upon whom they are to look."[109] Sin necessitates that God, the Creator, be known also as Redeemer "in the person of the Mediator."[110] This twofold knowledge of God as both Creator and Redeemer, essential for "true piety," came to humanity through prophets and apostles, whose teachings appear in texts that serve as "spectacles" to "clearly show us the true God."[111]

The Old and New Testaments present a unified voice, the latter making clear what the former foreshadowed in prophecy and symbols.[112] On this subject, Calvin notes, "[Old Testament believers] participated in the same inheritance and hoped for a common salvation with us by the grace of the same Mediator.... The covenant made with all the patriarchs is so much like ours in substance and reality that the two are actually one and the same. Yet they differ in the mode of dispensation."[113] Differences between New and Old include ceremonial and judicial parts of the law fulfilled in Christ or passing away with Israel's ancient theocracy, as well as the Holy Spirit's role in the church's understanding of scripture "with unveiled hearts" (2 Cor. 3).[114] Regarding the latter, the Spirit utilizes scripture to awaken and nurture the elect, calling and uniting them to Christ. Calvin's *Short Treatise on the Lord's Supper* (1541) describes this regeneration and feeding: "As the life into

106. *Inst*. IV.1.4 (*OS* 5:7).
107. *Inst*. IV.1.1 (*OS* 5:43–44).
108. *Inst*. I.6.2–3 (*OS* 3:62–63).
109. *Inst*. I.6.1 (*OS* 3:60–61).
110. *Inst*. I.6.1 (*OS* 3:60–61).
111. *Inst*. I.6.1 (*OS* 3:60–61); also *Inst*. I.2.1–2; I.3.3 (*OS* 3:34–37, 39–40).
112. *Inst*. II.10.1–3; II.11.1 (*OS* 3:403–5, 423–24). Augustine famously observed, following his mentor Ambrose's appropriation of Origen's hermeneutic: "The New Testament is concealed in the Old, the Old is revealed in the New." Augustine, *Seven Questions Concerning the Heptateuch* 2:73 (PL 34:623).
113. *Inst*. II.10.1–2 (*OS* 3:403–4).
114. *Inst*. II.11.8 (*OS* 3:430–31).

which [God] has regenerated us is spiritual, so the food for preserving and confirming us in it must be spiritual."[115] He goes on:

> The spiritual bread by which our souls are maintained is the same Word by which our Lord regenerated us. But [scripture] often adds the ground of this, that in it Jesus Christ, who alone is our life, is given and administered to us. For we must not think that there is life anywhere else but in God. But just as God has set all fulness of life in Jesus, in order to communicate it to us by means of him, so he has ordained his Word as instrument by which Jesus Christ, with all his benefits, is dispensed to us.[116]

For Calvin and other mainstream reformers, the connection between Spirit and Word ensured an objective, written standard against which claims about the Spirit's teaching could be evaluated. They critiqued Rome's presumption to have the Spirit's authority apart from scripture and refuted Spiritualists who claimed ongoing revelation from God that contradicted the Bible. Scripture is the standard, its interpretation essential for discerning and obeying God's voice—a conviction that Calvin clothes beautifully in the language of nurture: "Our souls have no other pasture than Jesus Christ. Therefore the heavenly Father in his care to nourish us, gives us nothing else, but rather recommends us to take our fill [in Christ offered in scripture], as from a refreshment manifestly sufficient, with which we cannot dispense, and beyond which it is impossible to find any other."[117]

How does God open "his own hallowed lips" through the church in a manner both intelligible and relevant to God's people in exile?[118] The *Institutes* assigns elements of this task to four church offices: pastor, elder, deacon, and teacher. These distinct roles complement one another to support the preaching of God's Word in a community gathered to receive and obey its teaching.[119] "In order that the preaching of the gospel might flourish," Calvin writes, "[God] deposited this treasure in the church. He instituted 'pastors and teachers' through whose lips he might teach his own; he furnished them with authority; finally, he omitted nothing that might make for holy agreement of faith and for right order."[120] Yes, God could have chosen any institutional safe house for this gospel "treasure." Yet God prefers to utilize a "ministry of ordinary

---

115. John Calvin, *Short Treatise on the Lord's Supper* (1541), in John Calvin, *Calvin: Theological Treatises*, trans. J. K. S. Reid, LCC (Westminster, 1954), 143 (CO 5:435).
116. Calvin, *Short Treatise*, 143 (CO 5:435).
117. Calvin, *Short Treatise*, 143 (CO 5:435).
118. *Inst.* I.6.1 (OS 3:60–61).
119. *Inst.* IV.3.1–9 (OS 5:42–51).
120. *Inst.* IV.1.1 (OS 5:1).

men" to interpret the Bible for others. To those who would criticize a model that hangs such grave responsibility on imperfect pastors, Calvin responds:

> This is the best and most useful exercise in humility, when [God] accustoms us to obey his Word, even though it be preached through men like us and sometimes by those of lower worth than we. . . . When a puny man risen from the dust speaks in God's name, at this point we best evidence our piety and obedience toward God if we show ourselves teachable toward his minister, although he excels us in nothing.
>
> It was for this reason, then, that he hid the treasure of his heavenly wisdom in weak and earthen vessels in order to prove more surely how much we should esteem it.[121]

For Calvin, the church is the locus of nurture in exile by God's design. Its gathered worship is a kind of oasis in the wilderness. Through the ministry, God distributes to Calvin's weary contemporaries sustenance for their journey home. Preaching and sacraments convey the same spiritual food—Christ, who enlivens and strengthens those who feed on him by faith: "[God] instituted sacraments, which we who have experienced them feel to be highly useful aids to foster and strengthen faith. Shut up as we are in the prison house of our flesh, we have not yet attained angelic rank. God, therefore, in his wonderful providence accommodating himself to our capacity, has prescribed a way for us, though still far off, to draw near to him."[122] God pastures his people on Christ through Word and sacrament in public worship as the Spirit seals God's promises held forth through a human ministry: "Believers have no greater help than public worship, for by it God raises his own folk upward step by step."[123]

This is an ecclesiology attuned to the needs of spiritual exiles, who often enough were also political exiles. Centered on the task of delivering nurture effectively to God's people, church polity defined in the *Institutes* is well-suited to communities on the move or in hiding, such as those in France. In Protestant England, Presbyterians utilized the church structure of Calvin's *Institutes* to organize underground bodies of elders and pastors in protest of the episcopal state church.[124] Such invisibility extended beyond polity to other practices of ministry. A Reformed ministry of Word and sacrament requires no special liturgical devices beyond words spoken or sung, along with common elements such as water, bread, and wine. This simplicity is especially adaptable to the provisional, often unstable circumstances of life in political

---

121. *Inst.* IV.3.1 (*OS* 5:42–44).
122. *Inst.* IV.1.1 (*OS* 5:1).
123. *Inst.* IV.1.5 (*OS* 5:7–10).
124. Polly Ha, *English Presbyterianism, 1590–1640* (Stanford University Press, 2011).

exile. Indeed, the plainness of Reformed worship belies its extraordinary claim to deliver Christ himself—nourishment to spiritual pilgrims, a foretaste of home along their trek heavenward. In Geneva, in England, and in countless hidden assemblies in France and elsewhere, believers regularly enacted their exilic status in communities where they received assurance that they did not travel alone.[125] Gathered around them were "fellow-trekkers" experiencing the same conflict with the world as they journeyed toward their future rest.[126] More importantly, God appeared in their midst—taking on a "face" through preaching and sacraments—to guide and nurture them.[127] Sixteenth-century refugees and exiles heard, saw, touched, and tasted the promise that their circumstances, however unsettling, were not beyond God's control and would not be the last word for God's elect.

Conclusion

Calvin never called the *Institutes* a refugee manual or an exilic text. He aimed to give students of theology "the sum of religion in all its parts." Here we have focused on just three aspects of its teaching, which reflect the book's original setting in its author's political exile. Providence, predestination, and ecclesiology appear in Calvin's most famous book as doctrines with specific relevance to comfort and nurture in exile as both political and spiritual reality. My grandparents were not religious. I often wonder how they made sense of life in their adopted country, especially at first, when so much was strange, so little certain. Would Calvin's God have been a comfort to them? I wish I could ask them. In the face of similar realities, Calvin's teaching on providence assured God's elect that their pilgrimage was purposeful, as surely as it would one day come to an end. Not only their deliverance but also every step and turn of their journey through exile was held in the divine hands. God met these early modern exiles with assurances of God's accompanying presence in the regular gift of manna in the wilderness.

I am speaking, of course, about the practices of the Reformed church—where God's daily, providential care, God's nurture and sustenance, of the elect took on specific forms. The practical arrangements for this in Geneva are the focus of chapters 5 and 6. The present chapter has shown how Calvin's *Institutes* offered this vision of an alternative home, community, and belonging to pastors and teachers in training, priming them to look for it as they read

---

125. Barbara Diefendorf, *Beneath the Cross: Catholics and Huguenots in Sixteenth-Century Paris* (Oxford University Press, 1991), 107–44.
126. Oberman, *Refugees*, 67.
127. CO 8:411–13, 418, 426–27.

the Bible. Yet this was but one side of Calvin's multimodal teaching formula. The reformer's commentaries, to which we now turn, come alongside the *Institutes* and paint this teaching with a broader palette. His exegesis offers colorful portraits of providence, election, reprobation, and nurture in the church brought to life through the stories of biblical figures.

For Further Reading

In Calvin's Words

1559 *Institutes of the Christian Religion*

The following topics, covered in this chapter, are addressed by Calvin in the indicated sections of the *Institutes*:

Scripture: *Inst*. I.6–7; II.10–11.

Divine providence: *Inst*. I.16–18.

Christ's ascension: *Inst*. II.16.14–16.

Union with Christ: *Inst*. III.1–4.

Predestination: *Inst*. III.21–24.

Present and future life: *Inst*. III.9–10.

Church as means of nurture: *Inst*. IV.1, 3.

Calvin, John. *On the Christian Life: A New Translation*. Translated by Raymond A. Blacketer. Crossway, 2024. This is a translation of *Inst*. III.6–10.

For Digging Deeper

Lane, Anthony N. S. *A Reader's Guide to Calvin's "Institutes."* Baker Academic, 2009.

McNutt, Jennifer Powell, and Herman Selderhuis, eds. *The Oxford Handbook of the Bible and the Reformation*. Oxford University Press, 2024.

Muller, Richard A. *The Unaccommodated Calvin: Studies in the Foundation of a Theological Tradition*. Oxford University Press, 2000.

Sanchez, Michelle C. *Calvin and the Resignification of the World: Creation, Incarnation, and the Problem of Political Theology in the 1559 "Institutes."* Cambridge University Press, 2019.

Wendel, François. *Calvin: Origins and Development of His Religious Thought*. Translated by Philip Maret. Labyrinth, 1987.

Zachman, Randall. *John Calvin as Teacher, Pastor, and Theologian: The Shape of His Writings and Thought*. Baker Academic, 2006.

FOUR

Calvin's Commentaries

The Bible for Exiles

It is important to notice how [Abraham] unties this inextricable knot; namely, by taking refuge in Divine Providence. . . . Whenever the Lord gives a command, many things are perpetually occurring to frustrate our purpose: means fail, we are destitute of counsel, all avenues seem closed. In such straits, the only remedy against despondency is to leave the event to God, in order that he may open a way for us where there is none. Just as we act unjustly towards God when we hope for nothing from him but what our senses can perceive, so we pay him the highest honor, when, in affairs of perplexity, we nevertheless entirely rest upon his providence.

—Calvin, Commentary on Genesis 22:7 (1554)[1]

[Paul] is here describing how God clothes us twice, first with the righteousness of Christ and sanctification of the Spirit in this life and then after death with immortality and glory. . . . The groaning of believers . . . arises from their knowledge that here they are exiles from their native land.

—Calvin, Commentary on 2 Corinthians 5:3–4 (1548)[2]

Although the whole world rise up against us . . . they can be brought to nought in a moment, as soon as God shows himself favorable towards

---

1. CTS 1:568; CO 23:316.
2. CNTC 10:67–68; CO 50:61–62.

us. . . . God has more than enough . . . both of weapons and of strength, to preserve and defend his Church.

—Calvin, Commentary on Psalm 46 (1557)[3]

A Biblical Blueprint for the Exilic Life

This chapter introduces Calvin's biblical exegesis, focusing especially on his formal commentaries. These differ from academic lectures in Geneva and contributions to the pastors' weekly Bible study (the so-called *congrégations*) that became, in many cases, the basis for published commentaries.[4] Calvin's preaching, on the other hand, was never intended for international audiences and was more narrowly directed to local congregations as part of his pastoral ministry.[5] We will consider the theology expressed across the commentaries and lectures here and focus more specifically in chapter 6 on how the sermons adapt these themes to local concerns. The last chapter surveyed how Calvin's *Institutes* integrated themes of providence, predestination, and ecclesiology into a vision of comfort for exiles. His commentaries flesh out this same vision through direct engagement with the biblical text. Calvin preferred a *lectio continua* (continuous reading) approach to exegesis because this forced interpreters to take up issues as they appear in scripture, rather than selecting only topics that suited them. Beginning with the appearance of his Romans commentary in 1540, Calvin wrote scholarly expositions of nearly every book of the Bible.[6] Like the *Institutes*, Calvin's commentaries explain the church's exilic condition and illustrate God's provision for believers. This chapter highlights four lessons Calvin's commentaries presented to sixteenth-century readers: (1) Adam's excommunication establishes the conditions for human existence, (2) David's exilic experiences define his example of faith for believers, (3) Israel's exile frames predestination as both comfort and warning, and (4) Paul unveils God's design for the church as nurturing mother to believers in exile. In each case, Calvin's commentaries treat themes already present in the biblical text and, in many instances, also examined in the *Institutes*. Together with the *Institutes*, they convey a biblical blueprint for spiritual exile that pilgrims in Calvin's day could use to make sense of their experiences.

3. Comm. Ps. 46:6, 10 (CTS 9:201, 205; CO 31:463, 465).
4. Erik de Boer, *The Genevan School of the Prophets: The Congrégations of the Company of Pastors and Their Influence in 16th Century Europe* (Droz, 2012).
5. See chap. 6, below.
6. T. H. L. Parker, *Calvin's New Testament Commentaries*, 2nd ed. (T&T Clark, 1993); and Parker, *Calvin's Old Testament Commentaries* (T&T Clark, 1986; repr., Westminster John Knox, 1993).

Adam's Excommunication and Ours: Exile as the Human Condition

In the Bible's opening chapters, Calvin sees stories of exile in the lives of Adam (Gen. 3), Cain (Gen. 4), and Abraham (Gen. 12). He takes each example of literal migration in these stories and relates it to spiritual exile.[7] Adam's banishment is a paradigm for humanity's spiritual condition. The exilic experiences of Cain and Abraham illustrate two sides of predestination. These lessons appear in both Calvin's preaching on Genesis and his commentary, which was published in 1554, as Geneva's population surged with émigrés.[8] We consider Calvin's commentary on Adam's exile here, returning in chapter 6 to how the reformer portrayed Cain and Abraham in his sermons on Genesis.

Adam appears twice in scripture in the context of exile, both in Genesis 3: the first couple's attempt to hide from God (3:7–10) and their subsequent expulsion from the garden (3:22–24).[9] In Calvin's commentary on John, this source material informs his description of "the whole human race" as "exiles," "complete strangers to the kingdom of God" due to our "corruption . . . in the person of Adam."[10] It also explains the *Institutes*'s language for the world as a "place of exile" from which people are "recalled" only by death. For Calvin, Genesis 3 establishes two critical characteristics of humanity's situation in spiritual exile: (1) its universality and (2) the presence of both divine judgment and divine mercy. Calvin trains readers to discern sin's effects everywhere. Just as ubiquitous, however, is evidence of God's intervention.

Consider humanity's short-lived self-exile in Genesis 3:7–10. Adam and Eve, naked and ashamed, attempt to flee from God. Calvin, as he does in the *Institutes*, attributes the first sin to both human responsibility and divine sovereignty: "Whatever sin and fault there is in the fall of our first parents remains with themselves; but there is sufficient reason why the eternal counsel of God preceded it, though that reason is concealed from us . . . [in] the secret counsel of God—[which is] to us like a labyrinth."[11] Calvin's exegesis reflects the views of earlier interpreters such as John Chrysostom (d. 407) and Nicholas of Lyra (d. 1349). Eating forbidden fruit "opened the eyes" of humanity to evil, corrupting heart and mind so that Adam and Eve

---

7. See Kenneth J. Woo, "Against 'Many Cains' and Fickle Travelers: Patterns of Exile in Calvin's Exegesis," in *Calvin, Exile, and Religious Refugees: Papers of the Thirteenth International Congress on Calvin Research*, ed. Arnold Huijgen and Karin Maag (Vandenhoeck & Ruprecht, 2024), 11–36.

8. Comm. Genesis (1554; CTS 1–2; CO 23:5–622).

9. Richard Stauffer, "L'exégèse de Genèse 1, 1–3 chez Luther et Calvin," in *Interprètes de la Bible: Études sur les réformateurs du XVIe siècle* (Beauchesne, 1980), 59–85.

10. Comm. John 3:3, 6 (1553; CNTC 4:63, 66; CO 47:54, 57).

11. Comm. Gen. 3:7 (CTS 1:157–59; CO 23:64).

(absurdly) presumed that they could hide even from God.[12] Nobody believed God actually lost track of them. Rather, thinkers like Augustine and the Jewish interpreter Rashi (Solomon ben Isaac; d. 1105) represent a consensus that takes God's question in verse 9—"Where are you?"—as an expression of mercy. Calvin agrees: God "with his voice alone recalls the fugitives . . . as physician rather than judge."[13] The serpent received no second chance, but God's punishment of the humans took a different turn. It had "the design of leading [them] to repentance."[14] Adam received mercy alongside God's judgment.

Next the plot moves from Adam's failed escape to his expulsion from the garden.[15] Calvin observes the same interplay of condemnation and forbearance toward humanity. Even death, rightly dreaded as "contrary to nature," was but a "more violent remedy" for sin.[16] God imposed death as the means through which Adam would regain "the life from which he had fallen."[17] Here Calvin follows traditional Christian interpretations of Genesis 3, which hold that Christ transforms, even for Adam, death into a doorway opening toward greater life.[18] Adam, however, was a slow learner. He named his wife "Eve," which means "life," simply out of relief that God did not strike them dead immediately.[19] Calvin reasons that God needed to drive home both sin's seriousness and God's kindness by consigning Adam to a new situation. Exile taught Adam, and humanity after him, to look out for God's mercy.

Calvin follows Augustine in taking Adam's expulsion from the garden as a precursor to church discipline. Adam was excommunicated. As in church discipline, this involved exclusion from a sacrament—in Adam's case, the tree of life.[20] Augustine describes the tree's sacramental nature as a "visible sign

---

12. Comm. Gen. 3:7–10 (CTS 1:157–62; CO 23:63–66); Chrysostom, *Homilies on Genesis* 17.1–44; Greek: "Homilia XVII," in PG 53:134–48; Nicholas of Lyra, *Biblia sacra cvm Glossis, interlineari & ordinaria, Nicolai Lyrani Postilla & Moralitatibus, Burgensis Additionibus, & Thoringi Replicis*, 5 vols. ([Ex Officina Gasparis Treschel], 1545), I:41v; and Augustine, *City of God* XIV.17 (Latin: *De Civitate Dei*, in CCSL 48:439–40).

13. Comm. Gen. 3:8–14 (CTS 1:159–67; CO 23:65–66, 68); also Rashi, *Pentateuch with Targum Onkelos, Haptaroth and Rashi's Commentary*, trans. M. Rosenbaum and A. M. Silbermann, 5 vols. (1929; repr., Silbermann Family, 1973), I:14; and Augustine, *Literal Meaning of Genesis* XI.34.45 (PL 34:448).

14. Comm. Gen. 3:14 (CTS 1:165–67; CO 23:68).

15. Comm. Gen. 3:16–23 (CTS 1:171–87; CO 23:72–81).

16. Comm. Gen. 3:22 (CTS 1:182–84; CO 23:78–79).

17. Comm. Gen. 3:22–23 (CTS 1:182–87; CO 23:78–81).

18. Comm. Gen. 3:22–23 (CTS 1:182–87; CO 23:78–81).

19. Comm. Gen. 3:20 (CO 23:77).

20. Augustine, *Literal Meaning of Genesis* XI.40.54 (PL 34:451).

... of invisible wisdom."[21] Adam had a "privileged bodily existence" before sin.[22] Calvin agrees that intimacy with God and easy access to eternal life, formerly signified by eating from a tree, were lost in exile.[23] Removal from the garden was a constant reminder that this sanction "was not for a moment, or for a few days, but that [Adam] shall always be an exile from a happy life."[24] Yet here, too, judgment included mercy. Life outside Eden was hard—wilderness in every sense—but never "cut off from all hope of salvation."[25] Adam's punishment retained a pedagogical aim: "We know what is the efficacy of sacraments.... The tree was given as a pledge of life. Therefore, that [Adam] might understand himself to be deprived of his former life, a solemn excommunication is added; not that the Lord would cut him off from all hope of salvation, but, by taking away what he had given, would cause man to seek new assistance elsewhere.... From the moment [Adam] became alienated from God, it was necessary that he should recover life by the death of Christ."[26] God took away the tree, a symbol of life before sin and death, to train Adam's eyes to look forward to Christ, the promised Redeemer who restores life out of death. Daily glimpses of God's favor reinforced this hope of salvation by mitigating "the rigor of [God's] judgment." Adam's "exile ... was mercifully softened" by gifts such as food, livelihood, and a dwelling. From such displays of God's liberality "Adam infers that the Lord cares for him, [receiving] proof of paternal love."[27] God's fatherly beneficence meant that "innumerable miseries," including "death itself," never left Adam without "hope of pardon."[28] Adam's "temporal exile" furnishes this lesson about exile as a spiritual reality: Mercy is never far off.[29]

Everyday events were not the only arena for beholding God's kindness. Adam's new situation included new sacraments to replace the one from which he was expelled.[30] Animal sacrifices radiated both the stench of death and the aroma of righteousness. These were visible signs encompassing both

21. Augustine, *Literal Meaning of Genesis* XI.40.54 (PL 34:451). Augustine's oft-quoted definition of a sacrament as a "visible sign of an invisible grace" is a summary of his comments in *On Catechizing the Uninstructed* XXVI.50 ("De Catechizandis Rudibus," in PL 40:344).
22. Augustine, *Literal Meaning of Genesis* XI.40.54 (PL 34:451).
23. Comm. Gen. 3:22 (CTS 1:182–84; CO 23:78–79).
24. Comm. Gen. 3:22 (CTS 1:184; CO 23:79).
25. Comm. Gen. 3:22 (CTS 1:184; CO 23:79).
26. Comm. Gen. 3:22 (CTS 1:184; CO 23:79).
27. Comm. Gen. 3:22–23 (CTS 1:184–85; CO 23:79–80).
28. Comm. Gen. 3:22–23 (CTS 1:184–85; CO 23:79–80).
29. Comm. Gen. 3:22–23 (CTS 1:184–85; CO 23:79–80).
30. Comm. Gen. 3:22–23 (CTS 1:184–85; CO 23:79–80); see also Augustine, *On Genesis Against the Manichaeans* II.22.34 ("De Genesi contra Manichaeos," in PL 34:213–14); Augustine, *Literal Meaning of Genesis* XI.40.55 (PL 34:451–52).

God's judgment and the promise of God's mercy. Sacraments were not for Adam's benefit alone. Exile had become the universal human condition, estranging all people from God as the consequence of Adam's sin. Animal sacrifices continued in different forms with Israel's worship, which pointed forward to the church's sacraments. In 1559 Calvin expounds upon this from the pulpit. Baptism and the Eucharist signify, with greater clarity, the blessing of life eternal that, after Adam's sin, comes only through Jesus Christ.[31] In exile, Adam had to learn a new way to approach God: by faith in God as Redeemer. Sacraments functioned for Adam just as they did for Adam's sixteenth-century children in exile, by holding forth the promise of salvation in Christ to awaken, guide, and strengthen faith.[32] As Calvin states in the *Institutes*, a sacrament involves "an outward sign by which the Lord seals on our consciences the promises of his goodwill toward us in order to sustain the weakness of our faith."[33]

Once more Calvin's exegesis puts differently what the *Institutes* also affirms about human experience.[34] Deprived of Adam's former intimacy with God, subject to hardship and the horror of death, the children of Adam encounter mercy in exile through daily displays of divine providence, but especially in formal sacraments that mediate God's presence. Unlike Augustine, whose account of Adam's excommunication also stresses the ongoing importance of sacraments, Calvin adds a polemical twist. Where Augustine concedes that sin taints all of life in exile, including sacraments, Calvin turns this logic into an attack on Catholic practices in ways that Augustine, a Catholic bishop, would not have.[35] Calvin criticizes Adam's false sense of security in a sacrament (the tree of life) as a reason for his expulsion into a situation that demands faith, admonishing hearers to be on guard against both false sacraments and improper use of true ones.[36] Misplaced confidence in rituals apart from faith in Christ was a stock complaint of Protestant polemic, appearing here as a criticism of both Rome and evangelicals who take sacraments too casually.[37] Sacraments, even as God's gifts, are subject to error and abuse. The same teaching about God's provision in exile could also distinguish God's faithful from those whom Calvin wanted to exile. We will return in chapter 6

31. Serm. Gen. 3:22–24, October 18, 1559 (*SC* XI/1:235).
32. *Inst*. IV.14.1–12 (*OS* 5:259).
33. *Inst*. IV.14.1 (*OS* 5:258–69).
34. See chap. 3, above.
35. Augustine, *City of God* XX.26 (CCSL 48:748–51).
36. Serm. Gen. 3:22–24, October 18, 1559 (*SC* XI/1:231–39).
37. Serm. Gen. 3:22–24, October 18, 1559 (*SC* XI/1:231–39). For views in Geneva that Calvin considered defective, see Christian Grosse, *Les rituels de la Cène: Le culte eucharistique réformé à Genève (XVIe-XVIIe siècles)* (Droz, 2008), 515–23.

to Calvin's teaching that Adam had two kinds of children in exile: elect and reprobate, represented (respectively) in Abraham and Cain.

Imitation of David: The Historical David as Pattern for Exile

King David has had a firm hold on the imaginations of readers from ancient times to the present day. Calvin was no exception. During an era that resulted in permanent changes for biblical interpretation,[38] reformers continued traditions that lifted up David as an exemplar of faith, while adapting him to the needs of their moment. For mainstream Protestants this meant styling David as the ancient forerunner of evangelical doctrines like justification by faith alone, or lifting up David's "theology" and practices to condemn Rome or radical reform movements. Though not always consistent in their own exegetical practices, evangelicals championed the Bible's "literal sense" (*sensus literalis*) against what they decried as excessive allegorizing prevalent in the medieval church.[39] They accused Rome of bending scripture to justify false teaching. This, too, was not exactly new. Centuries earlier, Jewish and Christian commentators already voiced preference for the literal meaning and historical circumstances of biblical texts. Medieval commentators such as Rashi, David Kimhi (d. 1235), Andrew of St. Victor (d. 1175), Herbert of Bosham, and Nicholas of Lyra laid the groundwork for Reformation-era "historical interpretation."[40] With the Psalms, this meant tempering the instinctive reflex to reach for christological allegories. For centuries Christian exegesis had favored interpreting David almost exclusively as a type or symbol of Christ.[41] The reformers' interest in recovering the historical David took many forms, including reconstructing David's life as a model for imitation. Along these lines, Calvin's approach stands out for making David's exilic status central to his identity and example for believers.

David's experiences, in the hands of the reformers, mapped seamlessly onto sixteenth-century doctrinal disputes and political changes. In Wittenberg,

---

38. David C. Steinmetz, ed., *The Bible in the Sixteenth Century* (Duke University Press, 1990).

39. David C. Steinmetz, "The Superiority of Pre-Critical Exegesis," *Theology Today* 37 (1980): 27–38.

40. Beryl Smalley, *The Study of the Bible in the Middle Ages* (Philosophical Library, 1952), 150–56, 186–95.

41. Henri de Lubac, *Medieval Exegesis: The Four Senses of Scripture*, trans. E. M. Macierowski, 3 vols. (Eerdmans, 2000), 2:1–9, 83–107. For Calvin's use of typology, which identifies how Christian teaching is prefigured symbolically in the Old Testament, see David C. Steinmetz, "John Calvin as Interpreter of the Bible," in *Calvin and the Bible*, ed. Donald K. McKim (Cambridge University Press, 2006), 282–91; and Wulfert de Greef, "Calvin as Commentator on the Psalms," in McKim, *Calvin and the Bible*, 85–106.

Lutherans Philip Melanchthon and Johannes Bugenhagen (d. 1558) reliably cited David's repentance after moral lapses to illustrate justification by faith alone.[42] Calvin similarly calls justification "the chief point of salvation" in his commentary on Psalm 32.[43] David uncovers "the partial righteousness" of "Papists," exposing their failure to grasp that "we are accounted righteous before God only by the free remission of sins." This same teaching was later "attested by the mouth of Paul," which "utterly destroys the righteousness of works."[44] Martin Bucer's exegesis of Psalm 24 sets David's piety against Rome's. David, Bucer explains, esteemed sacraments yet confessed that they do not convey God's grace apart from faith.[45] Calvin observes how David correctly appraised tabernacle ceremonies as "ladders" for worshipers to ascend, by faith, to God. With David, Calvin's contemporaries had a "mirror" in which to behold the function of preaching and sacraments in their own day.[46] This was one of several ways Bucer and Calvin, along with other reformers, came to depict the historical David as a precursor to early modern "Protestant piety."[47]

Calvin's teaching finds additional lessons in the historical David. Calvin's David consistently reinforces the *Institutes*'s teaching on providence and the present life as exile. The Psalms, for example, model the kind of "providential faith" that Calvin commends in the *Institutes* when they depict how David attended to daily signs of "God's activity as creator and sustainer of nature and history."[48] "David acted wisely," Calvin notes regarding Psalm 9:3, "when, upon seeing his enemies turn their backs, he lifted up the eyes of his mind to God to perceive that victory flowed to him from no other source than . . . God's incomprehensible aid."[49] In like manner, believers should differ from "ungodly men" who are "blind" and oblivious to God's presence apart from "what is

---

42. Philip Melanchthon, *Commentarii in Psalmos, 1535–1555*, ed. C. G. Bretschneider, Philippi Melanthonis Opera quae supersunt omnia, vol. 13 (Halle, 1846), 1065–66; and Johnannes Bugenhagen, *In librum Psalmorum interpretatio* (Basel, 1524), 74r. See also Luther, "First Psalms Lectures, 1513–1515," Ps. 32:8 (*LW* 10:147; *WA* 3:175–76).

43. Comm. Ps. 32 (CTS 8:521; CO 31:314); this is reminiscent of how the *Institutes* characterizes the doctrine as "the chief hinge upon which faith turns" (*Inst.* III.2.16 [OS 4:26]).

44. Comm. Ps. 32:1 (CTS 8:522–26; CO 31:314–17).

45. Martin Bucer, *Sacrorum Psalmorum libri quinque* (Strasbourg, 1529), 137r–v.

46. Comm. Ps. 9:11 (CTS 8:120–22; CO 31:101–2).

47. G. Sujin Pak, *The Judaizing Calvin* (Oxford University Press, 2010), 87–94. Besides justification and worship, reformers also put the historical David squarely within debates of their time as the archetypal "godly ruler." Bucer and Beza, e.g., exhorted Protestant leaders to remain steadfast in pursuing reform. See R. Gerald Hobbs, "Bucer's Use of King David as Mirror of the Christian Prince," *Reformation & Renaissance Review* 5 (2003): 102–28; and Scott M. Manetsch, *Theodore Beza and the Quest for Peace in France: 1572–1598* (Brill, 2000), 112–13.

48. Barbara Pitkin, *What Pure Eyes Could See: Calvin's Doctrine of Faith in Its Exegetical Context* (Oxford University Press, 1999), 98–130; and *Inst.* I.16.6–9 (OS 3:196–201).

49. Comm. Ps. 9:3 (CTS 8:113; CO 31:97–98).

visible to the eye."[50] Though Calvin does not attribute this psalm to David, his comments on Psalm 46 similarly contrast sight with faith in God's providence: "Although the whole world rise up against us, and confound all things by their increased madness, . . . God has more than enough, both of weapons and of strength, to preserve and defend his Church which he has adopted."[51]

Like others, Calvin tapped into traditions that held David to be a prophet who saw with perfect clarity the sweep of God's plan for history. Yet the reformer could just as often portray David's faith operating in a more mundane, but no less comforting, register. Even the mighty King David, Israel's storied prophet, often had only a partial, obscured view of God's activity in this life. Psalm 73 depicts David struggling, as early modern believers might, with the prosperity of the wicked (73:16). David "reflected on this subject on all sides, and yet . . . could not comprehend how God, amidst so great disorders and confusions, continued to govern the world."[52] Like ours, David's faith in God's providence failed to explain difficult experiences. Nowhere was this more evident than in exile.

In Calvin's 1557 commentary on the Psalms, David repeatedly appears as a fugitive in exile. Specific psalms of exile recount details from the books of Samuel regarding David's removal from Israel's religious and political centers. These include David's fleeing Saul (1 Sam. 21–24) and his own son Absalom (2 Sam. 15–17). Calvin thus cannot be accused of imposing exile onto David's story. The reformer's exegesis takes what he finds in scripture and holds up David prominently as an exile whose life speaks to early modern political exiles. Calvin, we know, drew autobiographical connections between the exiled David and his own story.[53] In his introduction to his commentary, Calvin likewise commends the Psalms to others: "This book holds forth this benefit, which is desirable above all others: that not only do we possess familiar access to God, but also that we are allowed and free to spread out before God our infirmities, which we would be ashamed to confess before men."[54] The Psalms beckon readers to learn from biblical examples how to pray, especially in times of hardship, which Calvin more narrowly defines in his life as related to his flight and exile from France. In this exilic context, Calvin learned prayer by following David's "footsteps" as a refugee reformer. All that David "suffered," Calvin states with gratitude, "God set before me as an example to imitate."[55]

50. Comm. Ps. 9:3 (CTS 8:113; CO 31:98).
51. Comm. Ps. 46:6, 10 (CTS 9:201, 205; CO 31:463, 465).
52. Comm. Ps. 73:16 (CTS 10:141; CO 31:682).
53. See chap. 1, above.
54. "Author's Preface," Comm. Psalms (CTS 8:xxxviii; CO 31:16–18).
55. "Author's Preface," Comm. Psalms (CTS 8:xl, xliv; CO 31:21, 27).

Anecdotes from his flight from France and struggles to establish his ministry in Geneva tell us that Calvin followed not a generic David but David the refugee, whose displacement and betrayal mirrored Calvin's own. Conforming "myself to the example of so great and so excellent a person," Calvin writes, has been "of much service in enabling me to understand the Psalms, so that in my meditation upon them, I did not wander . . . in an unknown region."[56] The exilic David was Calvin's hermeneutical key to the Psalms. This calls to mind how Calvin, in his exegesis, channeled Paul or prophets like Jeremiah. Like other Renaissance authors, such as Erasmus, Calvin engaged in a form of rhetorical "imitation," echoing an ancient writer's style to convey their thoughts.[57] Close identification with biblical writers gives Calvin's exegesis its confident tone, though he never admits to mimicking Paul's authority or claims to be a prophet.[58] Not so with David. Writing about David's struggles in exile is second nature: "I discourse upon them as matters of which I have familiar experience."[59]

How did Calvin depict this historical David as an example for others? He repeatedly focuses on David's awareness of spiritual deprivation and eagerness to be reunited with God's means of nurture. Commenting on Psalm 27, Calvin acknowledges historical distance while insisting on continuity between Christians' and David's hunger in exile: "We are in very different circumstances from the ancient fathers; but so far as God still preserves his people under a certain external order, and draws them to him by earthly instructions, temples still have their beauty, which deservedly ought to draw the affections and desires of the faithful to them. The Word, sacraments, public prayers, and other helps of the same kind, cannot be neglected, without a wicked contempt of God, who manifests himself to us in these ordinances, as in a mirror."[60] From this depiction of David, Calvin draws two conclusions for his readers. First, the church's ministry and worship are necessary for believers' spiritual well-being. David's pining for the "house of the Lord" (v. 4) while in exile arises from his knowledge that, through specific means, "God raises us to his presence, descending from his inconceivable glory to us, . . . furnishing us on earth with a vision of his heavenly glory." Calvin addresses readers who may encounter others (or find themselves) in situations where access to biblical teaching and pure worship are difficult or impossible

---

56. "Author's Preface," Comm. Psalms (CTS 8:xlviii; CO 31:33).
57. G. W. Pigman III, "Versions of Imitation in the Renaissance," *Renaissance Quarterly* 33 (1980): 1–32.
58. Bruce Gordon, *Calvin* (Yale University Press, 2009), 110–11.
59. "Author's Preface," Comm. Psalms (CTS 8:xlviii; CO 31:33).
60. Comm. Ps. 27:4 (CTS 8:454–55; CO 31:274).

to come by. This was no excuse to settle for deprivation. Not even David thought himself above this. In Psalm 61, David likens "[deprivation] of hearing the word and the administration of the sacraments" to being banished to "the ends of the earth."[61] Believers must, even at great cost, learn from "the example of David to persevere in crying out to God" for access to spiritual sustenance when this is lacking.

At the same time, David was not so foolish as to confuse God, as Rome does, with things like sacraments. The "papists," Calvin says, make this mistake by "wickedly transform[ing] God into whatever shapes please their fancy."[62] David valued sacraments within proper limits. He longed for them as spiritual lifelines without confusing symbols of Christ for the Lord himself. Calvin repeats this argument in his commentary on at least ten of the many psalms set during David's seasons of exile: Psalms 4, 18, 27, 42, 52, 61, 63, 84, 118, and 119.[63] Two themes appear across Calvin's exegesis of these psalms: (1) David's longing and sense of deprivation when denied access to preaching and sacraments in the earthly sanctuary; (2) David's refusal to reduce or bind God even to legitimate means of spiritual provision. No other reformer focuses as much on David in exile. Calvin's David repeatedly calls on contemporary believers to seek biblical preaching and sacraments in public worship.[64] This reinforces the same teaching about the church found in book IV of the *Institutes*—that it is the locus of nurture—by vividly connecting the reality of spiritual exile to the question of political exile in Calvin's day.[65] Sometimes it is necessary to leave one's homeland to find the provision David hungered for in exile.[66] Chapters 6 and 8, below, return to how Calvin made this case forcefully in his sermons, insisting on the benefits of Reformed worship and defending his ministry against various detractors in Geneva.

The Psalms have a long history of beloved reception in Judaism and Christianity. Calvin's contribution to this tradition reflects how violence, migration, and exile in his day accentuated believers' longing for a home beyond the power of rulers and powers to pillage or take away. To a church dispersed across borders, Calvin's teaching commends the Psalms as a pattern for imitation

---

61. Comm. Ps. 61:1–4 (CTS 9:410–13; CO 31:580–81).
62. Comm. Ps. 27:8 (CTS 8:458; CO 31:276).
63. Kenneth J. Woo, "Abraham, David, and the Problem of Exile in Calvin's Theology," *Harvard Theological Review* 118 (2025): 326–27.
64. Kenneth J. Woo, "David Among the Reformers," in *The Oxford Handbook of King David*, ed. Lena-Sophia Tiemeyer and David Shepherd (Oxford University Press, forthcoming).
65. See chap. 3, above.
66. In general, Calvin's anti-Nicodemite writings present resistance in place and exile as equally faithful options, defending Calvin's own flight to Geneva as a matter of God's calling. See Kenneth J. Woo, *Nicodemism and the English Calvin, 1544–1584* (Brill, 2019), 30–37.

that he found useful and comforting, inviting others also to think, pray, and worship like David—but especially like the David one encounters in exile.

True or False Church: Election and Apostasy in Calvin's Exegesis of the Prophets

As grist for the mill of an exilic imagination, Adam and David taught readers of Calvin's commentaries the innate qualities of life in exile. While Adam helps explain the origin of hardship and suffering in humanity's spiritual exile, David demonstrates the singular gift of God's presence in ordinary and special provision for God's people. Both biblical figures reinforce the need for faith in God's providence and appointed means of nurture in the wilderness. We turn now to another part of the biblical canon: the Hebrew prophets, where the question of French reform emerges pointedly in the convergence of predestination and exile in Calvin's exegesis. His preface to his cousin Pierre-Robert Olivétan's French translation of the New Testament (1535) makes a striking observation about God's solidarity, as fellow exile, among the Israelites during the exodus: "Being like a fugitive, [the Lord] accompanied them night and day in their flight."[67] During years of wilderness wandering, as exiles, the elect people received God's special care; this theme likewise pervades the later history of Israel's successive domination by foreign powers in the days of the prophets. We also focus here on Calvin's exegetical lectures, delivered to students and fellow pastors in Geneva. Those lectures frequently formed the basis for future publications, either as revised lectures or as formal commentaries for an international readership. This was true of Calvin's lectures delivered to pastors preparing to serve Reformed congregations in France, a situation he found mirrored in Israel's exilic experiences. Here we consider Calvin's lectures and commentaries on the prophets together as expressions of his ministry as doctor of the church, offering specialized training to others.[68]

The reformer's lectures on Jeremiah, published in 1563, appeared with a dedication to Frederick III, Elector Palatinate. Calvin praises Frederick's advocacy for Reformed refugees, whose plight mirrored the anxious realities Jeremiah addressed in Judah.[69] French Reformed believers are the dedicatees

---

67. John Calvin, "Épître à tous amateurs de Jésus-Christ (1535)," in *La vraie piété, divers traités de Jean Calvin et Confession de foi de Guillaume Farel*, ed. Irena Backus and Claire Chimelli (Labor et Fides, 1986), 27.

68. Peter Wilcox, "The Lectures of John Calvin and the Nature of His Audience, 1555–1564," *Archiv für Reformationsgeschichte* 87 (1996): 136–48.

69. Preface to Lect. Jeremiah (1563; CTS 17:xvi–xxiv; CO 20:72–79).

of Calvin's 1561 lectures on Daniel.[70] He points to their faith amid adversity as proof of their election. Calvin recounts his leaving France as a break from idolatry, like Daniel's. He elevates his refugee status by claiming to harbor no regrets for leaving "a region from which the truth of God, pure religion, and the doctrine of eternal salvation are banished, and the very kingdom of Christ laid prostrate." Employing violent imagery, Calvin urges French readers to similarly see their nation for what it has become. Daniel is a "mirror" of God's presence with them amid persecution and scattering. The preface arranges predestination, providence, and exile into a chorus of comfort. God's election is sure. Providence guarantees that God remains "master of the games," governing history for the sake of his elect even when this is not obvious. Similar themes appear in Calvin's commentary on Isaiah (1559), which likewise relates Israel's exilic past to the church's experiences.[71] Finally, Calvin's exegesis of the Minor Prophets reveals the ease with which his reading of these texts promoted a remnant theology of true church versus false church, seamlessly portrayed as combatants on the divided terrain of French religion and politics.[72]

Spanning a substantial portion of the Old Testament, the prophetic books showcase the anticipation, devastation, and long aftermath of Jerusalem's destruction and the people's exile. The plot was ready-made for Calvin's teaching as refugee theologian. Israel's political exile was a pointed expression of their spiritual exile. This backdrop makes the finality of predestination and its relationship to divine providence pop into sharp relief. Calvin treats these and related ideas in exegetical works on Isaiah (1559), Jeremiah (1563), Ezekiel (1565), Daniel (1561), and the Minor Prophets (1557, 1559).

Calvin carefully parses the prophets' pronouncements of blessing and condemnation by distinguishing between general election and special election. Not all words meant for Israel as a chosen nation apply to matters of individual salvation. Conversely, guarantees of deliverance point ultimately to salvation in Christ. As Calvin notes regarding Hosea 11:8–9, such promises cannot pertain to the reprobate, though they also were present to hear these words and benefited from being embedded among the elect: "Punishment was mitigated not only with regard to the elect, but also with regard to the reprobate, who were led into captivity. We must yet remember, that when God spared them for a time, he chiefly consulted the good of his elect. . . . The

---

70. Preface to Lect. Daniel (1561; CTS 24:lxiv, lxxiv–lxxv; CO 18:615, 623–24).

71. Barbara Pitkin, *Calvin, the Bible, and History: Exegesis and Historical Reflection in the Era of Reform* (Oxford University Press, 2020), 122–40.

72. Jon Balserak, *Establishing the Remnant Church in France: Calvin's Lectures on the Minor Prophets, 1556–1559* (Brill, 2011), 19–64.

Lord spared [Israel] for a time; for among them was included his Church, in the same way as the wheat is preserved in the chaff."[73]

This basic presupposition, that the prophets' audiences included both elect and reprobate persons, brings Calvin's doctrine of predestination to bear on his interpretation of the prophetic books in several ways.[74] First, Calvin reads double meaning into God's acts of judgment. During prolonged exile, the same action could function as both destruction of the reprobate and fatherly chastisement of God's children. Consider the terrifying announcement of Jerusalem's devastation. God's vow to make the city "a waste, . . . hissing, . . . and a curse" (Jer. 25:18) at once admonishes believers while hardening "the unbelieving who are in thick darkness," leaving them without excuse for failure to repent.[75] Second, the prophets' use of "Israel" for two groups mapped conveniently onto Calvin's context, where he juxtaposed the use of *church* for two groups: (1) the true church and (2) imposters who apostatized yet presumed upon God's favor.[76] Predictably, Israel's remnant in exile mirrored the French Reformed churches and evangelicals more broadly. They were elect according to God's mercy. The prophets called this remnant "Israel" out of the faithless assembly, even as the false church persecuted them. Calvin recasts Rome in the role of violent "bastards" who illegitimately claim the name "church," just as apostate Israel attempted to deny God's rejection of them.[77] Rhetoric depicting French Catholics as "incurable" with the "madness of idolatry" primed pastors training for ministry in France for the outbreak of religious war.[78]

A final implication of predestination in Calvin's exegesis of the prophets is reassurance that flows from the immutability of God's decree. God's commitment to the elect never wavers. The divine decree prevails despite the most convincing appearances to the contrary.[79] Israel's story teaches believers to

---

73. Lect. Hosea 11:8–9 (1557; CTS 26:400–407; *CO* 42:441–46); also Lect. Jer. 31:38–40 (CTS 20:147–52; *CO* 38:701–4); Lect. Zech. 1:17; 10:8 (1559; CTS 30:50–52, 294–95; *CO* 44:147–49, 294–95); and Lect. Mal. 1:2–6 (1559; CTS 30:463–82; *CO* 44:395–409).

74. Kenneth J. Woo, "Election in John Calvin," in *The T&T Clark Handbook of Election*, ed. Edwin Chr. van Driel (Bloomsbury, 2023), 220–24.

75. Lect. Jer. 25:18 (CTS 19:266–69; *CO* 38:487–88); also Lect. Ezek. 6:9 (1565; CTS 22:228–32; *CO* 40:144–47); and Lect. Zech. 10:2 (CTS 30:279–83; *CO* 44:285–88).

76. Balserak, *Remnant*, 19–64.

77. Preface to Lect. Dan. (CTS 24:lxiv, lxxiv–lxxv; *CO* 18:623–24); also Lect. Jer. 15:1–2 (CTS 18:247–53; *CO* 38:205–9); Lect. Ezek. 11:14–16 (CTS 22:362–68; *CO* 40:236–40); Lect. Hosea 1:10 (CTS 26:62–68; *CO* 42:216–19); Lect. Zech. 10:2 (CTS 30:279–83; *CO* 44:285–88); Lect. Mal. 1:2–6 (CTS 30:463–82; *CO* 44:403); and Comm. Isa. 11:12 (1559; CTS 11:390–91; *CO* 36:246–47).

78. Jon Balserak, *John Calvin as Sixteenth-Century Prophet* (Oxford University Press, 2014), 130–43.

79. Comm. Isa. 11:12 (CTS 11:390–91; *CO* 36:246–47); Lect. Jer. 13:13–14; 46:23–27 (CTS 18:169–75; 20:597–605; *CO* 38:159–62; 39:303–5); Lect. Ezek. 16:62 (CTS 23:178–80; *CO* 40:396–97); and Lect. Dan. 10:13 (CTS 25:251–54; *CO* 41:205).

expect the seemingly impossible: God will yet again gather outcasts scattered amid idolatrous nations. In commenting on Isaiah 11:12—"[God] shall assemble the outcasts of Israel, and gather together the dispersed of Judah from the four corners of the earth"—Calvin observes,

> The word "gather" is repeated.... He shows how efficacious God's calling will be; for as soon as he shall give the slightest indication that such is his pleasure, he will restore the people.... Under the same leader we ought at the present day to expect the restoration of a wretched and scattered Church; for there is no hope of gathering the remnant but by the elect looking to this ensign. We ought frequently, therefore, to call to remembrance those promises, that by relying on them we may more and more strengthen our hearts.[80]

How will this gathering of outcasts come about? Through the same ministry of God's Word. Both ancient prophets and modern pastors offer God's people in exile a steady diet of sound doctrine, "food for God's children."[81] This includes the sustaining word of comfort that God is bringing his saving decree to pass even when, by all accounts, the church seems hopelessly insecure, its members scattered, its future bleak with despair. For sixteenth-century evangelicals, Israel's exile encouraged them to stand firm in the cause of reform.

Honor Your Mother (and Pastors): Calvin's Pauline Ecclesiology of Nurture

Calvin's exegesis of Paul's letters abounds with reflections about the church's ministry as God's design for nurturing the elect in exile. As with other examples considered in this chapter, Calvin's interpretation of New Testament teaching concerning the church's situation and function addressed concrete realities of violence and displacement amid ecclesiastical reform.

Calvin's commentaries on 1–2 Timothy (1548) characterize the church's existence as one of perpetual calamity.[82] Taking up Paul's reflection on the "arduous and deeply anxious" nature of the "last days" (2 Tim. 3:1), Calvin applies this characterization not to some future apocalyptic crisis but to "the

---

80. Comm. Isa. 11:12 (CTS 11:390–91; *CO* 36:246–47); also Lect. Obad. 17 (1559; CTS 27:448–449; *CO* 43:195–96); Lect. Mic. 7:14 (1559; CTS 28:389–93; *CO* 43:422–24); Lect. Zeph. 3:14–15 (1559; CTS 29:299–301; *CO* 44:69–70); Lect. Hag. 2:21–23 (1559; CTS 29:384–88; *CO* 44:120–24); and Lect. Zech. 3:1–2 (CTS 30:80–85; *CO* 44:167–70).

81. Lect. Jer. 25:12 (CTS 19:256–57; *CO* 38:481); Comm. Isa. 49:1 (CTS 16:8–9; *CO* 37:3–5); Lect. Ezek. 20:40–44 (CTS 23:336–45; *CO* 40:508–14); Lect. Dan. 11:33–34 (CTS 25:326–34; *CO* 41:257–63); and Lect. Amos 9:14 (1559; CTS 27:411; *CO* 43:173–74).

82. Comm. 1 and 2 Tim. (1548; *CNTC* 10:179–344; *CO* 52:241–396).

universal condition of the Christian church," the lot of God's people since "the prophets and godly priests of old."[83] Calvin interprets old covenant and new covenant realities as a continuous history centered on salvation in Christ.[84] Differences between historical eras do not preclude claiming Paul for Calvin's side of contemporary disputes, especially against Rome.[85] At the same time, the church's exilic status means tolerating its imperfections: "If today there are mixed with us many whom we justly abhor, let us learn to groan patiently under that burden; . . . this is the lot of the Christian Church."[86] External threats include persecution promised to "all godly [people]" (2 Tim. 3:12).[87] Among these, Calvin singles out martyrdom, "exile, imprisonment, [and] flight." Yet not everyone will suffer overt violence. For some, "murmuring" and "slander" are enough to ensure that they "shall never be at peace and exempt from persecution." The elect, in particular, experience exile as "warfare." God's children live in a world that hates "Christ even in his members," where "Satan persecutes the servants of Christ."

Calvin was convinced that Paul grasped the church's exilic situation and oriented its faith accordingly. Specifically, the church's ministry awakens and nurtures faith like Abraham's. Calvin joined a long tradition, dating back to Paul, that sees the Hebrew patriarch as exemplar for Christian faith.[88] Like other reformers, Calvin took Paul's account of Abraham's righteousness in Romans 4 as a proof text for the evangelical doctrine of justification by faith alone.[89] Says Melanchthon, "Paul here as nowhere else refutes and rejects the righteousness of the Law. . . . The promise of grace . . . must be accepted *gratis*, by faith."[90] But there is more to Abraham's faith than its repudiation of Rome's reliance on works. It also possesses an unmistakable future orientation. Hebrews 11 celebrates Abraham explicitly for trusting God in exile. Calvin lifts up this distinctive quality in both the *Institutes* and the *Psychopannychia*.[91] In his commentary on Hebrews, a book he once attributed to Paul, Calvin identifies two aspects of Abraham's faith related to exile: (1) his

---

83. Comm. 2 Tim. 3:1 (*CNTC* 10:322; *CO* 52:375–76).
84. *Inst*. II.10.1–2 (*OS* 3:403–4).
85. Pitkin, *Calvin, the Bible, and History*, 49–50.
86. Comm. 2 Tim. 3:1 (*CNTC* 10:323; *CO* 52:376); see also *Inst*. IV.1.7 (*OS* 5:12).
87. Comm. 2 Tim. 3:12 (*CNTC* 10:327; *CO* 52:380).
88. David C. Steinmetz, "Calvin and Abraham: The Interpretation of Romans 4 in the Sixteenth Century," *Church History* 57 (1988): 443–555.
89. Comm. Rom. 4:1, 3 (1540; *CNTC* 8:82–84; *CO* 49:68–70); also Heinrich Bullinger, *In sanctissimam Pauli ad Romanos Epistolam Commentarius* (Zurich, 1533), 62r–63v; Luther, *Lectures on Romans* (*LW* 25:274–75); and Philip Melanchthon, *Commentary on Romans* (1540), trans. Fred Kramer, 2nd ed. (Concordia Publishing House, 1992), 106–7.
90. Melanchthon, *Romans*, 106–7.
91. *Inst*. II.10.11 (*OS* 3:411–12); and Calvin, *Psychopannychia*, 473 (*CO* 5:218).

willingness to depart into the unknown; and (2) his unwavering obedience over a lifetime of wandering as "a sojourner in the promised land," experiencing the opposite of what God had told him to expect.[92]

These themes appear as well in Calvin's exegesis of Romans 4. Abraham's faith, for Calvin, is recorded "not for his own sake alone. It does not refer to the individual calling of one particular person, but is a description of the way to obtain righteousness, which is one and unchanging among all believers."[93] Intrinsic to this universal calling is its forward-looking posture. Calvin glosses Paul's account of God's promise that Abraham would "inherit the world" (v. 13) by contrasting the present life and the life to come. The land of Canaan was, for Abraham, a type of the church's eschatological future.[94] Similarly, believers in the present life are given a "taste" of "the full and perfect blessing of God," while its "full possession" remains in the future.[95] The "very substance of Abraham's faith," says Calvin, is belief in God, "who gives life to the dead and calls into existence the things that do not exist" (v. 17). This is a "type and pattern of our general calling, by which our beginning is set before our eyes (not that which relates to our first birth, but which relates to the hope of the future life)."[96] Faith following in the footsteps of Abraham sees the present life as a journey toward homecoming, an arduous return from exile.

This eschatological orientation in Paul also surfaces in 2 Corinthians 5:3–4, about which Calvin says, "The apostle is here describing how God clothes us twice, first with the righteousness of Christ and sanctification of the Spirit in this life and then after death with immortality and glory. . . . The groaning of believers arises from the knowledge that here they are exiles from their native land and are shut up in the body as in a work-house."[97] This, unsurprisingly, is the same language the *Institutes* applies to believers' hope for the future.[98]

Paul, in Calvin's reading, further recognized that the kind of faith that truly grasps its exilic situation also struggles with this reality. In other words, in exile faith requires nurture. First Corinthians 12 relates spiritual gifts to roles in the church. In his comments, Calvin reflects on the logic of polity: "The natural order is that the gifts come before the actual office. . . . Offices are apportioned in such a way that by their combined efforts they may all build up the Church, each person making his own particular contribution at

---

92. Comm. Heb. 11:8–9 (1549; *CNTC* 12:167–68; *CO* 55:152–53).
93. Comm. Rom. 3:23 (*CNTC* 8:101; *CO* 49:86).
94. See note 41, above.
95. Comm. Rom. 4:13 (*CNTC* 8:91–92; *CO* 49:76–77).
96. Comm. Rom. 4:17 (*CNTC* 8:96; *CO* 49:81).
97. Comm. 2 Cor. 5:3–4 (1548; *CNTC* 10:67–68; *CO* 50:61–62).
98. See chap. 3, above; and *Inst*. III.9.5 (*OS* 4:175–76). See also Calvin, *Psychopannychia*, 442, 463–66 (*CO* 5:195, 211–13).

the same time."[99] God distributes gifts for diverse offices that complement one another to edify believers. Calvin notes that Paul describes both temporary and perpetual offices in the church, and he expresses his intent to take up this topic further in a forthcoming commentary on the book of Ephesians.[100]

Readers did not have to wait long. Calvin's commentary on Ephesians appeared two years later, in 1548. His interpretation of Ephesians 4:11–14 echoes the *Institutes*'s teaching about the church as nurturing mother to the elect. Once again picking up the subject of spiritual gifts, Calvin treats "five sorts of offices" that Paul catalogs here: apostle, evangelist, prophet, pastor, and teacher.[101] Of these, only the last two—pastor and teacher—are meant to exist at all times. By contrast, God raises up apostles, evangelists, and prophets for special seasons or tasks, such as founding the church initially. Calvin holds an especially high view of pastors in the church: "[Paul] commends the external ministry of the Word from the usefulness which it yields. The sum of it is that because the Gospel is preached by certain men appointed to that office, this is the economy by which the Lord wishes to govern His Church, that it may remain safe in this world, and ultimately obtain its complete perfection."[102] Next follow several comments anticipating objections to this teaching. Calvin opens his reflections on verses 11–14 by insisting that governance by men (like Calvin) called to teach and preach is Christ's design. It is no "human invention, the appointment of Christ. . . . As His own inviolable decree, it demands our assent. . . . That we have ministers of the Gospel is [Christ's] gift."

Ministers are therefore due honor and submission as Christ's gift to the church, which, through pastors, mothers God's children. God promises to "perfect" believers by uniting them with the one "Body of Christ," calling to mind similar language about union with Christ in the *Institutes*.[103] Calvin concedes that it is fair to ask why God, who "might Himself have performed this work," would delegate it to those less competent.[104] To this question Calvin attempts no further explanation than simply stating, "Paul teaches that a ministry is required, because such is the will of God." God ordained that the Spirit's "divine" work of effecting union with Christ occur through a human ministry. It is therefore "utter madness" that "those who neglect this instrument should hope to become perfect in Christ." Christ, the source of sanctification, rightly determines its means as well. "By the command of

---

99. Comm. 1 Cor. 12:28–31 (1546; *CNTC* 9:270–73; *CO* 49:506–8).
100. Comm. 1 Cor. 12:28 (*CNTC* 9:270–72; *CO* 49:506).
101. Comm. Eph. 4:11–14 (1548; *CNTC* 11:178–84; *CO* 51:196–202).
102. Comm. Eph. 4:11 (*CNTC* 11:178–80; *CO* 51:196–97).
103. Comm. Eph. 4:12 (*CNTC* 11:180–81; *CO* 51:198–99); and see chap. 3, above.
104. Comm. Eph. 4:12 (*CNTC* 11:180–81; *CO* 51:198–99).

Christ," Calvin continues, "no real union or perfection is attained, but by outward preaching. We must allow ourselves to be ruled and taught by men." No individual, from "the highest to the lowest," is excepted:

> The Church is the common mother of all the godly, which bears, nourishes and governs in the Lord both kings and commoners; and this is done by the ministry. . . . The use of the ministry is not temporal, as if it were a preparatory school, . . . but constant, so long as we live in the world. . . . Every day brings some nearer to others, and all approach together to Christ.
>
> The expression, "coming together," denotes that closest union to which we still aspire, and which we never reach until this flesh, which is always involved in many remnants of ignorance and unbelief, shall have been laid aside.[105]

In the church, the reality of spiritual exile as a lifelong homeward journey finds concrete institutional expression. Public worship offers sustenance for weary pilgrims. Stories of Adam's excommunication, David's spiritual hunger, and Abraham's future-oriented faith teach believers to look for God's provision. God accompanies the elect, throughout their exile, in the church's preaching and sacraments, which offer Christ himself as food for the journey home. For some, such rich fare was hard to swallow.

Readers familiar with the *Institutes*, where Calvin treats the offense of hearing God's word from a "puny man" in no way one's "equal," would have recognized the same rebuke here.[106] At issue is not whether God is free to do as God pleases, but that God's choices might offend us:

> Those who neglect or despise this order want to be wiser than Christ. Woe to their pride! We do not deny that we can be perfected by the power of God alone without human assistance. But we are now dealing with what is the will of God and the appointment of Christ, and not what the power of God can do. In employing men's work for accomplishing their salvation, God has conferred on men no ordinary honour. And the best way to promote unity is to assemble to the common teaching as to the the standard of a leader.[107]

Across different forms of teaching, then, Calvin's insistence upon the church's role as nurturing mother to the elect rarely appears without an immediate defense of the same idea. On the one hand, Calvin's exegesis of Paul's teaching on church office and ministry bears the expected polemical edge against Rome. Protestants routinely condemned Catholic clergy for

---

105. Comm. Eph. 4:12–13 (*CNTC* 11:180–82; *CO* 51:198–200).
106. *Inst.* IV.3.1 (*OS* 5:42–44).
107. Comm. Eph. 4:12 (*CNTC* 11:180–81; *CO* 51:198–99).

lacking requisite gifts to fulfill the ministry's core teaching function.[108] But what about criticism emerging from within Protestant communities? With evangelical insistence on the Bible's final authority came the difficulty of navigating different, often contradictory, interpretations of scripture. Absent an authoritative pronouncement from the church, Protestant ministers were left to persuasion, sometimes appealing to civil authorities to make their case more compelling. Calvin did both over his career, especially when opposition to his teaching arose in Geneva and abroad. In one instance from September 1547, the Consistory intervened to deal with François Favre for protesting ministers' claims of spiritual authority. Favre called Calvin "the great Devil" and likened him to a "Bishop of Geneva."[109] Favre was the father-in-law of Calvin's nemesis, Ami Perrin, yet Favre's sentiments were by no means unique among Genevans. What about the opinions of evangelicals in France? What did the objects of Calvin's special concern, named in the prefaces of so many works, think about his teaching? Calvin's unyielding views on doctrine and worship, even with the goal of nurture in view, could provoke unsympathetic responses. A reform-minded French official, Antoine Fumeé, offered this feedback in 1543: "Most people [here in France] find what you preach wretched. They complain that you are harsh and exceedingly cruel toward the afflicted, saying that preaching and admonishing is easy for you, who are over there, but [you] might feel differently if you were here."[110]

Calvin's teaching thus met strong resistance all around. French readers accused him of sounding off callously from fortress Geneva, where prominent Genevans wished he would just go back to France. Within his broader message, Calvin's account of the church's ministry was especially fraught, since it required the reformer to defend the structures that gave him authority as pastor and teacher.

Conclusion

Calvin's *Institutes* and commentaries express his high sense of calling to expound the scriptures. They also responded to political exile by initiating fellow ministers into ways of reading the Bible that situated their communities within a shared context of spiritual exile. This theological vision had unifying potential. As a concept, exile tracked well across language and culture. It spoke to Reformed believers in diverse circumstances, whether scattered across Europe

---

108. See, e.g., Luther, *Concerning the Ministry* (1523; *LW* 40:3–44; *WA* 12:169–95).
109. *CO* 21:413.
110. *CO* 11:646.

or possessing different starting points within the same congregation. Regardless of one's background, spiritual exile meant hope that the present would give way to a brighter future. Calvin's teaching on providence, predestination, and the church is often considered without reference to the context of early modern violence, displacement, and resettlement. Yet his writings frequently connect such doctrines to these very realities. The scriptural narrative of humanity's expulsion from the garden and Christ's rescue mission to guide them homeward provides a theological framework that recasts experiences of marginalization by the world as markers of belonging to God, tokens of God's favor. In Calvin's day, the *Institutes* and commentaries worked together to situate the church in this plot of exile, eventual homecoming, and nourishment in between. Alongside the *Institutes*, Calvin's exegesis renders exile in the living color of the biblical past. Ancient figures serve as guides to faith, with their experiences mirroring God's present dealings with God's children.

Calvin the teacher wrote himself into this story in the concrete role his ministry played in God's economy of salvation. In his eyes, his vocation was nothing less than how predestination and providence conspire to make election visible in the church. Right doctrine, proclaimed in sermons and sacraments, leads spiritual exiles to the Christ who brings them safely home. This was true no less in Calvin's day than it had been in Paul's or David's. The consistency of these exilic themes across Calvin's teaching leaves little doubt that he believed this message. From God's daily providence, Calvin drew the same reassurance that he offered to others. It is no less clear that Calvin also felt the need to correct those who disagreed with him. His repeated insistence on the ministry as God's gift included stating, nearly as frequently, that receiving the church as nurturing mother meant listening to one's pastor, whatever one thought of him. Now we turn to Calvin's pastoral ministry, at the front lines of his ministry as refugee theologian, and how his efforts as a pastor in Geneva addressed God's community in exile.

For Further Reading

In Calvin's Words

1539 Dedication to Commentary on Romans, *CNTC* 8:1–4.

1540 Commentary on Romans 4, *CNTC* 8:82–103.

1548 Commentary on Ephesians 4:11–14, *CNTC* 11:177–84.

1554 Commentary on Genesis 3, CTS 1:137–87.

1557 Commentary on Psalms, CTS, vols. 8–12.

1557–59 Lectures on the Minor Prophets, CTS, vols. 26–30.
1561 Dedication to Lectures on Daniel, CTS 24:lxiv–lxxv.
1563 Dedication to Lectures on Jeremiah, CTS 17:xvi–xxiv.

For Digging Deeper

De Greef, Wulfert. *The Writings of John Calvin: An Introductory Guide*. Westminster John Knox, 2008.

McKim, Donald K., ed. *Calvin and the Bible*. Cambridge University Press, 2006.

Parker, T. H. L. *Calvin's New Testament Commentaries*. T&T Clark, 1971.

———. *Calvin's Old Testament Commentaries*. T&T Clark, 1986. Repr., Westminster John Knox, 1993.

Pitkin, Barbara. *Calvin, the Bible, and History: Exegesis and Historical Reflection in the Era of Reform*. Oxford University Press, 2020.

Steinmetz, David C., ed. *The Bible in the Sixteenth Century*. Duke University Press, 1990.

Thompson, John L. *Reading the Bible with the Dead: What You Can Learn from the History of Exegesis That You Can't Learn from Exegesis Alone*. Eerdmans, 2007.

PART THREE

Calvin as Pastor

FIVE

Schooling God's Children in Exile

Calvin's Writings on Church Organization and Worship

How much more necessary is it now, in the dreadful devastation of the Christian world, that those Churches, which worship God rightly, few and dispersed and hedged about by the profane synagogues of Antichrist as they are, should give and receive mutually this sign of holy fellowship . . . to gather by our writings what such remains of the Church as may persist or even emerge after our death. . . . This indeed was my chief reason for publishing this Catechism.

—Calvin, preface to *The Catechism of the Church of Geneva* (1545)[1]

Sincere believers do not always have the things they want. In quitting their country they experience all kinds of trouble. But let them take comfort in this thought: "Nevertheless, we are still in God's house." . . . Even if we were the most miserable outcasts the world has ever known, God allows us, as members of his church, intimate access to the deep and wonderful secrets of his wisdom, as a father might do when conversing with his children. We would be churlish in the extreme if such a reward failed to satisfy us.

—Calvin, Sermon on Psalm 27:8 (1552)[2]

---

1. In John Calvin, *Calvin: Theological Treatises*, trans. J. K. S. Reid, LCC (Westminster John Knox, 1954), 90.

2. In John Calvin, *Faith Unfeigned: Four Sermons Concerning Matters Most Useful for the Present Time with a Brief Exposition of Psalm 87*, ed. and trans. Robert White (Banner of Truth Trust, 2010), 91 (CO 8:439).

It always remains true that our souls have no other pasture than Jesus Christ. Therefore the heavenly Father, in his care to nourish us, gives us nothing else, but rather recommends us to take our fill there, as from a refreshment manifestly sufficient, with which we cannot dispense, and beyond which it is impossible to find any other.

—Calvin, *Short Treatise on the Lord's Supper* (1541)[3]

When Exilic Theology Meets Real People

It is a common experience among seminary graduates to discover incongruities between pastoral ministry and what their classroom learning had led them to expect. Even as theological education becomes more practically oriented, focused on imparting concrete skills and competencies, ideas continue to land with unpredictable footing "in the real world." This was no less true in Calvin's day, when pastors in Geneva struggled to communicate and embody theological ideals presented so eloquently in the pages of his academic works. Political and religious conflicts, often exacerbated by cultural differences and personality clashes, affected how others received Calvin's theology. Not everyone agreed with, understood, or even cared about Calvin's ideas. This, in turn, shaped the reformer's pastoral approach.

Notice the complexities encapsulated in the sermon on Psalm 27, quoted in the epigraph above. Calvin addresses political displacement with the theology of nurture for spiritual exiles that appears in his commentaries and *Institutes*. The preacher acknowledges refugees' discontent with their difficult experiences. He names the perplexing gap between refugees' standing in the world and God's assessment of them. Stripped of conventional markers of belonging and status, such believers need not despair. In Geneva, among God's people, they are "in God's house" despite their worldly losses. Some exiles remained unconvinced. These Calvin chides as "churlish in the extreme" for failing to esteem so great a privilege. His corrective tone is consistent with Calvin's preaching on other occasions to mixed audiences of émigrés and Genevans. He challenges newcomers frustrated by what they have found upon arriving in Geneva. For many years he also directed similar rhetoric against a native faction marked by distrust of their foreign-born pastors and other religious refugees.[4] These, too, were ungrateful for God's gift of a true church in Geneva.

---

3. In John Calvin, *Calvin: Theological Treatises*, trans. J. K. S. Reid, LCC (Westminster, 1954), 143 (CO 5:435).

4. William G. Naphy, *Calvin and the Consolidation of the Genevan Reformation* (Manchester University Press, 1994), 172.

Every pastor knows something of the challenges Calvin faced. God's nurture of spiritual pilgrims through Word and sacrament is, on one level, easy to describe. Biblical exegesis deals with historical texts depicting persons whose feelings cannot be hurt by interpreters and who, at any rate, cannot talk back. It was an entirely different matter to actually transform these ideals into the theological imagination of a community powerfully enough to alter attitudes and behaviors in light of such teaching. Calvin found that this required the daily effort of pastoral ministry among difficult people, ministry undertaken by similarly complicated persons. Anxiety, discontent, oversensitivity, and combativeness characterized pastors who pointed out the same faults in others. Such was the imperfect instrument of a human ministry. Calvin's sermon on Psalm 27:8 is a glimpse into layers that readers must excavate to fully appreciate his pastoral context. An untidy breach with Catholicism, international currents of violence and migration, the resulting diverse and divided local church, the preacher's own impatience with malcontents—all these were elements of Calvin's situation as a refugee pastor.

In 1554, Calvin reminded evangelicals in Poitou, "Our time in pilgrimage is short.... We must not allow fear of persecutions to hinder us from seeking the food of life and continuing under the guidance of our good Shepherd."[5] Christ, the Good Shepherd (John 10), gathers his flock in exile, even under threat of persecution, to receive the "food of life." Although Genevans faced no danger of persecution, they too were spiritual exiles and required the same spiritual food. Providing it was the heartbeat of Calvin's pastoral ministry. This chapter introduces ecclesiastical and liturgical documents that Calvin authored or helped produce that structured Geneva's corporate religious life: Geneva's *Confession of Faith* (1536) and *The Catechism of the Church of Geneva* (1542), along with prescriptions for church organization and worship. The latter include Geneva's *Ecclesiastical Ordinances* (1541) and Calvin's *Short Treatise on the Lord's Supper* (1541), *The Form of Church Prayers and Hymns* (1542), foreword to the *Genevan Psalter* (1543), and writings on baptism. Geneva also led the way in encouraging private reading of scripture with the production of Bibles (notably in French and English), with ample annotations to guide lay readers.[6] These works established institutions and practices through which God's Word could regularly nourish God's people in exile.

---

5. Calvin to Christians of Poitou (France), September 3, 1554 (Bonnet, 3:68–71; CO 15:222–24).

6. Francis M. Higman, "'Without Great Effort, and with Pleasure': Sixteenth-Century Genevan Bibles and Reading Practices," in *The Bible as Book: The Reformation*, ed. Orlaith O'Sullivan and Ellen N. Herron (Oak Knoll, 2000), 115–22.

Genevan officials did not abolish rituals as such; rather, they implemented a new ritual system centered on scripture and its exposition as expressions of God's presence.[7]

Calvin's Pastoral Context

The Reformation centered the Word in the church. Nowhere is this more apparent than the pastoral ministry. The reformers corrected what they saw as an egregious failure of the Catholic priesthood by insisting on a learned pastorate whose main function was teaching, the public and private instruction of believers in biblical doctrine.[8] This commitment, reflected in Geneva's *Ecclesiastical Ordinances*, structured the city's religious life. The *Ordinances* mandated ordination exams for pastors that consisted of two parts: (1) biblical knowledge and ability to communicate it and (2) conformity of life to doctrine.[9] In a nutshell, Geneva's clergy were to be the antithesis of the ignorant, immoral priesthood Protestants saw in Rome's ministers. As in other Reformation contexts, local realities influenced how this pastoral ideal took shape in Geneva, where people struggled to adapt their new Reformed faith to the presence of many newcomers and the strong personality of the city's lead pastor.

The city's official embrace of Protestantism in 1536, two months before Calvin's arrival, did not erase all vestiges of Catholicism. As in other cities, leaving Rome did not follow a neat and tidy path in Geneva. Some things stayed the same. The Cathedral of St. Pierre and the churches of St. Gervais and La Madeleine remained the main settings for congregational worship during Calvin's career, dividing the city into distinct parishes.[10] Yet significant renovations were made to the internal architecture of these buildings. These included centering the pulpit and adding bench seating where the congregations could sit and listen to sermons. In keeping with the austerity characteristic of Swiss Reformed churches, Genevans removed much of the artistic and ceremonial elements of Catholic worship, including altars and incense,

---

7. Christian Grosse, "'Docere et Movere': Preaching, Sacrament, and Prayer in the Reformed Liturgical System of 16th-Century Geneva," in *A Companion to the Reformation in Geneva*, ed. Jon Balserak (Brill, 2021), 166–89.

8. Luther, *Concerning the Ministry* (LW 40:3–44; WA 12:169–95); Amy Nelson Burnett, *Teaching the Reformation: Ministers and Their Message in Basel, 1529–1629* (Oxford University Press, 2006); and David Cornick, "The Reformation Crisis in Pastoral Care," in *A History of Pastoral Care*, ed. G. R. Evans (Cassell, 2000), 223–51.

9. Calvin, *Ecclesiastical Ordinances*, 59 (CO 10a:17).

10. Elsie Anne McKee, *The Pastoral Ministry and Worship in Calvin's Geneva* (Droz, 2016), 48–51.

though stained glass windows depicting biblical scenes remained. Walls were painted over, reliquaries (which housed relics) banished. Even crosses came down from atop church buildings. In place of images, Genevans installed depictions of the biblical text itself, such as stone tablets engraved with the Ten Commandments.[11] Repurposing existing structures this way made the experience of them both familiar and strange. It was like returning to one's childhood home as an adult and finding it painted, decorated, and landscaped differently by new owners. This dynamic, the old existing within the new, applied as well to the religiosity of Genevans. Many embraced official reforms with zeal because of the political independence they symbolized. At the same time, some converts would later balk at how much this new faith demanded of them. To Calvin and his pastoral colleagues, the people's persistent entanglement in Catholic practices and doctrine resembled a disease. Pastors invested much energy in diagnosing and treating "superstition." Its cure required realigning the people's practices to the religious convictions the city had already adopted in name.

Baptism was one area in which religious transformations felt especially dramatic. Cultural habits died hard, and immigration compounded misunderstanding. It was popular to choose baptismal names for children that honored saints and legends.[12] Ministers attempted to curb this custom, viewed as superstitious, by recommending biblical names instead. Under pressure from ministers, magistrates approved a list of banned names that included "Claude" and "Martin," popular saints' names among Genevans.[13] Riots erupted in cases where pastors unilaterally replaced names chosen by the family.[14] In one instance, a child, Claude, was renamed "Abraham" by his pastor without warning at the moment of baptism, prompting the boy's father to seize the infant and declare the baptism invalid.[15] The baptismal conflicts highlight Genevans' distrust of their immigrant pastors, since by then all of Geneva's ministers had been born elsewhere, mostly in France.[16] They were also better educated than most, including the Catholic priests they replaced.

---

11. Philip Benedict, *Christ's Churches Purely Reformed: A Social History of Calvinism* (Yale University Press, 2002), 497.

12. McKee, *Pastoral Ministry*, 391–436; and Karen E. Spierling, *Infant Baptism in Reformation Geneva: The Shaping of a Community, 1536–1564* (Ashgate, 2004).

13. CO 10a:49–50. Calvin led this effort to ban certain names; see Jeffrey R. Watt, "Childhood and Youth in the Genevan Consistory Minutes," in *Calvinus Praeceptor Ecclesiae: Papers of the International Congress on Calvin Research*, ed. Herman Selderhuis (Droz, 2004), 41–62.

14. William G. Naphy, "Baptisms, Church Riots and Social Unrest in Calvin's Geneva," *Sixteenth Century Journal* 26, no. 1 (Spring 1995): 87–97.

15. Naphy, "Baptisms," 89.

16. See chap. 2, above.

Many Reformed pastors came to their new faith later in life, some fleeing their homes for their beliefs. This correlated to a high degree of zeal that further alienated Genevans. People complained that their pastors were simply foreigners peddling "fables," dishonest and not to be welcomed as neighbors.[17] Such cultural divisions were a constant subtext that could inflame mundane annoyances common in every church, such as pastors preaching too long and parishioners sleeping, chatting, or flirting instead of listening.[18]

These tensions galvanized Calvin's enemies, such as the Perrinists, or *Enfants de Genève*, so-called Libertines who steadfastly opposed Calvin for the first two decades of his ministry.[19] Many of these were regarded as patriots who had led the successful fight for Genevan independence, only to find themselves under a new foreign oppression. As one contemporary, Antoine Froment, recounted, Calvin and his fellow pastors "found the table set and the soup made" when they arrived in Geneva.[20] Controversy and resentment put pressure on Calvin's pastorate in ways that call to mind how congregations today mirror divisions in society. The issues were different in Calvin's day, to be sure, but no less divisive. His attempts to unify the church encountered real resistance.

Also polarizing was Calvin's personality. Then as now, a pastor could determine the course a congregation travels through conflict. Calvin's inner life—its tensions, anxieties, and motivations—was a vital "interior context" for his ministry.[21] Yet, for obvious reasons, it is not easy to examine. A person's psychology is challenging enough to assess face-to-face. Much less are historians with limited evidence able to bridge vast chronological and cultural distances to probe a subject's interior life with certainty. A few things are apparent from Calvin's writings and actions, however. He exuded confidence, for example, when interpreting God's design for events in his day and how scripture spoke to these. This has led some to discern a "prophetic self-awareness" behind his sense of personal infallibility as a biblical exegete.[22] This went beyond

---

17. Thomas A. Lambert, "Preaching, Praying and Policing the Reform in Sixteenth-Century Geneva" (PhD diss., University of Wisconsin–Madison, 1998), 381, 383.

18. Scott M. Manetsch, *Calvin's Company of Pastors: Pastoral Care and the Emerging Reformed Church, 1536–1609* (Oxford University Press, 2013), 152–55.

19. See chap. 2, above.

20. Robert Wilbé, "Antoine Froment: Le 'Livre de la Sédition,'" *Bulletin de la Société d'histoire et d'archéologie de Genève* 15 (1974): 272 (cited in Lambert, "Preaching," 492).

21. See, e.g., William J. Bouwsma, *John Calvin: A Sixteenth-Century Portrait* (Oxford University Press, 1988); and Denis Crouzet, *Jean Calvin: Vies parallèles* (Fayard, 2000).

22. Alexandre Ganoczy, *The Young Calvin*, trans. David Foxgrover and Wade Provo (Westminster, 1966), 287–312; Max Engammare, "Calvin: A Prophet Without a Prophecy," *Church History* 67, no. 4 (1998): 643–61; Olivier Millet, "Calvin's Self-Awareness as Author," trans. Susanna Gebhardt, in *Calvin and His Influence, 1509–2009*, ed. Irena Backus and Philip Benedict (Oxford University Press, 2011), 84–101; Jon Balserak, *John Calvin as Sixteenth-Century*

confidence in the clarity of scripture and included adjudicating special exceptions to scripture's teaching, especially in relation to pursuing regime change in France. Yet, for all his confidence, Calvin could also behave in ways deeply insecure, especially when facing criticism. Although associates generally deferred to Calvin's opinions, he possessed what one author deems a "fretful sense of falling woefully short" of his calling as a reformer.[23] For instance, Calvin rarely changed his mind, yet he obsessively revised his teaching for greater clarity and precision.

In that same exacting vein, Calvin could be a ruthless foe, especially toward those who doubted him. Calvin was not exactly the model of charitable disagreement. He ensured Jerome Bolsec's banishment for challenging him on predestination.[24] Similarly, Calvin objected to the magistrate's leniency in Pierre Ameaux's 1546 trial for blasphemy, which included insulting Calvin, and insisted on Ameaux's public humiliation.[25] The reformer could also be as impatient toward incompetence as he was unforgiving of disloyalty. Sometimes he was simply mean. He once derided a man denied ordination in Geneva for possessing "the ignorance of an ass," having "somewhat less of Latin than a child of eight years."[26] Other glimpses inside Calvin's "psychological context" include his lifelong fixation on France and assumption of a common Renaissance persona, "the overworked intellectual," which he expressed in a tireless work ethic that drove him to the point of physical breakdown.[27]

Calvin's pastorate cannot be understood apart from the speed bumps described above, some of his own making, that slowed Geneva's progress into a new faith with new neighbors and new church leaders. Despite such setbacks, Calvin remained committed to creating structures to dispense spiritual nurture, the "food of life" that the Good Shepherd promised his flock during their "time in pilgrimage."[28]

Prophet (Oxford University Press, 2014), 130–43; and Balserak, "Geneva's Use of Lies, Deceit, and Simulation in Their Efforts to Reform France, 1536–1563," *Harvard Theological Review* 112 (2019): 76–100.

23. Bruce Gordon, *Calvin* (Yale University Press, 2009), 3.

24. Gordon, *Calvin*, 204–11.

25. Robert M. Kingdon, *Adultery and Divorce in Calvin's Geneva* (Harvard University Press, 1995), 63–67; E. William Monter, *Calvin's Geneva* (Robert E. Krieger, 1975), 74–75; and Naphy, *Consolidation*, 94–96.

26. Naphy, *Consolidation*, 53–79; Calvin to brethren in Lyons, May 1542 (Bonnet, 1:328; CO 11:400–401).

27. Max Engammare, "Une certaine idée de la France chez Jean Calvin l'exilé," *Bulletin de la société de l'histoire du protestantisme français: Études, documents, chronique littéraire* 155 (2009): 15–27; and Engammare, "Calvin the Workaholic," in *Calvin and His Influence, 1509–2009*, ed. Irena Backus and Philip Benedict (Oxford University Press, 2011), 67–83.

28. See note 5, above.

Geneva's Educational Program for All of Life in Exile

Geneva's *Ecclesiastical Ordinances*, approved in November 1541 by the city's General Assembly upon Calvin's return from Strasbourg, established structures of pastoral ministry. The General Assembly, which included all men of legal voting age from among native-born citizens and those granted *bourgeois* status, was one of several layers of a civil government that was by design "elective, participatory, . . . layered, and circumscribed by a rather intricate system of checks and balances."[29] Calvin had a hand in drafting Geneva's first and second postrevolutionary constitutions, which, along with the *Ecclesiastical Ordinances*, established the relationship between the city-state and its church. It was important to align these entities because certain tasks, such as the Consistory's work of church discipline, involved the civil authority in a spiritual matter.[30] As the church's "constitution," the *Ecclesiastical Ordinances* prescribed a form of church government, times and places for public worship, and institutions for instruction and pastoral care. Pastoral ministry in Reformation Geneva fell to the city's Company of Pastors who, along with the Consistory consisting of pastors and city officials, oversaw the rhythms of religious life for thousands of inhabitants.[31] Their guiding vision for pastoral care was Calvin's description of the church as "mother" of the elect, nurturing "both kings and commoners . . . so long as [they] live in the world."[32] Lifelong biblical teaching, from birth to burial, reflected the doctrine expressed in Geneva's *Confession of Faith* and Calvin's *Catechism*, which summarized the Reformed faith and provided a way to pass it from one generation to the next. We will briefly introduce these documents before returning to the *Ordinances*'s structures for teaching, worship, and church discipline.

Geneva's Confession *(1536) and* Catechism *(1542)*

The 1536 *Confession*, presented to the city in 1537, was mostly Guillaume Farel's work, though Calvin likely assisted his friend.[33] Despite Calvin's sense of the people's enthusiasm for it, he and Farel were unsuccessful in requiring

---

29. William G. Naphy, "Calvin's Church in Geneva," in Backus and Benedict, *Calvin and His Influence*, 107.
30. Naphy, "Calvin's Church," 102–18.
31. CO 10a:20, 29; Manetsch, *Calvin's Company*; McKee, *Pastoral Ministry*; and Karin Maag, *Lifting Hearts to the Lord: Worship with John Calvin in Sixteenth-Century Geneva* (Eerdmans, 2016).
32. Comm. Eph. 4:12–13 (*CNTC* 11:180–82; *CO* 51:198–200).
33. Jason Zuidema and Theodore Van Raalte, *Early French Reform: The Theology and Spirituality of Guillaume Farel* (Ashgate, 2011), 5–6.

all Genevans to swear loyalty to the *Confession*.[34] Reflecting the city's recent departure from Catholicism and Farel's combative style, the *Confession* lays out Geneva's new faith with clear boundaries and provocative anti-Catholic language.[35] It also displays the same language of nurture and high view of pastoral ministry that characterizes Calvin's later writings. The *Confession* rejects Roman teaching on the role of good works in salvation, prayers to the saints, and the "execrable blasphemies and superstitions" of the Mass. The "human traditions" of Catholic piety amount to satanic overthrow of Christian liberty. By contrast, the true church exists where faithful preaching and sacraments feed "the sheep of Jesus Christ." Believers should receive "true ministers of the Word as messengers and ambassadors of God" and heed them with the diligence one owes God.[36]

How would pastors initiate ordinary Genevans into these doctrinal expectations for the church and its ministry? Catechetical instruction provided the way. Among the Reformation's changes to long-established rhythms of piety was moving religious instruction for children out of the home. Previously, mothers like Calvin's own took the lead in introducing basic tenets of the faith; now this fell to professional clergy such as Geneva's pastors.[37] Catechesis was not something ministers were content to leave solely to parents. Modeled on Zurich's practice, established by Zwingli in the early 1520s, Geneva's catechetical program gave pastors primary responsibility for instructing children. Calvin wrote his first catechism for Geneva in 1537.[38] A second catechism was published in 1542.[39] The *Catechism* summarizes, in question-and-answer format, the main topics of the 1536 *Institutes*, which commends the practice of catechizing children "among the ancient Christians."[40] Such instruction should culminate in public profession of faith: "While the church looks on as witness, [the child] would profess the one true and sincere faith, in which

---

34. CO 5:320; and Robert M. Kingdon, "Confessionalism in Calvin's Geneva," *Archiv für Reformationsgeschichte* 96 (2005): 109–13.

35. *The Genevan Confession* (1536), in John Calvin, *Calvin: Theological Treatises*, trans. J. K. S. Reid, LCC (Westminster, 1954), 26–33 (CO 22:85–96).

36. *Genevan Confession*, 32.

37. Robert M. Kingdon, "Catechesis in Calvin's Geneva," in *Educating People of Faith: Exploring the History of Jewish and Christian Communities*, ed. John Van Engen (Eerdmans, 2004), 295–300.

38. This work, written in French, was also published in Latin translation in 1538; see I. John Hesselink, *Calvin's First Catechism: A Commentary* (Westminster John Knox, 1998).

39. Kingdon, "Catechesis," 303. See also Randall C. Zachman, *John Calvin as Teacher, Pastor, and Theologian: The Shape of His Writings and Thought* (Baker Academic, 2006), 131–46. Since no original copies of this 1542 edition survive, we treat the Latin 1545 edition in this chapter.

40. John Calvin, *Institutes of the Christian Religion: 1536 Edition*, trans. Ford Lewis Battles (1975; rev. ed., Eerdmans and Meeter Center, 1986), 130.

the believing folk with one mind worship the one God."[41] For Calvin, this picture beautifully represents how biblical doctrine, like that expounded in the *Institutes*, begins to take root in a person.[42] Calvin's *Catechism* is divided into fifty-five weeks of instruction and was used to initiate generations of Genevan children into the faith.[43] The Company of Pastors was so committed to it that they pleaded with the National Synod of the French Reformed Church in 1596 not to abandon Calvin's *Catechism*, "one of the greatest treasures that the Lord has bestowed on us."[44]

Calvin's preface to the *Catechism* heralds its publication as part of the recovery of a long-lost form of teaching. "Abolished some centuries ago under the papacy," the Catholic Church replaced catechesis with the rite of Confirmation, a "spurious" ritual consisting "in nothing but theatrical gesticulations."[45] Calvin draws a firm boundary marking Geneva's movement from defiled religion to the pure faith revealed in scripture. Unlike the 1536 *Confession*, however, the *Catechism* does not contain strident anti-Catholic rhetoric, though its emphasis on the Lord's Prayer and Ten Commandments is an implicit critique of Catholic prayers and teaching on virtue ethics. Calvin introduces the work by stating a more positive goal: to unite evangelical churches by setting forth "doctrine held by all the pious."[46] These persecuted and harassed true churches may be "few and dispersed and hedged about by the profane synagogues of Antichrist." Emerging from Rome amid such "devastation," the *Catechism* functions, like the tradition of letters from bishops in ancient times, as a "sign of holy fellowship."[47] Its contents commend believers to each other in the church's scattered state. This will also preserve their faith for the sake of communities that will yet "emerge after our death."[48] Once again, Calvin invokes exilic themes to relate doctrine to experience. The *Catechism* addresses the urgent need of identifying God's remnant in the world, both to encourage believers and to ensure the faith's survival under harsh conditions of spiritual and political exile.

41. Calvin, *1536 Edition*, 130.
42. "John Calvin to the Reader, 1559," in *Inst.* 4 (*OS* 3:6); Elsie Anne McKee, "Exegesis, Theology, and Development in Calvin's *Institutio*: A Methodological Suggestion," in *Probing the Reformed Tradition: Historical Studies in Honor of Edward A. Dowey, Jr.*, ed. Elsie Anne McKee and Brian G. Armstrong (Westminster John Knox, 1989), 154–56.
43. Kingdon, "Confessionalism," 110; and *The Catechism of the Church of Geneva* (1545), in John Calvin, *Calvin: Theological Treatises*, trans. J. K. S. Reid, LCC (Westminster John Knox, 1954), 88–139.
44. Manetsch, *Calvin's Company*, 246.
45. *Catechism of the Church of Geneva*, 90–91.
46. *Catechism of the Church of Geneva*, 89.
47. *Catechism of the Church of Geneva*, 89–90.
48. *Catechism of the Church of Geneva*, 89–90.

Such framing hearkens back to how the reformer's preface to King Francis I embeds the *Institutes* in a similar context of persecution and struggle, even while Calvin organizes a positive account of biblical faith and practices around the Apostles' Creed, the Ten Commandments, the Lord's Prayer, and a Reformed understanding of the sacraments. By these means, catechumens imbibed the pure religion that had supplanted what the 1536 *Confession* decries as diabolic superstition. Although Calvin does not emphasize the theme of exile here, attentive readers will notice that his catechism nevertheless includes echoes of exilic themes elaborated in the *Institutes*, commentaries, and lectures. As in those other works, providence, predestination, and the church as nurturing mother appear in the *Catechism* with reference to the present life as exile. This imbues the *Catechism* with an exilic flavor that, while understated, nevertheless initiated children into a way of thinking about doctrine. As Genevans grew up in the church, Calvin's sermons built on this foundation to flesh out a theological vision of life in exile. The *Catechism* guided children toward the church's ministry, where the elect receive assurance of God's favor and learn "to live in this world as foreigners, thinking continually of departure."[49] The *Catechism* was useful for teaching adults too. Besides being present for the catechizing of children, adults were frequently admonished by the Consistory to review the *Catechism*'s contents for remedial training in doctrine.[50] Life, though "full of hardship," is the arena of God's "paternal favor," always expressed in "nourishing and preserving" believers.[51] This is true not only generally but also in the specific gift of set times for "the hearing of Christian doctrine, for the offering of public prayers, and for the profession of their faith."[52] When expounding the law of God, Calvin invokes "this earthly pilgrimage" to highlight the need for vigilance and hope as pilgrims journey through life.[53]

The *Catechism* progresses from general reflections about nurture in the context of worship, under its teaching on the sabbath, to more specific statements in sections on prayer and the sacraments. As in the *Institutes*, the human ministry is tied to the purpose of nurture. Ministers appointed to deliver God's "beneficence" to believers are the "channels" for "blessings that flow from the inexhaustible spring of [God's] generosity."[54] Here, as elsewhere, Calvin admonishes the faithful to be grateful for pastors, lest they exhibit

---

49. *Catechism of the Church of Geneva*, 103–4.
50. See the example of a former monk, Thomas Sylvester, in Manetsch, *Calvin's Company*, 274; and see Zachman, *John Calvin as Teacher*, 139–40.
51. *Catechism of the Church of Geneva*, 113.
52. *Catechism of the Church of Geneva*, 112.
53. *Catechism of the Church of Geneva*, 118.
54. *Catechism of the Church of Geneva*, 120. Translation modified for clarity.

"ingratitude to God."[55] Communal worship, not private reading of scripture, is where God primarily nourishes believers through sacraments joined to preaching.[56] These are the means by which the Spirit accommodates human weakness, enlivening faith even while "vestiges of distrust" cling to faith as a symptom of spiritual exile. "Still pilgrims on earth," believers nevertheless feed on Christ in the Lord's Supper and are nurtured by preachers "with the doctrine of salvation."[57] The *Catechism* traverses the broad terrain of Christian doctrine while reinforcing the essential role that nurture in the church plays in supplying God's provision to hungry pilgrims.

Geneva's Ecclesiastical Ordinances (1541)

Geneva's *Ecclesiastical Ordinances* translated this ideal into concrete realities by picking up the work Calvin and Farel left unfinished when they were banished in 1538.[58] A key provision establishes a quasi-ecclesiastical "assembly of ministers and elders." Twelve lay elders, appointed from Geneva's governing councils, should meet with the city's pastors every "Thursday morning, to see if there is any disorder in the church and to discuss solutions together as needed."[59] This group, known as the "Consistory," played an important role in regulating behavior and exercised church discipline that included barring unrepentant sinners from the sacraments.[60] The task of upholding moral standards involved the Consistory in marriage and sex cases that occupied much of its time.[61] Other areas of attention included lax or inattentive church attendance and failure to provide religious education for children in the home, which remained an expectation alongside catechetical instruction by pastors. The Consistory also took on the role of settling conflicts between neighbors.[62] Lingering Catholic beliefs troubled the waters of Geneva's Reforma-

---

55. *Catechism of the Church of Geneva*, 120.
56. *Catechism of the Church of Geneva*, 129–35.
57. *Catechism of the Church of Geneva*, 131–39.
58. The friends had presented articles, written by Farel, that prescribe new ecclesiastical structures and practices to the city magistrates in 1537; "Articles Concerning the Organization of the Church and of Worship at Geneva Proposed by the Ministers at the Council, January 16, 1537," in John Calvin, *Calvin: Theological Treatises*, trans. J. K. S. Reid, LCC (Westminster, 1954), 48–55 (CO 10a:5–14); and see Gordon, *Calvin*, 72.
59. CO 10a:20, 29.
60. Robert M. Kingdon, "The Geneva Consistory in the Time of Calvin," in *Calvinism in Europe, 1540–1610*, ed. Andrew Pettegree et al. (Cambridge University Press, 1994), 21–34; and Jeffrey R. Watt, "Consistories and Discipline," in *John Calvin in Context*, ed. R. Ward Holder (Cambridge University Press, 2020), 103–10.
61. Kingdon, *Adultery and Divorce*.
62. Robert M. Kingdon (with Thomas Lambert), *Reforming Geneva: Discipline, Faith, and Anger* (Droz, 2012), 101–9.

tion. Though Calvin did not consistently insist on discipline as an essential mark of the church, he tended to treat it as such.[63] The work of oversight and discipline gave elders an important role in pastoral care alongside the teaching ministry of pastors.[64] The *Ordinances* defines two additional offices to support the church's ministry. Deacons collect and distribute material resources, especially caring for the poor.[65] In Calvin's day, the diaconate took the lead in assisting refugees.[66] Finally, doctors (teachers) interpret scripture and teach doctrine for specialized audiences, including other leaders called to teach and preach.[67]

The *Ordinances* describes four offices but clearly places one at the center. Pastors proclaim God's Word through catechesis, preaching, and administration of sacraments. They also participate in church discipline alongside elders. The *Ordinances* gives considerable space to the pastor's office, from qualifications and elections to accountability and specific tasks involved in their work. Though the Venerable Company of Pastors, as they came to be called, were employees paid by the state, they did not possess governmental authority. Theirs was an office limited to spiritual leadership in the church.

The *Ordinances* prescribed practices that set normal rhythms for pastoral ministry in Geneva. This included a weekly meeting to discuss scripture; it was called the *congrégation*, and it became a place for mutual encouragement and quality control for preachers.[68] Other arrangements include instructions for visiting the sick and incarcerated, as well as for administering sacraments. The *Ordinances* mandated monthly observance of the Lord's Supper. In practice, Geneva settled on quarterly observance, to mark greater contrast with the Catholic Eucharist, over Calvin's preference for weekly Communion. Times and places set for worship and catechetical instruction were similarly aspirational. It would take several years before the published plan was fully realized in practice. The *Ordinances* called for regular worship services in three locations: St. Pierre, St. Gervais, and La Madeleine. Saint Pierre and La Madeleine were located near each other in the upper and lower regions of Geneva's Old Town. Saint Gervais

---

63. Tadataka Maruyama, *Calvin's Ecclesiology: A Study in the History of Doctrine* (Eerdmans, 2022), 70–71.

64. Elsie Anne McKee, *Elders and the Plural Ministry: The Role of Exegetical History in Illuminating John Calvin's Theology* (Droz, 1988).

65. Elsie A. McKee, *John Calvin on the Diaconate and Liturgical Almsgiving* (Droz, 1984).

66. Jeannine E. Olson, *Calvin and Social Welfare: Deacons and the Bourse Française* (Susquehanna University Press, 1989); and Esther Chung-Kim, *Economics of Faith: Poor Relief in Early Modern Geneva* (Oxford University Press), 137–61.

67. See chaps. 3 and 4, above.

68. CO 10a:19; and see Erik de Boer, *The Genevan School of the Prophets: The Congrégations of the Company of Pastors and Their Influence in 16th Century Europe* (Droz, 2012).

was across the Rhône, in the city's west end. Word and sacrament were thus conveniently offered in different parts of the city, in churches that were assigned their own pastors. Calvin was based at St. Pierre and regularly served La Madeleine. For a time he also traveled to St. Gervais, on the opposite side of the city.[69] The *Ordinances* further required children to attend catechism classes on Sunday afternoons in their home parish, where the pastors would lead them through the *Catechism*.[70] Failure to bring one's children to catechesis was grounds for the Consistory to reprimand parents for neglect.[71] This educational program, centered on the Word, was thus delivered by ministers, required of the family, and enforced by elders. A similar structure was put in place for rural churches.[72]

Adults required regular instruction as well. Regardless of age, believers remain God's children and in need of nurture.[73] To provide for regular spiritual nourishment, the *Ordinances* scheduled services most working days and three times each Sunday. Lord's Day services in the three main church buildings were to take place at dawn, at midmorning, and in the afternoon.[74] By 1551 services were held every day in all three churches.[75] Calvin's participation in a preaching rotation meant that all Genevans had a chance to hear their celebrity pastor, though not all saw this as a benefit. According to city government records, the baker Amyed Alliod complained about the moralizing "guest preacher" one morning at St. Gervais.[76] Alliod found Calvin's criticisms directed at absentee parishioners to be overly harsh. Geneva's midweek Day of Prayer was a distinctive feature of the city's communal piety that ordered time by placing theological emphasis on God's providence in ordinary life.[77] This was a key element of the "providential faith" that Calvin's teaching repeatedly highlighted through its use of David as an example.[78]

Every worship service required a sermon. This, along with decentering the Eucharist, further disrupted familiar experiences. Instead of attending a ritual

---

69. Manetsch, *Calvin's Company*, 150; and McKee, *Pastoral Ministry*, 460–61.
70. Calvin, *Ecclesiastical Ordinances*, 62, 69 (CO 10a:20, 28).
71. Calvin, *Ecclesiastical Ordinances*, 69 (CO 10a:28).
72. "Draft Order of Visitation for the Country Churches, January 11, 1546" and "The Ordinances for the Supervision of Churches in the Country, February 3, 1547," in John Calvin, *Calvin: Theological Treatises*, trans. J. K. S. Reid, LCC (Westminster, 1954), 74–75, 77–82 (CO 10a:45–48, 51–58).
73. *Inst.* IV.1.4 (OS 5:7).
74. Calvin, *Ecclesiastical Ordinances*, 62 (CO 10a:20). In practice, Geneva would adopt more opportunities for hearing preaching than the *Ordinances* specify, amounting to over thirty sermons per week (Grosse, "'Docere et Movere,'" 183).
75. Lambert, "Preaching," 286–87.
76. McKee, *Pastoral Ministry*, 462.
77. McKee, *Pastoral Ministry*, 310–52.
78. See chap. 2, above.

offering by a priest spoken in an unfamiliar language (Latin), with no additional instruction expected (or, perhaps, desired), Genevans now faced greater expectations. Preachers expounded scripture in their hearers' native tongue. For most, this was French or the Savoyard dialect of Italian-inflected French common in Geneva. People were expected to listen attentively. The Consistory would summon for questioning those whose attendance at services was spotty or simply to inquire about their knowledge of doctrine. This might include asking a person to summarize a sermon or to recite the Apostles' Creed, Ten Commandments, or Lord's Prayer.[79]

Modern readers may find this kind of accountability overly scrupulous and intrusive. Geneva's pastors believed that people needed time, yes, but also a lot of support to throw off the oppressive yoke of Catholic errors. Put positively, such a detailed, compulsory program could more effectively distribute God's generous spiritual nurture to God's children in exile. These ecclesial structures gave Calvin's theology of pilgrimage and comfort a visible form for spiritual exiles. Daily preaching was a new practice with enforceable rules. But it was also a steady diet of manna in the wilderness. As Calvin's *Catechism* puts it, "The inexhaustible spring of [God's] generosity" and "paternal favor" flowed to Genevans through the "channel" of biblical teaching. He also calls it that "door by which we enter [God's] celestial kingdom."[80]

Worship in the Wilderness: Pasturing on Christ as Exilic Community

It may surprise modern students of the Reformation that Calvin's ideal for worship, while prioritizing the sermon, also favored frequent Communion. North American Presbyterian and Reformed churches, shaped by eighteenth- and nineteenth-century revivalism and debates over Calvin's position on the Eucharist, have historically placed less emphasis on the sacraments in worship.[81] The Presbyterian theologian Charles Hodge (1797–1878) of Princeton Seminary vigorously rejected John Williamson Nevin's (1803–86) account of Calvin's theology of Christ's mystical presence in the Eucharist—or at least what this means for worship.[82] Nevin, professor at the German Reformed seminary at Mercersburg, Pennsylvania, lamented modern Protestant undervaluing

---

79. Kingdon, "Geneva Consistory," 24–26; Watt, "Consistories," 109.
80. *Catechism of the Church of Geneva*, 113, 120, 129. Translation modified for clarity.
81. Linden DeBie and Bradford Littlejohn, "Reformed Eucharistic Theology and the Case for Real Presence," *Theology Today* 71 (2015): 429–39; and D. G. Hart, *Recovering Mother Kirk: The Case for Liturgy in the Reformed Tradition* (Baker Academic, 2003).
82. Charles Hodge, "The Mystical Presence. A Vindication of the Reformed or Calvinistic Doctrine of the Holy Eucharist," *The Biblical Repertory and Princeton Review* 20 (1848): 227–78.

of the sacraments: "The voice of antiquity is all on the side of the Sixteenth Century, in its high view of the sacrament. To the low view which has since come to prevail, it lends no support whatever."[83] Hodge's views carried the day, but Nevin was closer to Calvin, who preferred frequent Communion as a means of feeding regularly on Christ.

Controversy around Calvin's views did not begin in the nineteenth century. He had difficulty convincing fellow Genevans. Calvin consistently illustrated the benefits of worship with the image of feeding on Christ through Word and sacrament. This appears in his works on the sacraments as well as in his liturgical writings. The latter held together both the Swiss Reformation's characteristic austerity, which avoided elements of worship without express biblical warrant, and Calvin's notion that gathering around the Lord's Table remained central to the service. Word and sacrament were embraced as food in the wilderness and structured Geneva's order of worship.

But Calvin did not have his way regarding the frequency of Communion. Three years before his death, Calvin looked back on three decades of Communion in Geneva with this blunt assessment: "Our custom is wrong."[84] He complained about the city's decision to observe the Lord's Supper "only quarterly" despite a prescription for monthly Communion in the *Ordinances*. In fact, beginning with the first edition in 1536, the *Institutes* states a preference for weekly observance.[85] In 1537 Calvin and Farel proposed the same to Geneva's magistrates but conceded that "the frailty of the people is still so great."[86] Monthly Communion could help Genevans more clearly differentiate Protestant spiritual practices from the Mass. Calvin's later misgivings about quarterly Communion hearken back to his view in 1536: "Sweetness of spiritual consolation comes to believers" in the sacrament "set before the church very often, at least once a week."[87]

Calvin's understanding of what the Supper entails explains his insistence on its regular observance. The brief opening section of Calvin's *Short Treatise on the Lord's Supper* (1541) is dense with the imagery of food, nurture, and God's paternal care. "Jesus Christ, who alone is our life, is given and administered" to believers in the Lord's Supper as "food for preserving and confirming" them in "the life into which [God] has regenerated" them out of God's "fatherly goodness."[88] Through the sacrament God discharges "the of-

---

83. John Williamson Nevin, *The Mystical Presence* (Lippincott, 1846), 149.
84. Calvin to unnamed recipients, August 12, 1561 (CO 10a:213).
85. Calvin, *1536 Edition*, 122–23; and *Inst.* IV.17.43 (OS 5:409).
86. "Articles Concerning the Organization of the Church," 49–50.
87. Calvin, *1536 Edition*, 122–23.
88. John Calvin, *Short Treatise on the Lord's Supper* (1541), in John Calvin, *Calvin: Theological Treatises*, trans. J. K. S. Reid, LCC (Westminster, 1954), 143 (CO 5:434–35).

fice of a loving father" to "nourish us and provide all that is necessary to life." With Rome and the tradition, Calvin affirms the centrality of the sacrament.[89] Calvin's account takes a characteristically Protestant turn, however, by tethering the sacrament to the Word revealed in scripture.[90] Word and sacrament are complementary means by which "Jesus Christ, with all his benefits, is dispensed to us."[91]

Much has been written about the relationship between Word and sacrament in Calvin's theology, as well as about his views on the Lord's Supper, in particular.[92] Here I simply highlight how spiritual exile recurs throughout Calvin's teaching on the sacraments. The Word revealed in scripture is "spiritual bread" upon which believers' souls are both regenerated and nourished by the Holy Spirit. Biblical teaching is the "instrument by which Jesus Christ, with all his benefits, is dispensed to us."[93] Preaching is effective only when it conveys Christ, whom believers receive by faith. Calvin cites scripture's use of "bread and water" (e.g., Matt. 4:4; Ps. 1:3) to symbolize the Word. He applies the same analogy to the Lord's Supper, which complements the Word so that they are together the "means by which our Lord leads us to communion with Jesus Christ."[94] Though preaching should have been sufficient, God provides sacraments as another way to take hold of Christ: "Seeing we are so foolish, that we cannot receive [Christ] with true confidence of heart, when he is presented by simply teaching and preaching, the Father, of his mercy, not at all disdaining to condescend in this manner to our infirmity, has desired to attach to his Word a visible sign, by which he represents the substance of his promises, to confirm and fortify us, and to deliver us from all doubt and uncertainty."[95]

Sacraments, contrary to Catholic teaching, do not function apart from faith. Rather, they are aids to strengthen the faith that feeds on Christ. In the *Institutes*, Calvin describes the effect of spiritual eating:

> Though the apostle teaches that "Christ dwells in our hearts through faith" [Eph. 3:17], no one will interpret this indwelling to be faith, but all feel that

---

89. Edward J. Kilmartin, *The Eucharist in the West: History and Theology*, ed. Robert J. Daly (Liturgical Press, 1998), 155–68.
90. *Inst.* I.6.2–3 (OS 3:62–64).
91. Calvin, *Short Treatise*, 143–44 (CO 5:434–35).
92. See, e.g., the still-useful study of the topic in Ronald S. Wallace, *Calvin's Doctrine of the Word and Sacrament* (Eerdmans, 1957). See also Thomas J. Davis, *The Clearest Promises of God: The Development of Calvin's Eucharistic Teaching* (AMS, 1995); and Hughes Oliphant Old, *Holy Communion in the Piety of the Reformed Tradition*, ed. Jon D. Payne (Wipf & Stock, 2020), 13–180.
93. Calvin, *Short Treatise*, 143–44 (CO 5:434–35).
94. Calvin, *Short Treatise*, 143–44 (CO 5:434–35).
95. Calvin, *Short Treatise*, 143–44 (CO 5:434–35).

he is there expressing a remarkable effect of faith, for through this believers gain Christ abiding in them. In this way the Lord intended, by calling himself the "bread of life" [John 6:51], to teach not only that salvation for us rests on faith in his death and resurrection, but also that, by true partaking of him, his life passes into us and is made ours—just as bread when taken as food imparts vigor to the body.[96]

Calvin diverges from Zwingli's position that believers' communion with Christ in the Lord's Supper is simply another expression of faith, insisting instead that the sacrament actually conveys Christ.[97] It is more than a sign. It serves to "seal in our consciences the promises contained in [Christ's] gospel concerning our being made partakers of his body and blood."[98] This does not necessitate the Catholic or Lutheran views that the elements become or contain Christ's flesh and blood. Rather, Calvin repudiates the need to "drag Christ's body to earth" when the Lord could just as easily "lift us to himself."[99] It is instead through the "secret working of the Spirit" that believers truly feed on Christ's body and blood in the sacrament, such that "participation in life" might flow from Christ's humanity into theirs: "He is life since he is the eternal Word of God, who came down from heaven to us, but also that by coming down he poured that power upon the flesh which he took in order that from it participation in life might flow unto us. From this also these things follow: that his flesh is truly food, and his blood truly drink, and by these foods believers are nourished unto eternal life."[100]

Such high regard for the unique benefits of the Lord's Supper explains why Calvin remained insistent about weekly Communion. With the preached Word, the sacrament makes Christ available to believers in exile as sustaining food and drink. The Supper invigorates faith, deepens union with Christ, and stirs gratitude for God's grace. These experiences also lead believers to recognize one another as spiritual siblings united as one body in Christ.[101] In this way, the pilgrim community takes a visible form by enacting their need for nurture. Believers recognize one another in their hunger around the table God sets for them in exile.

In this same vein, baptism also played an important role in the theological and social cohesion of Reformation Geneva.[102] As with the Lord's Supper,

96. *Inst*. IV.17.5 (OS 5:346).
97. Davis, *Clearest Promises*, 48–49.
98. Calvin, *Short Treatise*, 144 (CO 5:435).
99. *Inst*. IV.17.31 (OS 5:389).
100. *Inst*. IV.17.8, 31 (OS 5:349–50, 389).
101. Calvin, *Short Treatise*, 144 (CO 5:435).
102. Spierling, *Infant Baptism*.

Calvin's view of baptism closely correlates the sign with the benefits signified. Baptism holds forth washing and renewal by Christ's Spirit, solidarity with Christ in his death and resurrection, and participation in all Christ's blessings through union with him.[103] These benefits must be received by faith.[104] Unlike the blessings of Communion, those of baptism—particularly for infants—are not tied to the moment of administration but are realized over time.[105] Infants cannot exercise faith but must not be deprived of baptism. Baptism's effectiveness consists in "future repentance and faith, . . . the seed of [which] lies hidden within [baptized infants] by the secret working of the Spirit."[106]

Sixteenth-century divisions over the sacraments were complex, pulling on theological and social threads that remain frayed even today.[107] To risk oversimplification, for Calvin sacraments were means by which God leads believers—in the case of baptism, even before they know how to believe—toward union with Christ and keeps them secure in this union. The notion of feeding regularly on Christ held sway in his thoughts on how the sacraments function. Calvin includes this statement in his 1557 summary of the Reformed faith for King Henry II of France: "The holy supper of our Lord is a testimony of the union which we have with Jesus Christ, inasmuch as not only he died and rose from the dead for us, but also truly feeds and nourishes us with his flesh, till we be one with him and his life be common to us. . . . By the secret and incomprehensible power of his Spirit, he nourishes and vivifies us by the substance of his body and blood."[108]

It is not difficult to appreciate reasons for Calvin's emphasis on Word and sacrament as food for the soul. The present life is spiritual exile, requiring sustenance from beginning to end. Supplying such manna in the wilderness elevates the importance of pastoral ministry. Preaching and sacraments anchored the liturgy in Protestant Geneva. In public worship Christ appealed to the congregation's ears and appeared to its eyes. For sixteenth-century worshipers living amid constant reminders of temporal insecurity and the elusiveness of a lasting home in this world, communal worship could be a boon. It was a way station for the hungry and displaced, a regular reminder of where they truly belong. It also reorientated their hope as God provided this regular foretaste of the home that awaits them.

103. *Inst*. IV.15.1–6 (*OS* 5:285–89).
104. *Inst*. IV.15.14–18 (*OS* 5:295–99).
105. *Inst*. IV.16.20–22 (*OS* 5.324–27).
106. *Inst*. IV.16.20 (*OS* 5:324–25).
107. Amy Nelson Burnett, *Debating the Sacraments: Print and Authority in the Early Reformation* (Oxford University Press, 2019).
108. Calvin to the King of France, October 1557 (Bonnet, 3:376).

Two documents orient modern readers to Calvin's thinking on organizing the worship service: his 1543 foreword to the *Genevan Psalter* and the liturgical handbook known as *The Form of Church Prayers and Hymns* (1542).[109] The *Psalter*, compiled under Calvin's supervision, contains metrical arrangements of the Psalms by authors such as Theodore Beza and Clement Marot. Calvin wrote a handful himself. Originally Geneva's songbook, it also became beloved in Reformed communities gathering for worship in other parts of Europe.[110] Read alongside Calvin's later preface to his commentary on the Psalms, the foreword to the *Psalter* puts into practice his advice to embrace the Psalms as a guide to prayer. Calvin briefly describes the three main parts of worship: preaching, prayers, and sacraments—each one instituted by God not "merely to amuse the world by spectacle," but that "from it profit should come to all His people."[111]

In this short introduction, Calvin's main concern is that all parts of the service remain intelligible to participants. He sharply criticizes the Catholic practice of using only Latin and says it produces superstition around rites people do not comprehend.[112] Sacraments should always be accompanied by teaching. Baptism and the Lord's Supper function as "visible words" that depict the doctrines taught in preaching.[113] Congregational singing is a form of corporate prayer. Care must be taken with music, however, lest it stir improper or distracting thoughts and emotions. Still, music is a powerful gift from God to delight the heart and intensify praise toward God.[114] For this reason, Calvin commends the use of psalms set to tunes of appropriate majesty and gravity for addressing God. Because they are words of scripture, which "the Holy Spirit made and spoke" through the psalmists, Calvin cannot think of more appropriate lyrics. "God puts his own words in our mouths," Calvin writes, "as if he himself were singing in us to exalt his glory."[115] Calvin does not expressly invoke exilic themes to introduce the Psalms as songs for

---

109. "Calvin's Foreword to the Psalter," in *John Calvin: Writings on Pastoral Piety*, ed. Elsie Anne McKee, Classics of Western Spirituality (Paulist Press, 2001), 91–97 (*OS* 2:12–18); and *The Form of Church Prayers and Hymns with the Manner of Administering the Sacraments and Consecrating Marriage According to the Custom of the Ancient Church*, in *Liturgies of the Western Church*, trans. and ed. Bard Thompson (World Publishing, 1961), 197–224 (*CO* 6:173–210). Thompson includes a comparison of editions of Calvin's liturgy published in Geneva (1542) and Strasbourg (1545). For helpful reconstructions of worship in Calvin's Geneva, see Maag, *Lifting Hearts*; and McKee, *Pastoral Ministry*, esp. 177–267.
110. Benedict, *Christ's Churches*, 496; Grosse, "'Docere et Movere,'" 177.
111. "Foreword to the Psalter," 91 (*OS* 2:12).
112. "Foreword to the Psalter," 93 (*OS* 2:13–14).
113. "Foreword to the Psalter," 93 (*OS* 2:13–14).
114. "Foreword to the Psalter," 94–95 (*OS* 2:15–17).
115. "Foreword to the Psalter," 96 (*OS* 2:17).

worship. Yet his invitation to "sing these divine and celestial hymns with the good King David" identifies the worshiping community with the voice of the biblical poet-king, whom Calvin characterizes throughout his teaching as an exemplar for faith in the context of David's exile.[116]

After initially following Farel's service, Calvin implemented his own liturgical vision upon his return to Geneva in 1541. *The Form of Church Prayers and Hymns* first appeared in early 1542 and contains liturgies for regular worship services as well as special services for sacraments, marriage, and the midweek service of prayer. Geneva's service book was a guide for those leading worship as well as a teaching tool for participants. Worshipers had to comprehend the service in order to benefit from it. Though the Lord's Supper was celebrated less frequently in Geneva than Calvin would have liked, the logic of the Communion service highlights the sacrament's importance.[117] Biblical teaching had pride of place every Sunday in the sermon, which was preceded by a prayer for illumination that asks the Spirit's assistance in the preaching and hearing of God's Word.[118] The liturgy holds space for the Lord's Supper after the sermon, with a supplement treating the manner of conducting the sacrament.[119] Readers will note language of both feeding and nurture in Calvin's liturgy, which instructs ministers to invite believers to feast on Christ, "the bread of heaven to feed and nourish us to eternal life."[120] It is a meal for the needy: "This sacrament is a medicine for the poor sick souls. . . . In giving himself to us [Christ] makes a testimony to us that all that he has is ours."[121] Comfort and assurance frame the service. The Supper invites pilgrims to feed on Christ today even as the church awaits his bodily appearing. Bread and wine are means by which "our souls shall be disposed to be nourished and vivified by His substance when they are lifted above all earthly things, attaining even to heaven, and entering the Kingdom of God where he dwells."[122] The Supper, in so many ways, brings a taste of the future to believers in exile.

Baptism and the Lord's Supper, when they take place, should follow the sermon in keeping with the conviction that such visible signs of God's promises must be explained for the benefit of faith. The Sunday liturgy conveys

---

116. "Foreword to the Psalter," 97 (*OS* 2:17); and for David, see chaps. 1, 4, 6, and 8 in this book.
117. Old, *Holy Communion*, 13–16; and Christian Grosse, *Les rituels de la Cène: Le culte eucharistique réformé à Genève (XVIe-XVIIe siècles)* (Droz, 2008).
118. *Form of Church Prayers and Hymns*, 199 (*CO* 6:175).
119. *Form of Church Prayers and Hymns*, 202–8 (*CO* 6:179–80, 193–200).
120. *Form of Church Prayers and Hymns*, 207 (*OS* 6:199).
121. *Form of Church Prayers and Hymns*, 206–7 (*OS* 6:199).
122. *Form of Church Prayers and Hymns*, 207 (*OS* 6:200).

this logic of moving from Word to sacrament even when a given service does not include the Lord's Supper. This allows for seamless transition from the pulpit to the table, where the gospel proclaimed finds immediate, tangible expression in the gifts of Christ's body and blood. The suggested prayer after the sermon characterizes the assembled church as Christ's flock. It is "gathered and restored" by ministers, as undershepherds, to "Jesus Christ, the chief Shepherd." This takes place in a world full of "ravening wolves" and hardships that include persecution, prison, and banishment.[123] The Genevan service is unremarkable for its stock biblical imagery. Yet, as an expression of Calvin's exilic outlook, it habituated the church to a pattern of expectation, nourishment, and comfort whenever it gathered.

Calvin replaced traditional seasons of fasting and prayer with a weekly Day of Prayer. This reordered time according to Geneva's Reformed commitments in ways that other communities would imitate.[124] The traditional calendar of liturgical feasts and holy days fell under scrutiny for not being biblical, prompting Geneva to join other Reformed churches in moving away from a fulsome recognition of such days. A limited number of customary feasts, such as Christmas, remained as civic holidays until 1550, while Sunday (on biblical grounds) became the single, weekly holy day.[125] Simplifying the church calendar amplified the significance of Geneva's Wednesday prayer service, which featured a sermon (of course) but focused on prayers of repentance and gratitude for God's providence in the daily circumstances of life.[126] Daily services were optional, though Genevans were expected to attend services on both Sundays and Wednesdays.[127] This constituted a dual stream of schooling to sustain life in exile with a durable rhythm of preaching, Communion, and prayer services.[128] Alongside the Lord's Day worship, focused on preaching and sacraments as manna in the wilderness, the weekly Day of Prayer located Genevans in the hard realities of exile, training faith to see providence in both blessings and affliction.

Conclusion

This chapter introduced the context and structures that defined Calvin's highest calling as pastor, or minister of the Word. Political exile, including

---

123. *Form of Church Prayers and Hymns*, 200 (CO 6:176).
124. McKee, *Pastoral Ministry*, 310–52.
125. McKee, *Pastoral Ministry*, 275–310; Grosse, "'Docere et Movere,'" 182.
126. McKee, *Pastoral Ministry*, 328–29.
127. See chap. 2, above.
128. Grosse, "'Docere et Movere,'" 186.

Calvin's own, shaped the way in which he conducted his pastoral ministry. The form of church organization and worship in Geneva imposed rhythms of religious life that trained all Genevans to think like exiles, regardless of their actual migration status. This included learning from childhood about the present life as spiritual exile and the need to receive nurture through the church in daily worship services. Sermons and sacraments were manna in the wilderness for weary pilgrims. The thread of this logic appears woven throughout Calvin's writings on the church and worship. It is unmistakable in his preaching, where teaching about the church's exilic identity appears explicitly and repeatedly in the form of sermons. Proclamation of biblical teaching from the pulpit was Genevans' main source of nurture in exile. We turn to this next.

For Further Reading

In Calvin's Words

1541 *Draft Ecclesiastical Ordinances*. In John Calvin, *Calvin: Theological Treatises*, translated by J. K. S. Reid, 56–72. LCC. Westminster John Knox, 1954.

1541 *Short Treatise on the Lord's Supper*. In John Calvin, *Calvin: Theological Treatises*, translated by J. K. S. Reid, 143–66. LCC. Westminster, 1954.

1542/45 *The Catechism of the Church of Geneva*. In John Calvin, *Calvin: Theological Treatises*, translated by J. K. S. Reid, 88–139. LCC. Westminster, 1954.

1542/45 *The Form of Church Prayers and Hymns*. In *Liturgies of the Western Church*, translated and edited by Bard Thompson, 197–224. World Publishing, 1961.

1543 Foreword to *Genevan Psalter*. In *John Calvin: Writings on Pastoral Piety*, edited by Elsie Anne McKee, 91–97. Classics of Western Spirituality. Paulist Press, 2001.

For Digging Deeper

Davis, Thomas J. *The Clearest Promises of God: The Development of Calvin's Eucharistic Teaching*. AMS, 1995.

Kingdon, Robert M. *Adultery and Divorce in Calvin's Geneva*. Harvard University Press, 1995.

Maag, Karin. *Lifting Hearts to the Lord: Worship with John Calvin in Sixteenth-Century Geneva*. Eerdmans, 2016.

Manetsch, Scott M. *Calvin's Company of Pastors: Pastoral Care and the Emerging Reformed Church, 1536–1609*. Oxford University Press, 2013.

Old, Hughes Oliphant. *Holy Communion in the Piety of the Reformed Tradition.* Edited by Jon D. Payne. Wipf & Stock, 2020.

Spierling, Karen E. *Infant Baptism in Reformation Geneva: The Shaping of a Community, 1536–1564.* Ashgate, 2005.

SIX

Stirring the Exilic Imagination

Calvin's Sermons and the Challenge of Faithful Exile

> The most foreign in the world are effectively our neighbors, even though they are neither parents, relatives, nor close friends to us. Why? We are all of one flesh. We bear one mark, which must lead us to do whatever we can for each other.
>
> —Calvin, Sermon on Galatians 6:9–11 (May 1, 1558)[1]

> Our Lord Jesus Christ said that if we wish to be children of Abraham, we must resemble him and be conformed to his life and example. So let us observe that his calling serves as a general example for all believers. When God says to him, "You will leave your country," it is not because God wants everyone to leave his country without some need to do so, but because he wants to show us that all of us are to be strangers in this world.
>
> —Calvin, Sermon on Acts 1:1–7 (1550)[2]

Unity and Urgency as Themes in Calvin's Preaching

Preaching was the centerpiece of Calvin's vocation as pastor in Geneva. Just as catechesis left nothing to chance in the arena of forming children in the faith, Calvin's vision for spiritual exile was not something he was content

---

1. CO 51:106.
2. Serm. Acts 7:1–4, September 7, 1550, in John Calvin, *Sermons on the Acts of the Apostles: Chapters 1–7*, trans. Rob Roy McGregor (Banner of Truth Trust, 2008), 370–71 (*SC* VIII:239–40).

for believers to catch in passing. It had to be taught explicitly. Every worship service required a sermon; Calvin frequently addressed contemporaries with the same imagery of comfort in exile that appears in his teaching elsewhere. Like preachers of any era, Calvin's pulpit ministry covered an impressive range of topics to help ordinary believers understand, retain, and apply biblical doctrine.[3] Addressing practical issues such as marriage or poverty, correcting defective theological views, and so on, Calvin connected the world of scripture to his context in ways irreducible to any single theme. Calvin was not, in other words, a "preacher of exile." Yet an unmistakable theology of exile undergirds his sermons.[4] Its presence is not hard to explain. Exile was a ubiquitous theme in the Bible as well as a lived reality for millions in Calvin's day, including both migrants themselves and those who regularly encountered them. These were the waters in which the church swam. Our survey of Calvin's sermons introduces how they deploy exile to stir the imagination. Specifically, his preaching pressed exile's implications for unity and the urgency this demanded. These themes, unity and urgency, gave shape to a diverse community and simultaneously differentiated Calvin's theology from competing views.

Calvin usually preached twice on Sundays, for a time traveling across Geneva, between St. Pierre and St. Gervais, and once each workday on alternating weeks, for a total of around twenty sermons per month.[5] His extemporaneous style did not rely on notes. Calvin's busy schedule of pastoral duties, teaching locally, and writing for publication left little time for composing sermons. This is not to say that he was unprepared in the pulpit. Calvin's sermons represent the fruit of hours spent each day preparing exegetical lectures and commentaries. Though surpassed by Protestant Hebraists such as Sebastian Münster (d. 1552) and Konrad Pellikan (d. 1556), Calvin's competence in biblical languages and exceptional memory were assets to his preaching.[6] This does not mean that Calvin never erred when translating or quoting scripture, though such mistakes did not diminish his confidence.[7]

---

3. Randall Zachman, *John Calvin as Teacher, Pastor, and Theologian: The Shape of His Writings and Thought* (Baker Academic, 2006), 147–72; and T. H. L. Parker, *Calvin's Preaching* (T&T Clark, 1992).

4. Max Engammare, "'Dass ich im Hause des Herrn bleiben könne, mein Leben lang': Das Exil in den Predigten Calvins," in *Calvin und Calvinismus*, ed. Irene Dingel and Herman Selderhuis (Vandenhoeck & Ruprecht, 2011), 229–42.

5. The next two paragraphs rely heavily on the reconstruction of Calvin's preaching ministry in Elsie Anne McKee, *The Pastoral Ministry and Worship in Calvin's Geneva* (Droz, 2016), 460–523.

6. Max Engammare, "Calvin connaissait-il la Bible? Les citations de l'Écriture dans ses sermons sur la Genèse," *Bulletin de la Société de l'Histoire du Protestantisme Français (1903–2015)* 141 (1995): 164–65.

7. Max Engammare, "Calvin: A Prophet Without a Prophecy," *Church History* 67, no. 4 (1998): 643–61.

Like his commentaries and lectures, Calvin's sermons move through entire books verse by verse. This differs from other approaches prevalent in Calvin's day. One alternative was to follow the lectionary of biblical texts that marked events of Christ's life according to the church's liturgical calendar. The Swiss reformers generally rejected lectionary preaching as Rome's practice. Another method prioritized specific theological topics (*loci*) over a running exposition of a biblical passage. These approaches were not mutually exclusive, as a preacher could focus on doctrinal themes within the lectionary.[8] Calvin followed neither. He typically preached from the New Testament and Psalms on Sundays, with workweek sermons taking up continuous exposition of Old Testament books. Calvin broke from this pattern for special occasions such as Christmas and Easter, when he took up texts from the Gospels focusing on the nativity, passion, and resurrection. From 1538 to 1550 Geneva retained the four traditional feast days observed in Bern—Christmas, Circumcision (January 1), Incarnation (March 25), and Ascension—though it observed no special liturgy for such days and eventually abolished feasts for good in November 1550.[9] After Calvin's three-year exile in Strasbourg, his commitment to *lectio continua* prompted him to pick up in 1541 exactly where he left off in 1538, with the very next verse.[10]

The verse in question remains a mystery because access to Calvin's sermons is limited for several reasons. As we have noted, the reformer himself was reluctant to have his sermons published and generally had no involvement preparing them for print.[11] Calvin did concede, however, that he might be more open to publishing his sermons if he had time to revise them for wider audiences.[12] Despite his reservations, Calvin permitted the fund for French refugees, the *Bourse Française*, to hire stenographers to transcribe his preaching.[13] The resulting manuscripts became volumes of published sermons that were sold, in part, to benefit Geneva's refugees.[14] Patrons such as Laurent de Normandie and the publishers Jean Girard and Conrad Badius supported efforts to print and smuggle Calvin's sermons into France as part of Geneva's efforts to influence French affairs. At the center of this story is

---

8. Max Engammare, "Reformed Preaching in the Sixteenth Century: The Use of Lectionaries in Zurich," *Zwingliana* 42 (2015): 195–224; and Amy Nelson Burnett, *Teaching the Reformation: Ministers and Their Message in Basel, 1529–1629* (Oxford University Press, 2006), 157–70.

9. Grosse, "'Docere et Movere,'" 182.

10. Calvin to an unknown recipient, January 1542 (*CO* 11:365–66).

11. McKee, *Pastoral Ministry*, 542–45. See chap. 2, above.

12. Jean-François Gilmont, *John Calvin and the Printed Book*, trans. Karin Maag (Truman State University Press, 2005), 76–81.

13. Gilmont, *Printed Book*, 76–81; and Jeannine E. Olson, *Calvin and Social Welfare: Deacons and the Bourse Française* (Susquehanna University Press, 1989), 37–49.

14. Olson, *Social Welfare*, 37–49.

Denis Raguenier, the exceptionally accurate stenographer who transcribed Calvin's sermons from 1549 until Raguenier's death in 1560 or 1561.[15] We have Raguenier most of all to thank for these examples of actual preaching from the sixteenth century. Other admirers also helped preserve Calvin's sermons. Many of the published volumes appeared in English translations beginning in the 1550s.[16] Unfortunately, not all of Calvin's sermon manuscripts made it into print. Natural disasters and careless preservation have resulted in the destruction and discarding of many original manuscripts.[17] Some were recovered through the years, but many are feared to be lost forever. This makes the extant sermon manuscripts all the more valuable for their insight into how Calvin went about what he considered to be his most important activity. Sermons are a good index of the concerns and character of communities of faith in any era; Calvin's sermons are no different.

The remainder of this chapter samples how Calvin's sermons portray exile along two subthemes that frame the church's identity in relation to its present circumstances: unity and urgency. First, Calvin utilized the theme of spiritual exile to foster unity between groups in tension or facing potential estrangement. In so doing, he continued Christianity's long-standing tradition (going back to the New Testament) of appropriating exilic themes to shape the theology and practices of a faith community. This becomes even more evident in another way: Calvin employed exile in scripture to stoke urgency around external displays of faith. Not all forms of exile in the sixteenth century were equal. For Calvin, scripture prescribes a way to live in spiritual exile that, unsurprisingly, fell into lockstep with elements of his theology that others disputed. Calvin persistently taught that biblical examples such as Abraham and David modeled an urgency in their exilic faith. For his congregation's present situation, this meant an unqualified and even combative approach to the principles of Reformed doctrine and worship in Calvin's Geneva.

A Unifying Vision of Home and Neighbor: Redefining Place and People in Exile

Though Calvin was trained in rhetoric, his pulpit style did not always follow the rhetorical conventions of his day. He believed that preachers should

---

15. Olson, *Social Welfare*, 47–48.
16. Francis M. Higman, "Calvin's Works in Translation," in *Calvinism in Europe, 1540–1620*, ed. Andrew Pettegree et al. (Cambridge University Press, 1994), 88–99; and I. M. Green, *Print and Protestantism in Early Modern England* (Oxford University Press, 2000), 168–238.
17. Parker, *Calvin's Preaching*, 68–75.

use "unpolished and ordinary speech," rather than striving for "fineness of words [and] clever speculations."[18] Paul, a famously untrained speaker, was Calvin's model for such "spiritual eloquence."[19] This does not mean that Calvin ignored rhetorical strategies that could help his listeners. He frequently relied on repetition, familiar address, and the use of imaginary dialogues with interlocutors.[20] But the goal remained clarity and piety, rather than impressive oratory. Calvin frequently opened sermons with a concise summary of the teaching to follow. As a preacher, Calvin targeted the heart. He disliked "frigid" doctrine or empty speculation. In the pulpit, Calvin focused not on concerns of wider audiences abroad but on particular issues impacting ordinary Genevans, which he often related to exile as spiritual and political realities.

The most reliable manuscripts of Calvin's sermons come from the 1550s and 1560s.[21] These display the preacher's regular concern to convince his hearers of their equal status as spiritual exiles. Here Calvin addresses real-life issues like persecution, migration, and the challenges of welcoming others with a spiritual account of people and place. God's election undermines the world's assessment of relationships, power, and hope. This means belonging to a new family with a new home. As with his academic writings, Calvin's sermons employ providence, predestination, and ecclesiology to depict the present life as a pilgrimage.[22] Examples from sermons on Acts, Paul's letters, and Genesis demonstrate how he cultivated solidarity between believers in diverse situations as God's elect in a hostile world.

United as God's Household in Exile

Calvin the preacher invited Genevans to imagine a shared identity that reoriented, or even inverted, their prior notions of home and belonging. He paints this picture in a sermon on Acts 1:1–7.[23] Abraham's exile (Gen. 12) is

18. Comm. 1 Cor. 1:17 (*CNTC* 9:31–35; *CO* 49:319–22).
19. Bruce Gordon, *Calvin* (Yale University Press, 2009), 109–11; and Olivier Millet, *Calvin et la dynamique de la parole: Étude de rhétorique réformée* (Slatkine, 1992), 225–56.
20. Scott M. Manetsch, *Calvin's Company of Pastors: Pastoral Care and the Emerging Reformed Church, 1536–1609* (Oxford University Press, 2013), 156–81; McKee, *Pastoral Ministry*, 523–54; and Parker, *Calvin's Preaching*, 131–49.
21. The *Supplementa Calviniana* project, begun in 1936, has contributed critical editions of Calvin's sermons from surviving manuscripts to supplement the ones collected in CO; see T. H. L. Parker, *Supplementa Calviniana: An Account of the Manuscripts of Calvin's Sermons Now in Course of Preparation* (Tyndale, 1962).
22. Richard Stauffer, *Dieu, la création et la providence dans la prédication de Calvin* (Peter Lang, 1978).
23. Serm. Acts 1:1–7, September 7, 1550 (*SC* VIII:239–40).

"a general example for all believers"—not that everyone experiences migration or political exile, but "all [believers] are strangers in this world."[24] Identifying refugees and natives in his audience, Calvin points beyond these differences with a theological claim: All are spiritual exiles. Following Abraham is not a matter of "changing countries for the sake of switching residences," but being "prepared to leave this world when God calls us."[25] Calvin's sermons repeat this theme of spiritual pilgrimage often, even when exile is not explicit in the biblical text. Like passengers on a tumultuous "sea voyage," believers "press toward heavenly life" as "pilgrims" who are "passing through" this world.[26] "With no other refuge than in God's providence," believers find security neither in worldly attachments nor "home" as the world defines it.[27] For the forgetful or faint of faith, God constantly reminds the church of its true identity through preaching and sacraments. In public worship, Christ appears and "heaven is opened," as if "God extended his hand . . . to certify that life is among us" even while believers remain "strangers on earth."[28] Alienation from the world produces solidarity and generosity when believers recognize one another as fellow travelers and siblings in God's household.[29]

This was not always easy to see. Diversity created by the influx of refugees into Geneva prompted Calvin to call for patience and fraternity between people who found one another burdensome, strange, or otherwise unwelcome. Preaching on Galatians 6 in 1558, Calvin uses the language of "country," "kinship," and "household" to illustrate how people naturally associate goodwill with familiarity.[30] But spiritual bonds unite members of the church as "God's house" despite significant differences and lack of any obvious similarities. Believers "forsake themselves" if they do not welcome even those "most foreign" to them and receive such outsiders like family. One might expect such behavior of wild animals, Calvin says, not people who recognize the image of God in fellow humans and, beyond that, cherish the spiritual kinship that unites believers more deeply than political bonds of country, region, or kingdom. The church must repudiate natural suspicion of foreigners and

24. Serm. Acts 1:1–7, September 7, 1550 (SC VIII:239–40).
25. Serm. Acts 1:1–7, September 7, 1550 (SC VIII:239–40).
26. Serm. 1 Tim. 1:18–19, October 14, 1554 (CO 53:106–7; my dating of sermons follows the chronology presented in McKee, *Pastoral Ministry*, 823–921); Serm. 2 Tim. 3:6–7, July 7, 1555 (CO 54:240); Serm. 2 Tim. 2:8–10, May 26, 1555 (CO 54:126); and Serm. 2 Tim. 4:7–8, August 4, 1555 (CO 54:339).
27. Serm. 1 Tim. 3:3–5, December 2, 1554 (CO 53:273).
28. Serm. 2 Tim. 1:9–10, May 5, 1555 (CO 54:63–64); and Serm. Titus 1:1–5, August 25, 1555 (CO 54:416).
29. Serm. 2 Tim. 2:8–19, May 26, 1555 (CO 54:135–36).
30. Serm. Gal. 6:9–11, May 1, 1558 (CO 51:106–7).

instead express a "common brotherhood" as "God's children . . . together in his house." Calvin makes similar remarks in his commentary on Hebrews, which identifies hospitality to "refugees for the name of Christ" as a mark of solidarity among God's children. This was especially true in the case of the poor and afflicted, who could be viewed as burdensome by Genevans: "Since you are members of the same body, you ought to have a common feeling for one another's troubles, so that you are not divided amongst yourselves."[31]

Other sermons make the point that a new identity means new priorities and counterintuitive relationships. Those grumbling and causing division after city elections in 1555 should remember the church's exilic identity and future homecoming: "We are even better confirmed in our hope of eternal life when things in this world don't go according to our desires."[32] Another sermon relates spiritual exile to class divisions.[33] Rich and poor alike require "daily bread" from God's hand. The Lord's Prayer is not "for the poor only." God provides both spiritual and material benefits to all God's children, who must learn to rely entirely on their heavenly Father, regardless of their station in life.

Solidarity in the experiences of spiritual exile also united Genevans with other evangelicals, including the persecuted: "The fires are lit everywhere, we know what is done against the children of God. . . . Are we moved?" The preacher rebukes the callousness of talking about such atrocities while doing little more. "If there is no further humanity in us," Calvin warns, "we should not think God will claim us as his children, because we ought to have compassion for the whole church."[34] In another sermon, he commends the faith of those who cannot flee persecution but remain steadfast under threat: God sees them and is with them.[35] This awareness of God's active concern would have comforted refugees who left others behind to get to Geneva. A sermon on 2 Timothy 4:5–6 takes up martyrdom and relates it to God's providence: "[God] desires to water us like earth that is half-dry. When he sees such dryness and barrenness among us, that we don't bear fruit abundantly enough, he waters us with the blood of the martyrs."[36] While perhaps jarring to most people who do not regularly think about martyrdom, Calvin speaks of the violence that was producing martyrs and refugees in early modern Europe as no anomaly to God's plan. It is a symptom of spiritual exile that results from rejecting the world's account of power,

---

31. Comm. Heb. 13:2–3 (*CNTC* 12:204–5; *CO* 55:187).
32. Serm. Titus 2:15–3:2, October 6, 1555 (*CO* 54:555–62).
33. Serm. 1 Tim. 6:17–19, April 14, 1555 (*CO* 53:636–37).
34. Serm. 2 Tim. 4:8–13, August 11, 1555 (*CO* 54:355).
35. Serm. 1 Cor. 3:12–15, December 29, 1555; cited in McKee, *Pastoral Ministry*, 528–30.
36. Serm. 2 Tim. 4:5–6, August 4, 1555 (*CO* 54:327).

wealth, and success. True faith is costly, and Calvin's preaching recalibrated his listeners' imaginations to God's economy.

This recalibration meant learning to value how the church's ministry provides for God's household in exile. God uses biblical doctrine to bring his children "into his house," a privilege worth more than "all of this world's goods and benefits." Even King David wanted only to be "in the courts of the LORD" (Ps. 84) and counted "among the least in God's church."[37] Calvin's preaching vigorously defended pastors against their detractors. He was fond of insisting that God speaks through preachers, putting "his speech" into "the mouth" of the pastor.[38] A pair of 1558 sermons on Ephesians 4 mirrors the argument of his commentary, while insisting even more forcefully on submission to pastors. It is God's will that "one man should teach the rest," so that all "might have one same faith" and "be gathered together under" Christ.[39] Believers need to be nurtured in the church's bosom "as long as we are in this world." God's Word directs and strengthens the faithful as they "advance more and more" on pilgrimage: "When God set this order in his church, that his Word should be preached, it is so that as long as we are on this earthly pilgrimage, we will always come to the school where God teaches us, for we walk by faith (says St. Paul) and not by sight."[40] In the church, common doctrine joins old and young, weak and strong, learned and unlearned, and so also establishes a deeper spiritual unity. All are "God's children," equally called to pay diligent attention to preaching, so that "faith begins and . . . continues day by day until it is entirely perfected."[41]

Calvin criticizes those who despise such tokens of God's fatherly beneficence. "As a good father cares for his children," God provides gifts to believers through daily providence, but especially through pastors who feed the flock with biblical teaching.[42] Thus, preachers are appropriately honored as "fathers" in God's household because they function as instruments of God's paternal care: "God is Sovereign Father, men inferior to him. And yet [ministers] don't cease to be fathers to us, and we their children, when they bring to us the incorruptible seed by which we are regenerated to become children of God, as well as when they feed us with this same teaching."[43] Calvin likens those who refuse to submit to the ministry to hungry people who reject

37. Serm. Acts 5:40–42, August 3, 1550 (*SC* VIII:194).
38. Serm. 1 Tim. 1:3–4, September 23, 1554 (*CO* 53:22).
39. Serm. Eph. 4:11–12, August 28, 1558 (*CO* 51:563). For the commentary, see chap. 4, above.
40. Serm. Eph. 4:11–14, August 28, 1558 (*CO* 51:567–68).
41. Serm. Eph. 4:11–14, August 28, 1558 (*CO* 51:568).
42. Serm. 1 Tim. 3:3–5, December 2, 1554 (*CO* 53:272–73).
43. Serm. 2 Tim. 1:1–2, April 21, 1555 (*CO* 54:10–11).

food.[44] Word and sacrament are manna in the wilderness. In the Lord's Supper, "Christ testifies that he takes us to himself, and that he desires that we are fed by his very substance, . . . passing through this world as strangers."[45] Instead of taking it for granted, believers should guard the ministry, with "hand to the sword," as they would protect their food from robbers.[46] Even Satan grasps the ministry's value. He attempts to poison the church's teaching with "spicy sauce" that harms God's children by leaving them without nourishment in exile.[47]

United Against God's Enemies in Exile

Another way to foster unity between God's children was to distinguish them from God's enemies. For Calvin's theology of the church in exile, this meant clarifying the boundaries between those who could count on God's care and nurture and those who were excluded from such benefits. Geneva's high-profile execution of the Spanish physician Michael Servetus in 1553, for heresy, required Calvin to defend going to such lengths to protect doctrine.[48] God's honor and the well-being of spiritual pilgrims, who depend on sound teaching to nurture their faith, are imperiled by false belief.[49] The French Reformed theologian Sebastian Castellio called for toleration. Theodore Beza countered with *On Punishing Heretics* (1554), to which Castellio replied with *On Not Punishing Heretics* (1555).[50] Calvin preached on the Pastoral Epistles amid these disagreements and did not mince words from the pulpit: "Magistrates affirm—when they raise the sword against those who trouble the church, against all heretics, and those who sow errors and false opinions, and those Satanic fanatics who today argue for liberal impunity toward those who invert the truth and tear the unity of the faith and peace of the church—that all these show themselves to be at war against God and that it is Satan who leads them."[51] Castellio, that "Satanic fanatic," was not in attendance. But Calvin is not speaking to him. He wants Geneva's leaders to heed Paul by upholding "all godliness" (1 Tim. 2:2), with "the sword" if necessary. Dereliction

---

44. Serm. 2 Tim. 1:1–2, April 21, 1555 (CO 54:12).
45. Serm. 2 Tim. 2:8–10, May 26, 1555 (CO 54:125–26).
46. Serm. 2 Tim. 1:13–14, May 12, 1555 (CO 54:66).
47. Serm. 2 Tim. 1:13–14, May 12, 1555 (CO 54:65, 67).
48. Roland H. Bainton, *Hunted Heretic: The Life and Death of Michael Servetus, 1511–1553* (Beacon, 1960).
49. Serm. 1 Tim. 2:1–2, October 28, 1554 (CO 53:139).
50. Michael W. Bruening, *Refusing to Kiss the Slipper: Opposition to Calvinism in the Francophone Reformation* (Oxford University Press, 2021), 153–79; and George Huntston Williams, *The Radical Reformation*, 3rd ed. (Sixteenth Century Journal Publishers, 1992), 959–62.
51. Serm. 1 Tim. 2:1–2, October 28, 1554 (CO 53:139).

of this duty "won't go unpunished." Pastors, for their part, must confront false teaching just as vigorously. If they kept silent, no distinction would remain between truth and error, "the gospel" and "Muhammad's Qur'an."[52] By defending heretics, Castellio is "unworthy to be called [God's child], for who allows a person to mock their father?"[53] Calvin calls on city authorities to support the beleaguered pastors: "We don't need to depart from the city of Geneva to be persecuted on account of the gospel!"[54]

By late 1555, Calvin was still complaining. In sermons on Titus, he again rebukes Genevans challenging pastoral authority, calling on private citizens to support ministers and officials to enforce laws protecting the free speech of preachers.[55] "Those who despise our teaching," Calvin inveighs, "which is to say that which we bring in God's name, will find that they aren't waging war against us." He continues: "In the end they will know that God is their opponent, because they have taken up a battle against his Word."[56] It appears that not everyone knew what was good for them. The Servetus affair left plenty wondering about Geneva's hard-line approach to doctrine.[57] Some actively resisted their pastors. Not all people found comfort in God's method for nurturing spiritual pilgrims in exile.

Calvin's preaching employed exile in other adversarial ways besides turning a critical eye toward ungrateful pilgrims. He used predestination to distinguish the elect from other groups by identifying three kinds of spiritual exile: (1) exile common to all, (2) exile belonging to the reprobate, and (3) the pilgrim status unique to the elect. Regarding the first, Adam's exile symbolizes the human condition of estrangement from God and conflict with creation that result from sin.[58] On this point, Calvin's preaching on Genesis follows his 1554 commentary, depicting the present life as exile under God's penal sanction, yet with the ongoing possibility of mercy.[59] "The gospel," Calvin tells Genevans in 1559, "brings with it the law because we cannot be prepared to receive the grace of our Lord Jesus Christ unless we have become well-acquainted with our condemnation."[60] For us who come after Adam,

52. Serm. 2 Tim. 1:6–8, April 28, 1555 (CO 54:47).
53. Serm. 2 Tim. 4:14–22, August 11, 1555 (CO 54:361–62).
54. Serm. 1 Tim. 2:1–2, October 28, 1554 (CO 53:142).
55. Serm. Titus 1:1–5, August 25, 1555 (CO 54:413–15); Serm. Titus 2:15–3:2, October 6, 1555 (CO 54:554).
56. Serm. Titus 2:15–3:2, October 6, 1555 (CO 54:554).
57. Williams, *Radical Reformation*, 924–34.
58. See chap. 4, above.
59. Calvin preached on Genesis in 1559 and 1560, after having produced a commentary on the book in 1554. See Serm. Genesis, 1559–60 (SC XI/1–2); and Comm. Genesis, 1554 (CO 23:5–622).
60. Serm. Gen. 3:7–10, October 5, 1559 (SC XI/1:183); and see chap. 4, above.

"the excommunication of our father Adam is also ours. . . . We must know that God has deprived us of his blessings and declares that while we yet live in this world as the inheritance he gave us, we are strangers and pilgrims here and need to hold out for more, . . . like people banished from earth, who were formerly blessed."[61] Similarly, he tells his congregation in 1559 that God's "double lesson," judgment and mercy, turns exile (by which Calvin means the present life) into a place where they should look expectantly for God's comfort. Christ, through preaching and sacraments, "presents himself and declares that we find life in him—that it is not necessary for us to search for it far off, because he has descended here below to make us feel, by the power of the Holy Spirit, that he will never be separated from us."[62]

Adam's children will experience various forms of hardship in this life, including political exile. Yet this teaching might have been scant comfort to believers experiencing such suffering alongside their enemies in an age when violence and migration discriminated little between confessional groups. What made their exile different? Calvin taught his congregation how divine predestination demarcates two divergent paths for Adam's children in exile. The elect exist in the wilderness of spiritual exile alongside the reprobate. For Calvin, Cain's wandering (Gen. 4) exemplifies the reprobate person's experience in spiritual exile. Here Calvin follows an exegetical tradition that distinguishes Cain's exile from that of his parents. Cain was doubly exiled as "fugitive and wanderer," removed from both the garden and "the face" of God (Gen. 4:16). Some interpreters, like Ambrose and Zwingli, took Abel and Cain as allegories for Christ and the Jewish authorities who called for his crucifixion.[63] Calvin rejects this view, being far more interested in the Bible's psychological portrait of Cain's wandering in exile. Interreligious conflict is not the point, for Calvin, but neither is banishment to a specific place. No, Cain's exile reveals the reprobate mind: always unsettled and never at peace. Calvin the preacher presents this as comfort to his hearers. Although it may appear for a time that God's enemies flourish, Calvin assures Genevans that this is but an illusion masking the relentless inner turmoil of Cain's double estrangement. The reprobate already share humanity's estrangement from God on account of sin, but they also have no hope of God's mercy—a hopelessness believers never experience.[64] The elect never cease to belong to the "city of God."[65]

---

61. Serm. Gen. 3:22–24, October 18, 1559 (*SC* XI/1:235).
62. Serm. Gen. 3:22–24, October 18, 1559 (*SC* XI/1:236).
63. Ulrich Zwingli, *Farrago Annotationum in Genesin*, 1527, ed. Emil Egli et al., Huldreich Zwinglis sämtliche Werke 13 (Theologischer Verlag, 1982), 12:35–36; Ambrose, *De Cain et Abel* II.9.31 (PL 14:375–76); Augustine, *City of God* XV.7 (CCSL 48:459–62); and Augustine, *Contra Faustum Manichaeum* 12.9 (PL 42:258–59).
64. Serm. Gen. 4:10–12, October 30, 1559 (*SC* XI/1:287).
65. Serm. Gen. 4:12–14, October 31, 1558 (*SC* XI/1:293).

Calvin knew that such teaching was hard for refugees to believe, especially for those who had left loved ones behind. His sermons trained listeners to imagine Catholics who persecuted evangelicals as being like Cain. In autumn of 1559, Calvin devoted the better part of four sermons on Genesis to inveighing against those who dragged believers (likened to Abel) "to the fire," where they were burned in city after city "by enemies of our Lord . . . enflamed with rage."[66] Calvin says that, like Cain, the reprobates of his day are blinded by sin, flee from God, and must "keep running." At this point, Calvin sets aside his usual circumspection about reprobation in preaching.[67] Although only God ultimately knows the elect, Calvin has no problem identifying "many Cains living today." These "beasts," "dragons," and "dogs" include rulers and officials, like those in France who serve as "the Pope's executioners." This echoes language that Calvin applies to Rome and its agents in other sermons.[68] Believers must not be deceived. Despite appearances, God torments their tormentors. The ostensible power and ease of these latter-day "Cains" belies the inner turmoil of double exile. They have been driven from the face of God, with no hope of reconciliation. Like Cain, who lamented his plight (Gen. 4:13–14), the reprobates of Calvin's day carry "hell around" with them, their consciences being "100,000 executioners" that preview God's final rejection. Not all spiritual exile is the same. With the example of Cain, Calvin uses exile to comfort believers with a psychological analysis of their most violent enemies. God has no concern to nurture the reprobate. Their exile, Calvin emphasizes, will never give way to joyful homecoming.[69]

Problematizing Exile: Urgency in Resistance and Hunger

Through portrayals of inclusion and exclusion, Calvin's preaching sought to unite a diverse church around a common identity as spiritual exiles, regardless of migration status. God's people find common belonging around shared doctrine and communal worship. Such teaching had limited appeal,

---

66. Serm. Gen. 4:8–10; 4:10–12; 4:12–14; and 4:15–18, October 21 to November 1, 1559 (*SC* XI/1:264–411).

67. Paul Jacobs, *Prädestination und Verantwortlichkeit bei Calvin* (Kreis Moers, 1937), 158–59; and Wilhelm H. Neuser, "Calvin the Preacher: His Explanation of the Doctrine of Predestination in the Sermon of 1551 and in the *Institutes* of 1559," *Hervormde Teologiese Studies* 54, nos. 1–2 (1998): 60–103.

68. Serm. 1 Tim. 4:14–15, January 20, 1555 (CO 53:424).

69. In making a point about Ishmael and Hagar (Gen. 21) as outside God's election, e.g., Calvin demurs from Luther's more positive portrayal of the pair as exiles banished by Sarah and Abraham. See John L. Thompson, "Hagar, Victim or Villain? Three Sixteenth-Century Views," *Catholic Biblical Quarterly* 59, no. 2 (1997): 220–30.

however, for people who resisted such visible expressions of unity. Reasons for this included political rivalry in Geneva, the silent dissent of Nicodemism, or the fact that some people simply did not like their pastor. How could Calvin make his teaching on unity and comfort more compelling? On the one hand, consistorial discipline could police practices. But Calvin did not rely on corrective measures alone. He made a positive case in his preaching, particularly through its use of Abraham and David. The Bible's portrayal of these figures gave Calvin a ready-made template for the church's behavior in spiritual exile. Both examples, for Calvin, focus on the proper behavior of God's elect with respect to the church's ministry. Abraham in exile teaches the combative posture of confronting false religion. David's exilic experiences, as we saw in chapter 4, depict his intense spiritual hunger for Word and sacrament. Together, these biblical examples summon believers to communal worship, whether in Catholic France or Reformed Geneva. Abraham and David in exile appear in Calvin's sermons (even where one would not ordinarily expect to encounter them) to goad believers to action. Faithfulness for God's elect means a restless and determined approach to God's means of nurture in the church. It is about hungering for such nourishment and rejecting all alternatives. The tempestuous sea of early modern religious options only sharpened the contours of Calvin's movement against others. His use of Abraham and David had another important function: policing his own community of faith. Calvin depicted spiritual exile as a time of restless hunger and confrontation with unbelief. Believers who could not muster such zeal were deemed less faithful, even if they ostensibly rejected false teaching and became Reformed. They also had to mean it.

We see this articulated in Calvin's advice to political exiles. His friend Jaques de Bourgogne, lord of Falais, eventually sided against Calvin during the doctrinal conflicts of the 1550s.[70] But 1544 was a different time. Falais and his wife had fled France and were living for a time in Cologne. Calvin responded to their request for a chaplain from Geneva by invoking Abraham and David in exile. It is striking that Calvin mentions these figures not to commend the couple for the path they chose but to prepare them for the road ahead. Even fugitives for Christ remain prone to backsliding. God's Word is a "spur to goad us onward."[71] By this Calvin does not mean a particular geographical destination but ever-increasing vigilance in the practices of Reformed worship. David resisted the idolatry of the Philistines because he pined for true

---

70. Françoise Bonali-Fiquet, ed., *Jean Calvin: Lettres à Monsieur et Madame de Falais* (Droz, 1991), 7–30; and Uwe Plath, *Calvin und Basel in den Jahren 1552–1556* (Helbing & Lichtenhahn, 1974), 87.

71. Calvin to Falais, 1544 (Bonnet, 1:424–25; CO 11:735–36).

sustenance in preaching and sacraments. Abraham did not stop at leaving Ur but built altars to rebuke idolaters in Caanan and "exercise himself in the service and worship of God."[72] Monsieur and Madame de Falais should comport themselves similarly in exile, rather than "like crawfish" who step forward only to scamper back.[73] This means remaining true to why they left France. Pure worship is not something discovered only to be neglected. It must be sought constantly.

Calvin's preaching taught that not all instances of political exile are equivalent, not even among those who leave their country for religious purity. How refugees conduct themselves in exile is just as important. It is not coincidental that Calvin mentions both David and Abraham in his letter to Falais. Both appear throughout his preaching to drive home the same lessons about the urgency that all believers must maintain in spiritual exile. Their stories render Calvin's theology of exile in living color.

Abraham's Combative Faith in Exile

Jewish and Christian exegetical traditions celebrate Abraham's departure, at God's summons, from the familiar into parts unknown (Gen. 12). Calvin's interpretation follows suit in praising Abraham's obedience.[74] As we noted in chapter 4, Calvin's New Testament commentaries accent how exile shaped Abraham's faith and its lessons for others. This appears as well in Calvin's sermons. His preaching on Genesis lifts up Abraham for his hearers as a guide through the complex realities of exile. Election is important for this portrait. Unlike Adam, whose exilic experience is paradigmatic for all people, or Cain, who illustrates the double exile of reprobation, Abraham embodies God's election. His exile is the precise model for believers to imitate as the elect in spiritual exile. In Calvin's reading of Abraham in exile, two areas stand out and set his interpretation apart from earlier tradition. First, he bothers to ask if Abraham's exile was legitimate. Second, Calvin makes Abraham's altars in Canaan expressly about rejecting his neighbors' religion and deliberately provoking them.

In both his commentary and his sermons, Calvin problematizes the question of political exile in his day by assessing Abraham's departure from Ur, when he was still called Abram. For nearly all other past interpreters, Jewish and Christian, the simple fact that God called him meant Abram was right to

---

72. Calvin to Falais, 1544 (Bonnet, 1:425; CO 11:736).
73. Calvin to Falais, 1544 (Bonnet, 1:425; CO 11:736).
74. Kenneth J. Woo, "Against 'Many Cains' and Fickle Travelers: Patterns of Exile in Calvin's Exegesis," in *Calvin, Exile, and Religious Refugees: Papers of the Thirteenth International Congress on Calvin Research*, ed. Arnold Huijgen and Karin Maag (Vandenhoeck & Ruprecht, 2024), 21–23.

leave.⁷⁵ There was no need to examine this further. Here Calvin departs from tradition not by disagreeing but by spending a lot more time establishing this view. He raises the question of why people leave home in the sixteenth century and applies this to Abram. Contrary to other kinds of migrants, Abram was not "fickle," nor did he leave out of "disgust with [his] own country," nor "on account of crime, . . . foolish hope, or . . . any allurements." No, Abram "was guided by the word of God."⁷⁶ Calvin ends up where other interpreters did, but he is clearly fixated on the choices Europeans faced in an era when people changed locations for widely varied motives.⁷⁷ This leads his exegesis to pause here. For Calvin, not all migration is equal in an age of exile. Leaving is complex, and Abram's decision exemplifies the right kind of departure. God commanded it. And this carried further obligations.

In a sharper turn from tradition, Calvin's preaching depicts Abram's initial wandering in Canaan as a rebuke of Nicodemism, or the attempt to hide one's faith to avoid persecution.⁷⁸ Abram built altars at Shechem and near Bethel, knowingly provoking his neighbors because he refused to behave like a cowardly Nicodemite.⁷⁹ Luther's more common take on the passage simply sees the altars as expressions of piety.⁸⁰ Calvin agrees while taking their meaning further. His use of Abram for a lengthy critique of Nicodemism is not an intuitive reading of Genesis 12, but it reflects what was on Calvin's mind. In 1560, he tells Genevans that Abram should "prick [those] who [are] sluggish" and try to sidestep persecution.⁸¹ The "sum of Abram's altar" (its main lesson) is that God must be worshiped "in body as well as soul." This, Calvin insists, is "the duty of all and their responsibility toward God."⁸² No other historical interpreter made Abram's altars about rejecting hidden faith. But few were as preoccupied with Nicodemism as Calvin, a subject we will revisit in chapter 8. For him, Abram's combative posture in exile exemplifies how God's elect should behave in all circumstances. Piety must be visible. Calvin's commentary on this passage adds the claim that undergirds his anti-Nicodemite writings: "Piety has its appropriate seat in the heart, but from this

---

75. Woo, "'Many Cains,'" 21–23.
76. Serm. Gen. 12:1–3, January 27, 1560 (SC XI/2:591); and Comm. Gen. 12:1, 1554 (CO 23:173). This quote is from his commentary.
77. Nicholas Terpstra, *Religious Refugees in the Early Modern World: An Alternative History of the Reformation* (Cambridge University Press, 2015), 112.
78. For Nicodemism, see the introduction and chap. 8 in this book.
79. Serm. Gen. 12:5–9, February 6, 1560 (SC XI/2:612); also Comm. Gen. 12:7 (CTS 1:353–56; CO 23:181).
80. Luther, *Lectures on Genesis*, 12:7 (LW 2:284–85); see also Ambrose, *De Abraham* 1.2.5 (PL 14:422).
81. Serm. Gen. 12:5–9, February 6, 1560 (SC XI/2:612).
82. Serm. Gen. 12:5–9, February 6, 1560 (SC XI/2:612).

root confession emerges afterwards as fruit."[83] Moreover, outward confession, as repudiation of idolatry, is not an activity performed just once. It is a constant expression that identifies the church in spiritual exile. So Calvin reminds Falais, who has already fled compulsory Roman idolatry, that Abram's leaving was just the beginning.[84]

David's Restless Longing in Exile

For modern readers, it might be surprising that Calvin's rejection of crypto-religion so deeply colors his interpretation of Abraham's story. Yet Calvin's lived experience could not but shape his engagement with scripture. Nicodemism, an abiding scourge for Calvin, also features prominently in his preaching about the historical David. If Abraham's behavior models the importance of outward religion to distinguish true from false worship, David's actions illustrate the necessity of these same practices for obtaining spiritual nurture. For Calvin, David exemplifies the exilic form of the present life better than any other biblical figure. David, portrayed as a fugitive in exile, grounds Calvin's approach to the Psalms.[85] As we have noted with his commentaries, Calvin's sermons about David also apply David's fugitive experience broadly. Its lessons are not limited to migrants in political exile but apply to all God's elect as spiritual exiles. Like Abraham, David's conduct in exile models urgency, but in the register of spiritual deprivation and hunger rather than confrontation with unbelief. This second emphasis is no less useful for challenging Nicodemites.

Preaching on the Psalms and 2 Samuel, Calvin paints a vivid portrait of David that stresses the importance of public worship for reasons beyond God's hatred of idolatry or demand for outward faith. David's chief concern was spiritual nurture and sustenance. Preaching on Psalm 27, Calvin describes David's pining for the "house of the LORD" (v. 4), to "seek his face" (v. 8), during a time when Saul drove him from Jerusalem. Israel's communal worship, where God "takes on a face" through the ministry of Word and sacrament, was a "ladder" David climbed to enter God's presence.[86] David knew "the need to be taught by sermons, confirmed by the sacraments, and brought up in public prayers and confession of faith."[87] This requirement, Calvin tells Genevans, "we share with the patriarchs." Why did Nicodemites settle for less, as if they were better than David?[88] Calvin calls such dissemblers to come out of hiding

---

83. Comm. Gen. 12:7 (CTS 1:353–56; CO 23:181).
84. Calvin to Falais, 1544 (Bonnet, 1:425; CO 11:736).
85. See chaps. 1 and 4, above.
86. *Four Sermons* (CO 8:411–13, 418, 426–27).
87. *Four Sermons* (CO 8:413, 418).
88. *Four Sermons* (CO 8:419–24).

and find sustenance in a true church. They are malnourished without this. Curiously, Calvin delivered this message in Geneva, of all places, where the Reformed church already possessed the kind of ministry David sought and Nicodemites lacked. Once again, Calvin addresses those who disrespected Geneva's refugee pastors. David challenges their ingratitude for the spiritual food that Calvin and his fellow ministers provide. Dissenters get little from church because they take its ministry for granted.[89] Calvin does not spare fellow refugees who behave badly among their hosts. Speaking about those who act entitled when the Genevan church does not meet their expectations, Calvin declaims, "It would have been better that they broke their necks than ever set foot in this church."[90] Thus David's hunger for preaching and sacraments applies not only to Nicodemites but universally, to believers in all circumstances. God's people in exile should always be known for restlessly longing after true worship.

Sustenance in exile is also a theme in Calvin's preaching on 2 Samuel. These 1562 sermons reconstruct the exilic situations behind David's longing in the Psalms. In one case, David fled Jerusalem with the ark of the covenant only to send the ark back while he remained in exile (2 Sam. 15:25–29). This was a curious decision. Given his longing for its presence, why did David willingly part with the preeminent sacrament of God's presence in his day? Why would David, in other words, amplify his own pain? Calvin takes up this dilemma in two September sermons. David loved the ark. He desired nothing greater than "to gaze upon the Ark of God to worship him there."[91] From this the preacher contends, "We who have access to the sacraments should prize this more than anything." Calvin's commentaries and preaching on Psalms also make this point.[92] Yet for Calvin, David's decision in 2 Samuel to restore the ark to its proper place, prompting the misery of the Psalms, also proves his wisdom. Unlike Catholics, who attribute too much to sacraments—presuming that they work apart from faith—David respected divinely sanctioned limits. Sacraments are not replacements for God; they are means by which God reliably brokers access to the divine. Calvin points out Rome's failure to maintain the symbolic nature of the sacraments, veering into idolatry by substituting created things for God.[93] David in exile models the nuanced faith Calvin wants from his congregation. David refused to make

---

89. *Four Sermons* (CO 8:422).
90. *Four Sermons* (CO 8:422–23).
91. Serm. 2 Sam. 15:16–26, September 23, 1562 (SC I:439).
92. See above and chap. 4.
93. Serm. 2 Sam. 15:16–26, September 23, 1562 (SC I:439–40); and Serm. 2 Sam. 15:25–32, September 24, 1562 (SC I:442).

too much of the ark. But neither did he despise it. In exile, he pined for the ark. This is the aspect of David's faith that Calvin commends to Falais while his friend made his way into exile. Faithfulness is not achieved by leaving Catholic France. It requires ongoing commitment to the church's ministry of Word and sacrament, prompted by real hunger for God. Like Abraham, David reveals how a lack of commitment to these gifts falls short of God's mark for faithfulness in exile.

Suffering and the Exilic Faith of David

Samuel and the Psalms are natural places to reflect on the exilic David, but David appears also in less intuitive locations in Calvin's exegesis. Susan Schreiner notes how "David accompanies Job on almost every page of [Calvin's] Job sermons."[94] It is indeed striking how often Calvin reflexively reaches for David in his preaching on Job. David is not just an example for sixteenth-century believers but also someone from whom Job could learn to suffer well. David appears in 62 of the 159 sermons on Job that Calvin preached in Geneva from February 26, 1554, to March 6, 1555. That is an extraordinary amount of teaching about David from texts not obviously about him.[95] Again, the power of David's example is obvious for Calvin, who, for his congregation, repeatedly uses David to supplement lessons from Job's suffering. David joins Job and others, including Abraham, as models for believers facing intense affliction, especially when God's goodness and intentions are hidden: "Was Job not human? Abraham? David, too? How did they endure trials? . . . Is God not the same today?"[96] The question of human righteousness in light of God's righteousness leads Calvin to focus more on David's inner piety, humility, and awareness of sin.[97] David is a case study for how God's providence comforts the elect.

David appears with Job most often as a fellow sufferer. As in Calvin's teaching elsewhere, his preaching on Job favors portraying the historical David as an exile, implying that political exile is part of God's just punishment for David's

---

94. Susan E. Schreiner, *Where Shall Wisdom Be Found? Calvin's Exegesis of Job from Medieval and Modern Perspectives* (University of Chicago Press, 1994), 101.

95. Students interested in Calvin's Job exegesis should consult Schreiner, *Wisdom*; and also Derek Thomas, *Calvin's Teaching on Job: Proclaiming the Incomprehensible God* (Christian Focus, 2004).

96. Serm. Job 1:13–19, March 12, 1554 (*CO* 33:85); see also Serm. Job 17:6–16, August 15, 1555 (*CO* 34:59–60); and Serm. Job 20:1–17, August 29, 1554 (*CO* 34:135).

97. See, e.g., Serm. Job 5:17–18, May 9, 1554 (*CO* 33:269); and Serm. Job 13:23–28, July 17, 1554 (*CO* 33:646–52).

past sins.[98] The David of these sermons on Job is also deeply aware of the present life as spiritual exile. Like the David of the Psalms, he finds comfort in the spiritual food God provides in communal worship. But he especially treasures the daily provision of God's providence. David knows that God "has placed us in this world to the end that we might be in a great theater to contemplate his works and confess that he shows himself wise, righteous, and powerful." Yet David often struggles to see this clearly. Even so, Calvin insists, David teaches believers, "We must still affirm that [God] does nothing without reason."[99] Transparent understanding awaits a future, "final renewal" in the "kingdom of heaven." The preacher tells his congregation that the stories of Job, David, and "our Lord Jesus Christ" teach believers to be patient for this future. These figures experienced suffering as a precursor to vindication, which assures the faithful that the same path awaits them: Renewal will follow affliction.[100] In another sermon on Job, Calvin reminds hearers that David and Abraham were mercilessly mocked only later to be vindicated. God's children rest in the sure hope that justice will prevail.[101] David modeled pilgrim faith that trusts God's providence as it awaits this future.

Other sermons on Job teach hearers to look for God's fatherly care in ordinary food and drink, as well as in the special provision of sacraments that "nourish hope."[102] The preacher highlights the brevity of life for "pilgrims" who rely on God's provision. Spiritual exile forms faith when believers learn to "take refuge in [God]" in a hostile environment that Calvin likens to a "battle."[103] As a conscientious father, God utilizes this "earthly pilgrimage" to demonstrate love for the elect.[104]

Calvin brings David back into focus to highlight the same regard for preaching and sacraments that appears in his exegesis of the Psalms and 2 Samuel. Like Abraham, David teaches believers that faith must be confessed, never

---

98. Calvin occasionally highlights David's exilic circumstances explicitly. See, e.g., Serm. Job 2:1–6, March 14, 1554 (*CO* 33:106); Serm. Job 4:7–11, March 29, 1554 (*CO* 33:193); and Serm. Job 16:1–9, August 4, 1554 (*CO* 34:9–10).

99. Serm. Job 11:7–12, June 29, 1554 (*CO* 33:539); and Serm. Job 38:12–17, February 12, 1555 (*CO* 35:382–83).

100. Serm. Job 14:13–15, July 20, 1554 (*CO* 34:689–90); and Serm. Job 42:9–17, March 6, 1555 (*CO* 35:510).

101. Serm. Job 18:12–21, August 17, 1554 (*CO* 34:85–86); Serm. Job 19:17–25, August 28, 1554 (*CO* 34:124); and Serm. Job 19:26–29, August 29, 1554 (*CO* 34:135).

102. Serm. Job 1:2–5, February 27, 1554 (*CO* 33:41–42); and Serm. Job 1:5, February 28, 1554 (*CO* 33:48).

103. Serm. Job 2:11–13, March 16, 1554 (*CO* 33:140); Serm. Job 14:1–4, July 18, 1554 (*CO* 33:663–64); and Serm. Job 14:13–15, July 20, 1554 (*CO* 33:691–92).

104. Serm. Job 7:1–6, May 24, 1555 (*CO* 33:337); and Serm. Job 10:18–22, June 23, 1554 (*CO* 33:509–10).

hidden.[105] David understood how the Holy Spirit uses pastoral ministry: "When [pastors] speak, God desires to be heard through [them]."[106] Doctrine, for David, was "comfort" to one who knew he was "only en route" in the world and looked to God "for refuge."[107] Such teaching, together with ordinary food and drink, constituted David's daily bread.[108] In these sermons on Job, Calvin's portrait of David corroborates the lesson that preaching is "spiritual food" for souls, "medicine" that "heals" as well as "feeds." "Bread always has its normal use," says the preacher, "but the word of God should not only nourish us, but it should also heal our diseases and purge them from us."[109] It is no wonder that Calvin's David hungered for this food with such urgency.

Conclusion

The previous chapter outlined Geneva's program of doctrinal education, from cradle to grave, intended to serve the needs of spiritual exiles of all stripes. At its center was worship, where God encountered the people through Word and sacrament, manifestations of God's presence to strengthen and guide them along their pilgrimage. This chapter has demonstrated how Calvin's teaching in this setting drew consistently on biblical imagery of exile, pilgrimage, and nurture to locate the church in the world. More specifically, the exilic identity Calvin imposed from the pulpit was intended to unite believers and call them to greater zeal in practice. The preacher drew heavily on providence and predestination to paint pure worship as a great privilege: This is how God feeds God's children in exile. The same remarkably consistent vision appears in Calvin's sermons, especially in connection with Abraham and David. Their experiences render Calvin's exilic theology in case studies that illustrate how the elect should live as exiles in this world. Calvin's teaching constantly addressed violence and migration in Geneva's context, taking up topics ranging from refugee neighbors to persecuted brothers and sisters in Christ abroad to the despicable behavior of cowardly Nicodemites. These concerns bent Calvin's exegesis in unique directions. His preaching also reveals that not all found his account of exilic faith persuasive. As much as he tried to include diverse experiences in an inclusive vision of God's comfort for the elect, navigating dissent required him to exclude others as well. We turn now to this matter.

105. Serm. Job 20:1–7, August 30, 1554 (CO 34:141).
106. Serm. Job 33:1–7, December 12, 1554 (CO 35:43).
107. Serm. Job 15:11–16, July 31, 1554 (CO 33:720–21).
108. Serm. Job 33:14–17, December 17, 1554 (CO 35:68–69).
109. Serm. Job 13:1–10, July 6, 1554 (CO 33:608); Serm. Job 15:1–10, July 30, 1554 (CO 33:707); and Serm. Job 33:29–34:3, December 21, 1554 (CO 35:129–30).

For Further Reading

In Calvin's Words

A number of recent translations from Banner of Truth Trust have made Calvin's sermons more accessible to today's readers in English. These include the following:

1552 *Faith Unfeigned: Four Sermons Concerning Matters Most Useful for the Present Time with a Brief Exposition of Psalm 87*. Translated by Robert White. Banner of Truth Trust, 2010.

1554–55 *Sermons on Job*. Translated by Rob Roy McGregor. 3 vols. Banner of Truth Trust, 2022.

1554–55 *Sermons on 1 Timothy*. Translated by Robert White. Banner of Truth Trust, 2018.

1555 *Sermons on 2 Timothy*. Translated by Robert White. Banner of Truth Trust, 2018.

1559–60 *Sermons on Genesis*. Translated by Rob Roy McGregor. 2 vols. Banner of Truth Trust, 2009–12.

For Digging Deeper

McKee, Elsie Anne. *The Pastoral Ministry and Worship in Calvin's Geneva*. Droz, 2016.

Parker, T. H. L. *Calvin's Preaching*. T&T Clark, 1992.

Schreiner, Susan E. *Where Shall Wisdom Be Found? Calvin's Exegesis of Job from Medieval and Modern Perspectives*. University of Chicago Press, 1994.

Woo, Kenneth J. "Abraham, David, and the Problem of Exile in Calvin's Theology." *Harvard Theological Review* 118 (2025): 314–36.

PART FOUR

Calvin as Polemicist

SEVEN

Herding God's Flock in Exile

Calvin's Polemical Works

When God raised up Luther and others, who held forth a torch to light us into the way of salvation, and on whose ministry our churches are founded and built, those heads of doctrine in which the truth of our religion, those in which the pure and legitimate worship of God, and those in which the salvation of men are comprehended, were in a great measure obsolete. We maintain that the use of the sacraments was in many ways vitiated and polluted. And we maintain that the government of the Church was converted into a species of horrible and insufferable tyranny.

—Calvin, "The Necessity of Reforming the Church" (1543)[1]

It is enough for me that it behooved us to withdraw from them that we might come to Christ.

—Calvin, *Institutes* IV.2.6 (1559)[2]

Just as the hungry dog catches at the shadow instead of the flesh, so Westphal feeds on his own imagination.

—Calvin, *Last Admonition to Joachim Westphal* (1557)[3]

---

1. *Tracts*, 1:125 (CO 4:459). The Latin title of this work is *Supplex exhortatio ad Caesarem*, a direct translation of which would be *Sincere Exhortation to the Emperor*.
2. OS 5:37.
3. *Tracts*, 2:365.

Establishing a Perimeter: Defining God's People amid Religious Controversy

Imagine the following book review: "Your book struck me as so cheap and trivial that I felt profoundly sorry for you, defiling as you were your very elegant and ingenious style with such trash." This was Luther's assessment of Erasmus's *Diatribe Concerning Free Choice* (1524).[4] The reformers and their opponents did not mince words in theological debate. Many people today remember the Reformation primarily for such disagreements about ideas that divided the Western church and European nations with it. It is easy to laugh at the hyperbole and name-calling. Disputes about theology and the authority to determine doctrine certainly defined the era. But there was always more than sparring over ideas. And the consequences were more serious than hurt feelings or loss of an argument.

Many people died for their beliefs. Others killed. Millions left home, whether by their choice or another's.

Like other theologians of his day, Calvin relished a good takedown of theological opponents. This chapter introduces how his polemical writings reveal his situation as a refugee. Specifically, Calvin's concern to distinguish his community from others reflected the high stakes of knowing where one stood before God. In a sea of competing options claiming to be the true church, not all claims were valid, not all exiles were faithful, and not everyone could count on God's favor. Calvin's polemical writings refuted error to give his community greater confidence that they were truly God's people in exile. It was a matter both of herding God's flock away from error and of pointing them toward true spiritual food.

The theological divisions that emerged during the Reformation were closely connected to notions of social purity. The body of Christ (*Corpus Christi*) was a powerful metaphor for church and society, which led to anxiety about impurities within these bodies. Nicholas Terpstra uses the categories "purity," "contagion," and "purgation" (informed by medieval medical manuals) to describe how early modern religious communities dealt, often violently, with difference in their midst. Religious difference, often deemed "heresy," was a disease to be contained and expunged to restore health to the body of Christians (*Corpus Christianum*).[5] Indifference was costly. Famine, plague, poverty, and natural disaster expressed divine displeasure for tolerating those whom

---

4. Martin Luther, "The Bondage of the Will, 1525," in *The Annotated Luther*, vol. 2, *Word and Faith*, ed. Kirsi I. Stjerna (Fortress, 2015), 160.

5. Nicholas Terpstra, *Religious Refugees in the Early Modern World: An Alternative History of the Reformation* (Cambridge University Press, 2015), 1–73.

God opposed. Catholics and Protestants alike justified violence in God's name with rhetoric that dehumanized opponents and styled their punishment as divine justice.[6] Religious polemic thus contributed to cycles of persecution and exile that affected so many Europeans, beginning with the expulsion of Jews and Muslims from Iberia before the Reformation. Christians also mischaracterized Jews and alleged witches in especially egregious terms, depicting the rituals of these already marginalized groups as perversions of Christian rites. A "blood libel" tradition, for instance, held that Jewish Passover observance required Christian blood.[7] Calvin himself was caught in the fallout from religious violence and purged from France with fellow evangelical "heretics." From Geneva, Calvin contributed to the Protestant counteroffensive, diagnosing Rome as the disease. Living, as it were, in a rotting corpse, evangelicals had no choice but to depart Rome to "come to Christ."[8]

On such logic, political exile was an act of preserving the church's purity and asserting one's identity on the right side of widening divisions. Calvin's polemic against Rome was a form of identity construction. He redrew boundaries around God's elect by redefining the terms upon which the church exists. In a sea of competing claims to be the "true church," it became necessary to define God's people in exile with precision. This involved exposing the misguided confidence of others. Such confrontation clarified who, exactly, could expect the nurture and care reserved for God's own by calling out imposters. Calvin and Farel attempted, unsuccessfully, to enforce Reformed identity by imposing subscription to Geneva's *Confession*.[9] Other Swiss cities, such as Catholic Fribourg, required all residents to swear loyalty to a confession. In Calvin's Geneva, however, such oaths were limited to church officers and students. Broader community definition (and control) had to be reinforced by other means, such as consistorial discipline and teaching that marked clear boundaries, particularly around the nature and practice of the sacraments.

Catholics were not the only wolves against whom Calvin herded God's people into a distinctive flock. Fellow Protestants also required confrontation. These included Lutherans, some of whom despised Calvin more than he disliked them. Even more pernicious were certain Anabaptist and Spiritualist sects, such as so-called Libertines and thinkers who denied the Trinity. These were among

6. Natalie Zemon Davis, "The Rites of Violence," in *Society and Culture in Early Modern France: Eight Essays* (Stanford University Press, 1975), 152–87.

7. Edwin Muir, *Ritual in Early Modern Europe*, 2nd ed. (Cambridge University Press, 2005), 233–45.

8. *Inst*. IV.2.6 (OS 5:37).

9. Robert M. Kingdon, "Confessionalism in Calvin's Geneva," *Archiv für Reformationsgeschichte* 96 (2005): 109–13.

the groups that Calvin cast out of the true church. The reformer portrayed these people as contagions that needed to be purged along with Rome. This illustrates how violence could go both ways. In the case of the antitrinitarian Michael Servetus, for instance, Geneva killed a man in the name of religious purity. Within the broader French-speaking evangelical movement, disagreement on topics such as crypto-religion, predestination, and religious toleration required Calvin to take up the pen to defend his account of comfort for exiles.

Reprobating Rome: Rewriting the History of God's Elect in Exile

Calvin's rejection of Roman Catholicism, christening the pope as "Antichrist," and characterizing those loyal to Rome as reprobate (exemplified by figures like Cain)—these were standard-issue Reformation-era Protestant polemics.[10] Others, like Luther, said similar things just as colorful (sometimes more so). The body of Christ, Luther reasoned, had no need for the opinions of "popes and bishops," whom he likened to the church's "urine, excrement, or filth." "Not part of the body," they were instead "snot on the sleeve and dung itself; for they persecute the true gospel."[11] Yet, also like other reformers, Calvin realized that there was an art to rejecting the church that administered one's baptism, especially in an age when theological innovation was not a measure of virtue. Protestants, after all, were already accused of inventing their religion out of whole cloth. Who was more trustworthy in matters of salvation? Cardinal Jacopo Sadoleto asked the inhabitants of Geneva in 1539 to be loyal to their spiritual mother, who had nurtured saints in her bosom for one-and-a-half millennia. Could they trust a sketchy start-up less than twenty-five years old?[12] Basic math and chronology were on Sadoleto's side.

Calvin knew this. But there were reasons why he did not simply retort that God was doing a new thing and move on. For one thing, mainstream Protestants like Calvin received the historic Catholic tradition sympathetically despite claims, then and now, that they derived their theology *sola scriptura*. They looked to church fathers and medieval thinkers as doctrinal authorities, insofar as they judged such authors to accord with the Bible's teaching.[13]

---

10. *Inst.* IV.2.11–12. For Cain, see chap. 4, above. On the general topic of Calvin's relationship to Roman Catholicism, see Randall C. Zachman, ed., *John Calvin and Roman Catholicism: Critique and Engagement, Then and Now* (Baker Academic, 2008).

11. Serm. John 7:39–44 (*LW* 23:287).

12. John C. Olin, ed., *A Reformation Debate: Sadoleto's Letter to the Genevans and Calvin's Reply* (Harper & Row, 1966), 40–41.

13. R. Ward Holder, *Calvin and the Christian Tradition: Scripture, Memory, and the Western Mind* (Cambridge University Press, 2022); Esther Chung-Kim, *Inventing Authority: The Use*

Reformers found support for their views in thinkers like Cyprian, Chrysostom, Ambrose, and especially Augustine, even as Rome claimed the same backing for theirs. Overlapping authorities called for disentanglement from error rather than rejecting the tradition outright. Mainstream Protestants, in fact, agreed with Rome regarding many central tenets of Christian theology. The Trinity and Christology, for instance, were not at issue. Where they disagreed most sharply, on the nature of the church and its sources of authority, represents a relatively small, if powerful and incendiary, part of the tradition.

To address the charge of novelty, it was important for Protestants to show that they were the more faithful heirs of past teachers and not making up their theology. They were actually to thank for righting a ship that had gone terribly off course amid medieval Christianity's excess and hubris. The widening of papal power after the model of secular monarchs was especially egregious. Establishing historical links was important to reformers for another reason: It connected them to the biblical apostles and prophets. Despite his stature with Protestants and Catholics alike, Augustine was a man who could err. For example, Calvin chides him for being "involved in the common" misreading of Romans 7 as the struggle of a nonbeliever.[14] Church fathers were valuable authorities only insofar as they reflected biblical doctrine, the teaching of the prophets and apostles. Thus, the endgame of Protestant appeals to tradition was to establish continuity with the faithful of Christian history, and through them to communities depicted in the Old and New Testaments. This would ground the reformers' teaching upon scriptural as well as historical precedent.

Sadoleto intimated correctly that the stakes were high. Nothing less than salvation was on the table at a time when Europeans had looked for centuries to the Roman Church for this most lofty gift. Convincing people to invest their eternal inheritance in an apparent startup was a tall order. It required an immense transfer of trust. To be sure, some people were already looking for reasons to jump ship, whether over doctrinal disagreements or political rivalry with Rome. Many others were fairly indifferent, or perhaps simply drawn to the excitement of change. Still, for countless Europeans, including the reformers themselves, choosing to change sides could be a costly proposition in a time still dominated by an established and powerful old religion. It had to be worth the risk.

Calvin carefully related biblical events to contemporary realities as part of a continuous sacred history, without flattening historical differences between

---

of the Church Fathers in Reformation Debates over the Eucharist (Baylor University Press, 2011); and David C. Steinmetz, "Calvin and Abraham: The Interpretation of Romans 4 in the Sixteenth Century," *Church History* 57 (1988): 454–55.

14. Comm. Rom. 7:15 (CO 49:130). Calvin argues that Paul depicts himself as struggling with sin even as a mature believer.

them.[15] This required him to show how the exilic theology of comfort he found in scripture applied equally to biblical figures and sixteenth-century evangelicals, whom Rome dismissed as heretics. To accomplish this, Calvin wrote Rome into a new role in his plotting of church history. He demoted Rome from true church to false church, from elect to reprobate, from God's pilgrim people in exile to this community's tormentors (or, as Luther would have it, the church's excrement). Rome was not spiritual mother but a failed imposter. This did not mean there was no good in the Roman Church's past. Calvin distinguished the invisible church of God's elect from the visible church, which contains a mixture of elect and nonelect, truth and error.[16] Historically, God preserved pockets of true teaching in the visible church through the likes of the church fathers, medieval thinkers like Bernard of Clairvaux, and many nameless faithful in between. The church held to true doctrines such as the Trinity and promises of God's covenant. Calvin calls these "traces of the church" (*vestigia ecclesiae*), among which he also includes the sacrament of baptism.[17] Yet such traces had become so faint that Protestants had no choice but to leave the Roman Church. This was not an act of schism or lack of forbearance with the visible church, both of which Calvin criticizes in the *Institutes*.[18] No, leaving was acknowledging what Rome had become: an apostatized false church. Even if Catholics did not (at least at first) kick Protestants out, Rome had already banished Christ. Calvin took this argument to Sadoleto, reversing the cardinal's charge. Rome, not Geneva, was late on the scene, arrogant, and power-hungry. Rome, the imposter, had introduced countless errors, burying the teaching of the apostles and prophets. Thus, Calvin reframed history to show how the members of his community, persecuted and scattered, were the true followers of Christ in spiritual exile.[19] Part of this involved showing how Protestants recovered biblical teaching and right use of the sacraments, essential marks of God's presence, to accompany and nurture the church in exile.

Those interested in Calvin's anti-Catholicism can open to almost any page in his works. Two examples from early in Calvin's ministry as a reformer are his *Reply to Sadoleto* on behalf of the Genevans (1539) and a 1543 assessment of the divide between Protestants and Rome, his *Supplex exhortatio ad Caesarem* (*Sincere Exhortation to the Emperor*).[20] Calvin did not formally distinguish

---

15. Barbara Pitkin, *Calvin, the Bible, and History: Exegesis and Historical Reflection in the Era of Reform* (Oxford University Press, 2020), 122–40.
16. *Inst*. IV.1.7–9 (*OS* 5:12–14).
17. *Inst*. IV.2.12 (*OS* 5:41–42).
18. *Inst*. IV.1.10–16 (*OS* 5:14–21).
19. See chap. 6, above.
20. Olin, *A Reformation Debate*, 49–94; *Supplex exhortatio ad Caesarem* appears as "The Necessity of Reforming the Church" in *Tracts*, 1:123–234.

between polemical and doctrinal writings, and he frequently polemicized in his preaching. Correcting error was a part of his overall teaching ministry. In the writings against Catholics that we examine here, Calvin does not pull punches in giving a sophisticated answer for why evangelicals legitimately hold the title "true church," with all its benefits. The same critique of Rome speaks to Protestants as well, inviting them to envision a new reality and reimagine their old church as an enemy of God's true people.

Sadoleto's appeal to the Genevans centers on a classical definition of the church that identifies it with an institution: the Catholic Church and its visible succession of bishops, beginning with the apostle Peter. This church cannot err because it possesses the Holy Spirit: "To define it briefly, the Catholic Church is that which in all its parts, as well as at the present time in every region of the world, united and consenting in Christ, has been always and everywhere directed by the one Spirit of Christ."[21] The reformers, Sadoleto insists, forsake this church, putting before innocent people a road that "breaks off in two directions, . . . one of which leads us to life, . . . the other to everlasting death."[22] Envy, licentiousness, and pride headline Sadoleto's exposé of their motives. He accuses Protestants of inventing new institutions and rewards to compensate for their lack of talent. Genevans should bet, instead, on the safe, established option. The Catholic Church, guided by the Spirit, cannot err. But even if it did, God would not fault believers for trusting this church as generations before them had done.[23] At bottom, he charges evangelicals with two crimes: (1) heresy, or "false religion," resulting in "depraved worship" and "the most immediate peril of eternal death," and (2) schism, or endeavoring to "tear the spouse of Christ in pieces."[24] These were serious charges that the church historically leveled against those considered to be outside the Christian faith.

Calvin agreed that such accusations were grave indeed. However, Rome was the guilty party. Taking pains to defend himself and other reformers from Sadoleto's personal attacks, Calvin asserts his calling as pastor and teacher in the true church. Next, Calvin reverses the charges of heresy and schism by challenging Sadoleto's definition of the church:

> When the Genevese, instructed by our preaching, escaped from the gulf of error in which they were immersed, and betook themselves to a purer teaching of the gospel, you call it defection from the truth of God; when

---

21. Olin, *A Reformation Debate*, 41.
22. Olin, *A Reformation Debate*, 42.
23. Olin, *A Reformation Debate*, 45.
24. Olin, *A Reformation Debate*, 39, 46.

they threw off the tyranny of the Roman Pontiff, in order that they might establish among themselves a better form of Church, you call it a desertion from the Church. . . . What comes of the Word of the Lord, that clearest of all marks, and which the Lord himself, in pointing out the Church, so often recommends to us?[25]

Sadoleto had omitted the most important mark of the church. Calvin grants that possession of the Holy Spirit distinguishes the true church, but then he immediately adds that the Spirit works through scripture: "Seeing how dangerous it would be to boast of the Spirit without the Word, [Christ] declared that the Church is indeed governed by the Holy Spirit, but in order that that government might not be vague and unstable, He annexed it to the Word."[26] Christ rules the church by his Spirit through the written Word—a distinctively Protestant conviction that upended claims to church authority apart from scripture. The true church is manifest not in any particular institutional form, but rather in the purity and unity of biblical teaching "spread over the whole world, and existing in all ages, . . . bound together by the one doctrine and one Spirit of Christ."[27] By missing this point, Rome wrongly presumed its standing as the true church, when it had actually departed from scriptural doctrine, polity, and sacraments.

Far from eclipsing biblical teaching, Calvin continues, Protestants in fact recovered the doctrine and practices of Christ and his apostles. This includes justification by faith alone, the pastoral ministry's central teaching function, and the proper understanding and use of sacraments. Rome not only denies these elements of true faith but also persecutes those who resist such corruption. This leaves evangelicals with no choice. Not Geneva but Rome embodies the classical definition of heresy, which delivers "a soul . . . deprived of the Word of God . . . unarmed to the devil for destruction."[28] Moreover, by abandoning biblical teaching and misusing the sacraments, those true marks of the church, Rome is guilty of schism, of rejecting Christ and dividing his body. Leaving the Roman Church is thus a Christian duty because "the light of divine truth had been extinguished, the Word of God buried, the virtue of Christ left in profound oblivion, and the pastoral office subverted."[29] Far from innovating, the reformers restored the faith "back to its fountainhead, . . . its original purity."[30] Truth and history side with Calvin against Sadoleto.

25. Olin, *A Reformation Debate*, 57, 60.
26. Olin, *A Reformation Debate*, 57, 60.
27. Olin, *A Reformation Debate*, 62.
28. Olin, *A Reformation Debate*, 78.
29. Olin, *A Reformation Debate*, 75.
30. Olin, *A Reformation Debate*, 88.

Calvin began writing *Supplex exhortatio ad Caesarem* at Martin Bucer's request while Protestants and Catholics pursued a series of (ultimately unsuccessful) meetings in 1540–41 to explore the possibility of reconciliation. The work covers similar ground as the *Reply to Sadoleto*. Calvin insists that Protestants simply recovered biblical teaching.[31] Once again treating doctrine, church government, and the sacraments, Calvin focuses on two issues: "legitimate worship of God" and "the ground of salvation."[32] One cannot exist without the other; worship requires reconciliation with God. Truth ushers God's children into proper worship, where God dispenses spiritual nourishment: "The uniform characteristics of a well-ordered Church are the preaching of sound doctrine and the pure administration of the Sacraments. . . . We mean a Church which, from incorruptible seed, begets children for immortality, and, when begotten, nourishes them with spiritual food (that seed and food being the Word of God), and which, by its ministry, preserves entire the truth which God deposited in its bosom."[33] With no nourishment to offer in its defective teaching, priesthood, and sacraments, Rome has abdicated its responsibility to gather and nurture God's elect—the function of the true church. Here the theme of nurture in exile frames Calvin's argument for the Reformed church's identity over against Catholicism.

Around this same time, the 1543 edition of the *Institutes* added considerable material contrasting the true church and the false church, reflecting Calvin's response to the failed religious colloquies.[34] Evangelicals could be confident in leaving a body no longer entitled to the name *church*. Although Rome's apostasy does not preclude the possibility of true believers in her midst, the marks of the true church have been so thoroughly "erased" under the papacy that "every one of their congregations and their whole body lack the lawful form of the church."[35]

For Calvin, one must not confuse the Catholic Church for God's true spiritual pilgrims. Calvin's exegesis of the prophetic books drives home this point by tracing a line from God's exilic people in history to the struggles facing Reformed churches. Both experience the same pattern of exile and restoration that marks the true church in every age.[36] Calvin essentially writes Rome out of

---

31. *Tracts*, 1:146.
32. *Tracts*, 1:146.
33. *Tracts*, 1:214.
34. Wilhelm H. Neuser, "The Development of the *Institutes* 1536 to 1539," in *John Calvin's "Institutes," His Opus Magnum: Proceedings of the Second South African Congress for Calvin Research, July 31–August 3, 1984* (Potchefstroom University for Christian Higher Education, 1986), 44–47.
35. *Inst.* IV.2.12 (*OS* 5.41–42).
36. Pitkin, *Calvin, the Bible, and History*, 122–40.

the story as God's elect, rescripting Catholics into the role of God's forsaken. Beginning in 1559, his lectures for expatriate pastors preparing to return to France distinguish two varieties of "church" in the present. This mirrors how the prophets addressed both the faithful remnant and the apostate nation under the name *Israel*.[37] Evangelicals facing persecution and political exile can receive the same consolation that the prophets offered Israel's remnant in exile. Both groups are expressions of the one true church, whose status as God's elect will be vindicated by restoration, homecoming, and rest. For the apostate "church," that other Israel, centuries of prosperity and influence will not alter its final destruction.

Lutherans, Anabaptists, and Libertines: Drawing the Line Between Error and Heresy

Calvin further defined his movement by turning his polemics against fellow Protestants. Lutherans disagreed with Calvin and the Reformed over matters that included worship and sacraments. While Luther, Melanchthon, and their colleagues in Wittenberg focused especially on justification by faith alone, Reformed theology developed differently through the contributions of men such as Zwingli, Bucer, Bullinger, and Calvin. The Reformed highlighted pure worship and resistance to idolatry. Outside the mainstream Lutheran and Reformed camps, proponents of more radical reform viewed tradition with suspicion as human invention. These favored a literal interpretation of the New Testament to govern faith and practice.[38] Among such radicals were Anabaptists, Spiritualist thinkers such as Libertines, and antitrinitarians whose readings of scripture led them to reject traditional doctrines shared by Catholics and mainstream Protestants. Calvin did not want to be confused with any of these others.

In each case, Calvin distinguished adherents of Geneva's brand of Reformed theology from those who differed along a continuum of error. Lutherans were misguided in their sacramental theology but (with increasing caution) should be treated as siblings in Christ despite their errors. The radicals were another story. Calvin placed Spiritualists and antitrinitarians with Rome, outside the true church. It did not help that Catholics and Lutherans associated radical views with Reformed theologians. For his part, Calvin

---

37. Jon Balserak, *Establishing the Remnant Church in France: Calvin's Lectures on the Minor Prophets, 1556–1559* (Brill, 2011), 19–64. See also chap. 4, above.

38. George Huntston Williams, *The Radical Reformation*, 3rd ed. (Sixteenth Century Journal Publishers, 1992), 1255–60.

rejected radical reformers by defending established tradition and authorities in ways reminiscent of how Sadoleto had addressed Calvin himself. It was not merely about winning arguments. Calvin was modeling how to read scripture and tradition in ways that reinforced his theology and its account of God's elect in exile.

Answering Lutheran Critics

Calvin's relationship with Zurich, ground zero of the Swiss Reformation, and with Wittenberg, birthplace of Lutheranism, at turns exhibited affinity, potential, and strain. He sought ecumenical consensus but struggled with theological differences. The Zurichers were important allies, but Calvin had less regard for their forebear, Zwingli. He even revised debts to Zwingli's ideas out of the *Institutes* and stated his preference for Luther's theology.[39] Yet it was with the Zurichers that Geneva succeeded in forging common doctrinal ground. Calvin worked with Zwingli's successors, most notably Bullinger, to find shared language regarding the Lord's Supper. Known much later as the *Consensus Tigurinus* (1549), or Zurich Consensus, this agreement consolidated one side of the Protestant divide over the sacrament. Disputes between Lutherans and the Swiss Reformed dated to the Marburg Colloquy of 1529, where Luther insisted on Christ's physical presence in the Eucharist while Zwingli countered that the Communion elements are merely symbolic.[40] It took some time, but the Swiss found common ground, due in no small part to Calvin's political savvy. To reach consensus they had to overcome lingering suspicion that Calvin was too close to Luther's view. They also had to surmount Calvin's own contempt for Zwingli's position.[41] The Lutherans took longer to reach internal concord, and some (notably Melanchthon) even privately affirmed Calvin's views. Luther despised "Sacramentarians" for denying Christ's bodily presence in the Eucharist and affirming only its sacramental efficacy. Luther saw little difference between this view and those of radical Spiritualists who rejected all external religious rites. He frequently lumped the Reformed with Spiritualists and Anabaptists, deriding them all as "dunces" for insisting that Christ is seated "at the Father's right hand" and thus "cannot be present in the Lord's Supper."[42] Luther's negativity was

---

39. Bruce Gordon, *Calvin* (Yale University Press, 2009), 167.
40. For the complex theological issues involved in disagreements over the Eucharist, see Amy Nelson Burnett, *Debating the Sacraments: Print and Authority in the Early Reformation* (Oxford University Press, 2019).
41. R. Ward Holder, "The Pain of Agreement: Calvin and the Consensus Tigurinus," *Reformation & Renaissance Review* 18 (2016): 85–94.
42. Serm. John 6:41–42 (*LW* 23:80).

unfortunate for Calvin, who respected Luther and viewed his own theology as compatible with the German reformer's. Calvin believed his account of the Lord's Supper satisfied Luther's insistence on receiving Christ's body without making the mistake of ascribing divine attributes to a human body.[43] Some Lutherans, alas, viewed things differently. Others, like Melanchthon, were more sympathetic.

The Zurich Consensus coincided with debates within Lutheranism after Luther's death in 1546. Strict Lutherans, later known as "Gnesio-Lutherans" (i.e., genuine Lutherans), derided "Philippists," followers of Philip Melanchthon, for failing to uphold Luther's distinctive legacy. Gnesio-Lutherans sought to inoculate the Wittenberg reformer's thought against impurities, chief among which was Reformed theology like Calvin's.[44] The Genevan reformer's most vocal Lutheran critic was Joachim Westphal (d. 1574) of Hamburg, who produced several works assailing Calvin in the 1550s. Despite similarities between his own views and Calvin's, Westphal took Calvin's agreement with Zurich as denial of Christ's bodily presence in the sacrament.[45] Calvin disagreed. He shared Luther's belief that one must feed on the whole Christ in Communion. He saw himself differing with Lutherans only concerning the manner by which such eating occurs. For Calvin, God spiritually lifts communicants up to Christ, rather than requiring that Christ in some way descend bodily to them. There is no need to "drag him from heaven," Calvin insists.[46] For his Lutheran critics, such recourse to "spiritual eating" was simply Zwingli's "Sacramentarian" denial of Christ's body repeated in wordier form. The 1557 *Formula of Concord*, which synthesizes different streams of Lutheran theology, has Calvin in view when it describes "the most dangerous kind [of Sacramentarians], who . . . appear to use our language and who pretend that they also believe in a true presence of the . . . body and blood of Christ in the Holy Supper."[47]

Calvin, for his part, could not let this criticism go unanswered. His responses to Westphal also addressed the needs of political exiles. English refugees, who had fled the persecutions of "Bloody" Queen Mary beginning in 1553, were settling into exile communities across the European continent. These refugees found themselves in the crossfire of Lutheran polemic against

43. Thomas J. Davis, *The Clearest Promises of God: The Development of Calvin's Eucharistic Teaching* (AMS, 1995), 168–80.
44. Irene Dingel, "Calvin in the Context of Lutheran Consolidation," *Reformation & Renaissance Review* 12 (2010): 155–87.
45. Wim Janse, "Joachim Westphal's Sacramentology," *Lutheran Quarterly* 22, no. 2 (2008): 142–47; and Davis, *Clearest Promises*, 168–73.
46. *Inst.* IV.17.8, 31 (OS 5:350, 389).
47. Robert Kolb and Timothy J. Wengert, eds., *The Book of Concord* (Fortress, 2000), 504.

the Swiss.[48] Calvin spoke into this situation with several works refuting Westphal's mischaracterizations of his views on the Lord's Supper: *A Defense of the Sound and Orthodox Doctrine of the Sacraments* (1555); *A Second Defense of the Pious and Orthodox Faith Concerning the Sacraments in Answer to the Calumnies of Joachim Westphal* (1556); and *Final Admonition of John Calvin to Joachim Westphal* (1557).[49] The debate between Calvin and Westphal illustrates how both the Reformed and the Lutherans received tradition sympathetically. Both sides claimed Augustine's legacy against the other.[50] In works that spoke to exiles moved by doctrine to put their lives on the line, Calvin portrayed his theology as more faithful to Augustine's and, ultimately, to scripture. Here was, in other words, a pedigree English Protestants could trust.

Both political and spiritual exile appear in Calvin's responses. In his *Second Defense*, Calvin invokes his own foreigner status in Geneva, which Westphal had cited to discredit Calvin as a teacher: "Far am I from being ashamed of voluntary exile."[51] Exile, after all, is the spiritual identity of all believers, as Calvin states in his initial 1555 *Defense* against Westphal:

> Certainly if Paul could say, that so long as we are in the world we are absent as pilgrims from the Lord, we may say, on the same ground that we are separated from him by a certain species of absence, inasmuch as we are now distant from his heavenly dwelling. Christ then is absent from us in respect of his body, but dwelling in us by his Spirit he raises us to heaven to himself, transfusing into us the vivifying vigour of his flesh, just as the rays of the sun invigorate us by his vital warmth. [The Lutherans'] common saying, that he is with us invisible, is equivalent to saying that though his form is treasured up in heaven, the substance of his flesh is on the earth.[52]

Like a bookend, Calvin's final rebuttal of Westphal reiterates this idea. Though Christ's body is absent, spiritual exiles get nothing less than the full benefit of Christ's flesh in the holy sacrament: "We acknowledge in the Supper such a presence as is accordant with faith, and confine the absence to the real human nature. In this way believers recognize, in a manner which surpasses hope, that though they are pilgrims on the earth, they have life in common with their head."[53]

48. Chung-Kim, *Inventing Authority*, 61.
49. CO 9:5–36, 41–120, 137–252.
50. Holder, *Christian Tradition*, 115–19.
51. *Tracts*, 2:326 (CO 9:106–7).
52. *Tracts*, 2:240 (CO 9:33).
53. *Tracts*, 2:450 (CO 9:218).

In the *Institutes*, Calvin insists on the importance of Christ's ascension. Christ's bodily ascent through the sky proves that his humanity is bound to a circumscribed space, like ours. It also sets the parameters of our present existence as exile characterized, in part, by the absence of Christ's body. This makes Communion even more precious, insofar as it enables believers to feed on Christ's body even as it remains apart from them in heaven. Like Westphal, Calvin wants nothing to do with Zwingli's denial that Christ nourishes us with his body. As the *Institutes* puts it,

> "I am," he says, "the bread of life come down from heaven. And the bread which I shall give is my flesh, which I shall give for the life of the world." By these words [Christ] teaches not only that he is life since he is the eternal Word of God, who came down from heaven to us, but also that by coming down he poured that power upon the flesh which he took in order that from it participation in life might flow unto us. From this also these things follow: that his flesh is truly food, and his blood truly drink, and by these foods believers are nourished unto eternal life.[54]

Calvin maintains that Christ offers his flesh and blood as real food and drink to pilgrims but does so in a way that does not artificially resolve their exile. Homecoming awaits reunion with the ascended Christ at the end of this present age. Until then, Christ's body remains in heaven while we wait on earth. Still, believers enjoy the benefits of feeding on the body now, during their earthly pilgrimage:

> But greatly mistaken are those who conceive no presence of flesh in the Supper unless it lies in the bread. For thus they leave nothing to the secret working of the Spirit, which unites Christ himself to us. To them Christ does not seem present unless he comes down to us. As though, if he should lift us to himself, we should not just as much enjoy his presence! The question is therefore only of the manner, for they place Christ in the bread, while we do not think it lawful for us to drag him from heaven. Let our readers decide which one is more correct. Only away with that calumny that Christ is removed from his Supper unless he lies hidden under the covering of bread! For since this mystery is heavenly, there is no need to draw Christ to earth that he may be joined to us.[55]

Even if Westphal found Calvin's position unsatisfying, it is precisely Christ's bodily absence that grounds Calvin's understanding of why the Lord's Supper is comfort for exiles. It is a meal that points forward in hope to a reunion that

---

54. *Inst*. IV.17.8 (*OS* 5:350).
55. *Inst*. IV.17.31 (*OS* 5:389).

awaits, without making hope unnecessary with the Lutheran assertion that Christ's body appears to us now. Such overrealized eschatology detracts from the significance that, for the church, today remains a time of waiting, sojourn, and exile. Only in the wilderness is the manna that God offers through the sacrament so satisfying and astonishing. Today the elect receive as food the very thing they should not have until the eschaton. But they receive this only in a penultimate manner. For now, the Spirit mediates Christ's body; in the day of homecoming, believers will behold him face-to-face.[56] For Calvin, the best is yet to come.

Refuting Anabaptists, Libertines, and Antitrinitarians

Calvin further distinguished his own Reformed faith from Anabaptists and Spiritualist "Libertines," even though Lutherans commonly dismissed them all as "Sacramentarians." In 1544 Calvin published *A Brief Instruction for Arming All the Good Faithful Against the Errors of the Common Sect of the Anabaptists*, following this up with *Against the Fantastic and Furious Sect of the Libertines Who Are Called "Spirituals"* in 1545.[57] As polemical sources, they are more useful for studying how Calvin employs rhetoric against heresy than for reconstructing the beliefs and practices of his enemies.[58] Anabaptism was never a monolithic movement with a single creed or central organization. The term more accurately encompasses diverse communities who rejected infant baptism as a practice they believed to be foreign to scripture. With roots in groups like the Swiss Brethren in Zurich, Anabaptists of various stripes felt that mainstream reformers did not completely curtail nonbiblical teaching and practices.[59] Some embraced violence, like the radicals who seized Münster and established a communal government there in 1534–35. Violence was the exception, but suspicion that Anabaptist views led to social disruption persisted. This was, after all, an era when infant baptism was deeply woven into the social fabric. Baptism was a church rite with civil significance, marking a person's belonging to both church and society. As mainstream reformers, Lutheran and Reformed theologians relied on local and regional government to support church reform. They were, understandably, sensitive to being associated with sedition. It did not help that Lutherans cast Reformed

---

56. See chap. 3, above.
57. English translations of both texts can be found in John Calvin, *Treatises Against the Anabaptists and Against the Libertines*, trans. and ed. Benjamin Wirt Farley (Baker, 1982); COR IV/1:143–71; CO 7:49–142.
58. Mirjam van Veen, "'Supporters of the Devil': Calvin's Image of the Libertines," *Calvin Theological Journal* 40 (2005): 21–32.
59. Williams, *Radical Reformation*, 212–86.

teaching on the Lord's Supper as a dangerous form of Spiritualist theology akin to Anabaptism. In like manner, Calvin uses exaggeration as well as outright mischaracterization to distance himself from the Anabaptists.

Calvin's *Brief Instruction* takes aim at the *Schleitheim Confession of Faith*, which was written mostly by Michael Sattler for Swiss and South German Anabaptists in 1527.[60] Among other teachings, the *Schleitheim Confession* rejects infant baptism and oath taking. It also calls for practicing the ban (shunning), separation from the world, and nonviolence.[61] Calvin's response refutes each of the *Schleitheim Confession*'s seven articles in turn. But he first grants an important point of similarity: Anabaptists "receive the holy Scriptures, as we do."[62] From there, Calvin exposes how Anabaptists merely gesture at the Bible's authority. They instead mislead "the simple" by teaching false doctrine. They align "closely with the papists" on cardinal "points of Christianity," such as "free will, predestination, and the cause of our salvation."[63] Thus, with a few strokes of his pen, Calvin identifies Rome with radical reform: Neither takes the Bible seriously. For his part, Calvin argues at length that infant baptism does not depart from scripture.[64] More sinister than being wrong about baptism, however, is that Anabaptists keep company with historical heretics. After addressing the *Schleitheim Confession*'s seven articles, Calvin broadens his case by alleging that Anabaptists follow the likes of Marcion and the Manichaeans by denying Christ's humanity.[65] Calvin is responding specifically to the claims of Anabaptists, such as Melchior Hoffman (d. ca. 1543) and Menno Simons (d. 1561), that Christ possessed a heavenly body and gained nothing from being born of a woman. Time and again, he accuses Anabaptists of claiming adherence to scripture in order to cloak teaching that leads people away from salvation. Calvin warns the reader that one cannot believe all appeals to scripture. As we saw with his *Reply to Sadoleto*, Calvin's attempts to differentiate his Reformed community from Rome involved reversing the charges of schism and heresy. His handling of alleged radicals reads more like redirecting blame. He asserts his own movement's orthodoxy and loyalty to civil magistrates, pushing other groups to the margins as heretical and seditious: Here, he says, are the real threats to society. Such rhetoric from both Protestant and

60. Williams, *Radical Reformation*, 288–97.
61. See the translation in John C. Wenger, "The Schleitheim Confession of Faith," *Mennonite Quarterly Review* 19, no. 4 (1945): 243–54.
62. Calvin, *Treatises*, 39 (CO 7:53).
63. Calvin, *Treatises*, 43 (CO 7:56).
64. Calvin, *Treatises*, 44–55 (CO 7:56–64).
65. Calvin, *Treatises*, 115 (CO 7:108–9).

Catholic polemicists supported relentless persecution of Anabaptist groups in the sixteenth century.[66]

With Libertines, Calvin saw an even graver concern. He accused the movement of emerging from the devil himself to mislead believers at the precise moment when the reformers were recovering the gospel.[67] These Libertines were not the Perrinist faction that opposed Calvin in Geneva, whom he disparaged with the same name.[68] *Against the Fantastic and Furious Sect of the Libertines Who Are Called "Spirituals"* targets a diverse spiritual movement that included Catholics but is most associated with varieties of Anabaptism and other proponents of radical reform. As Spiritualists, they prioritize the inward work of God's Spirit.[69] External criteria for discerning God's will, including scripture, were less important. Unlike the Anabaptists whom Calvin attacks in his *Brief Instruction*, Libertines did not assert the Bible's sole authority. As Calvin's title suggests, they preferred the name "Spirituals," but Calvin dismissed them as "Libertines."[70]

Calvin had in view men like Claude Perceval, Bertrand des Moulins, Quintin Thieffry, and Antoine Pocquet. Bucer once welcomed them to Strasbourg, and their ideas were now making inroads in the Low Countries and France. Their extreme version of predestination held that God inhabits all things to carry out the divine intentions.[71] In their understanding, the human spirit has been reintegrated with the divine Spirit, which results in strict determinism. Free will is an illusion, an imaginary construct. So is the distinction between good and evil, the perception of spiritual imperfection, and Christ's resurrection. The resurrection simply illustrates the pattern of spiritual reintegration that pertains to all. Humanity is already one with God and thus cannot wander from God's will. Ethics are illusory; sin is a fiction.

Unsurprisingly, Calvin and his colleagues decried such beliefs as "libertine" and took measures to distance themselves from these claims. Calvin characterizes Libertines as arrogant, dishonest, and no better than animals—the same stock insults Westphal would use later against Calvin and the Swiss

---

66. Brad S. Gregory, *Salvation at Stake: Christian Martyrdom in Early Modern Europe* (Harvard University Press, 1999), 197–249.

67. Van Veen, "'Supporters of the Devil,'" 25.

68. See chap. 1, above; and also Gary W. Jenkins, *Calvin's Tormentors: Understanding the Conflicts That Shaped the Reformer* (Baker Academic, 2018), 77–92.

69. Allen Verhey and Robert G. Wilkie, "Calvin's Treatise 'Against the Libertines,'" *Calvin Theological Journal* 15 (1980): 190–219.

70. See Kenneth J. Woo, "Nicodemism and Libertinism," in *John Calvin in Context*, ed. R. Ward Holder (Cambridge University Press, 2020), 291–94.

71. Calvin, *Treatises*, 196–99 (CO 7:158–59).

Reformed.[72] Unfortunately, we know the views of Spiritualists like Thieffry and Pocquet only through the works of their critics, which are rife with stereotypes and therefore short on accuracy.

What Calvin's treatise lacks as a reliable source for understanding radical spiritualism it makes up for as an example of Reformed identity construction. Calvin's theology, of course, was also rooted in providence, predestination, and a spiritual account of the sacrament as elements of God's care for the church. Westphal thus tried to paint Calvin and the Libertines with the same brush. Calvin's main concern was not outward facing, however. He wrote not to convince Wesphal or Libertines. He wanted Reformed believers to see the difference between their beliefs and the "raving and fantastical" claims of other Protestants about the same doctrinal themes. For a time, Thieffry and Pocquet were ministers in the court of Marguerite de Navarre, a notable ally to French evangelicals.[73] Calvin wanted to defend Reformed francophone believers against the pernicious influence of such false teachers. His point was that not all those who suffered exile for their faith could be accounted members of the true church.

Closer to home, disputes about the Trinity continued in Geneva, where Servetus was put to death in 1553.[74] The city's Italian refugee community became a seedbed for similar antitrinitarian teaching. The Consistory labored to address the confusion caused by men such as Matteo Gribaldi (d. 1564), Giorgio Blandrata (d. 1588), and Valentino Gentilis (d. 1566). Calvin joined the fray with his *Response to the Questions of Giorgio Blandrata* (1558).

In some ways, Calvin's defense of the orthodox doctrine of the Trinity against the likes of Servetus and the Italians was a fitting coda to a career that began with Calvin himself denying charges of heresy. Pierre Caroli, onetime professor of theology at the University of Paris, criticized the absence of the word *Trinity* in Calvin's 1536 *Institutes*.[75] For decades reformers struggled to square aspects of traditional theology they took as indispensable, like God's triune nature, with their claim to ground all theology in scripture. Initially this meant avoiding words like "Trinity" that do not appear in the Bible.[76] However, this quickly put mainstream reformers in bad company

---

72. Van Veen, "'Supporters of the Devil,'" 27–29.

73. Wulfert de Greef, *The Writings of John Calvin: An Introductory Guide* (Westminster John Knox, 2008), 156–57.

74. Roland H. Bainton, *Hunted Heretic: The Life and Death of Michael Servetus, 1511–1553* (Beacon, 1960).

75. Jenkins, *Calvin's Tormentors*, 21–22. See also John L. Thompson, "Confessions, Conscience, and Coercion in the Early Calvin," in *Calvin and The Early Reformation*, ed. Brian C. Brewer and David M. Whitford (Brill, 2020), 155–79.

76. Kenneth J. Woo, "Trinity (Heb. 1:3/John 1)," in *The Oxford Handbook of the Bible and the Reformation*, ed. Jennifer Powell McNutt and Herman Selderhuis (Oxford University

with radicals who discarded the doctrine altogether. Changing tack by the 1540s, magisterial reformers such as Luther, Melanchthon, and Bullinger reversed their earlier reluctance to use classical creedal terms and began to assert that such language is defensible through biblical exegesis.[77] Calvin's exegesis of Hebrews and John, for example, argues that nonbiblical terms for describing the Trinity are useful when they merely clarify, rather than add to, the Bible's teaching.[78] This, too, was important for defining Calvin's Reformed community. On the one hand, they were trinitarians, claiming as their own the theology worked out in the fourth- and fifth-century ecumenical councils, such as Nicaea (325) and Chalcedon (451), because they believed these doctrines to be biblical.[79] This set them apart from antitrinitarians, but also from Jews and Muslims, who similarly rejected the Trinity and Christ's divine nature.[80]

But the Reformed were also distinctive among fellow trinitarians. Bucer derides Lutherans' inconsistent Christology in their application of divine attributes to Christ's body (which they claimed to be present wherever the Eucharist is celebrated) as "insanities posing as doctrine."[81] Calvin takes aim at Rome for being inconsistently trinitarian, undermining orthodox doctrine with nonbiblical teaching. "The papists," Calvin complains in his commentary on Hebrews, embrace Christ's divinity in words only to "rob Him of one-half His power" by denying how Christ's intercession renders lesser priests unnecessary.[82] Catholics might affirm the right things about Christ's nature, but their faulty grasp of Christ's priesthood "destroys the church of God rather than builds it."[83] Calvin's community must know that it is not enough to share similar doctrines or even the same Protestant commitment to the Bible's authority. Not all readings of scripture are equally valid. Reformed believers should check their sources, which is to say that the church in exile must be vigilant.

Press, 2024), 721–32.

77. Richard A. Muller, *Post-Reformation Reformed Dogmatics: The Rise and Development of Reformed Orthodoxy, ca. 1520 to ca. 1725*, 2nd rev. ed., 4 vols. (Baker Academic, 2003), 4:60.

78. Comm. Heb. 1:3 (*CNTC* 12:8–9; *CO* 55:12); Comm. John 1:1 (*CNTC* 4:7–10; *CO* 47:1–3); and Woo, "Trinity," 726–27.

79. On the fourth- and fifth-century debates about the Trinity and Christology, see Frances M. Young, *From Nicaea to Chalcedon: A Guide to the Literature and Its Background*, 2nd ed. (Baker Academic, 2010).

80. Comm. Heb. 1:3 (*CNTC* 12:8–9; *CO* 55:12); and Comm. John 1:1 (*CNTC* 4:7–10; *CO* 47:1–3).

81. Woo, "Trinity," 728–30.

82. "The Theme," Comm. Heb. (*CNTC* 12:2; *CO* 55:6).

83. Comm. Heb. 1:3 (*CNTC* 12:9–10; *CO* 55:13); and Comm. Heb. 3:6 (*CNTC* 12:37; *CO* 55:38).

Conclusion

Calvin's disputes with theological opponents on all sides set his views against a diverse backdrop of competing alternatives. Though he dismissed these alternatives as inferior, for Calvin it was never simply about winning arguments. He wanted to ensure that the community God promised to comfort and lead through exile knew exactly who they were. Not all forms of exile were equal. Catholics and Anabaptists could flee persecution, just as Italian antitrinitarians found refuge in Geneva. Yet none of these could count on God's favor. Calvin's harsh language toward outsiders as false, apostate, reprobate, and heretical contributed to a heated rhetorical climate that encouraged actual acts of violence. But it also served to unite and herd God's flock away from danger and toward nourishing pastures. Refuting error bolstered confidence in biblical doctrine and pure worship as refuges for God's elect. For those in Calvin's Reformed movement, this meant being sure that they were standing in just the right place, with the right people, amid the vicissitudes of religious disputes, violence, and migration.

For Further Reading

In Calvin's Words

1539 *Reply to Sadoleto*. In *A Reformation Debate: Sadoleto's Letter to the Genevans and Calvin's Reply*, edited by John C. Olin, 49–94. Harper & Row, 1966.

1543 *Supplex exhortatio ad Caesarem* (*Sincere Exhortation to the Emperor*), which appears as "The Necessity of Reforming the Church" in *Tracts*, 1:123–234.

1544 *A Brief Instruction for Arming All the Good Faithful Against the Errors of the Common Sect of the Anabaptists*. In *Treatises Against the Anabaptists and Against the Libertines*, translated and edited by Benjamin Wirt Farley, 36–158. Baker, 1982.

1545 *Against the Fantastic and Furious Sect of the Libertines Who Are Called "Spirituals."* In *Treatises Against the Anabaptists and Against the Libertines*, translated and edited by Benjamin Wirt Farley, 187–326. Baker, 1982.

1555 *A Defense of the Sound and Orthodox Doctrine of the Sacraments*, which appears as "Exposition of the Heads of Agreement" in *Tracts*, 2:221–44.

1556 *Second Defence of the Faith Concerning the Sacraments in Answer to Joachim Westphal*. In *Tracts*, 2:244–345.

For Digging Deeper

Chung-Kim, Esther. *Inventing Authority: The Use of the Church Fathers in Reformation Debates over the Eucharist*. Baylor University Press, 2011.

Holder, R. Ward. *Calvin and the Christian Tradition: Scripture, Memory, and the Western Mind*. Cambridge University Press, 2022.

Williams, George Hunston. *The Radical Reformation*. 3rd ed. Truman State University Press, 1992.

Zachman, Randall C., ed. *John Calvin and Roman Catholicism: Critique and Engagement, Then and Now*. Baker Academic, 2008.

EIGHT

Conformity and Commitment

Calvin's Anti-Nicodemite Writings

They gladly keep the heart for God (at least as they say so), but they have no trouble abandoning their bodies to profane and harmful things. . . . Can God be pleased with such a mixture? Can the one who said that every knee shall bow before him and every tongue confess his name suffer anyone to kneel before idols? . . . My teaching is not hard, but it is the hardness of their heart that leads them to find it so.

—Calvin, *Answer to the Nicodemites* (1544)[1]

Abram, the father of the faithful, showed us another path, and this is offered to us as a rule. . . . He was not exempt from persecution, conflict, or affliction when he erected his altar to God. But he overcame all these things that could hinder him, even those that could entirely corrupt him.

—Calvin, Sermon on Genesis 12:5–9 (1560)[2]

Crypto-Religion and the Question of Commitment

Another significant polemical campaign that Calvin took up energetically was his unrelenting attack on Nicodemism, or crypto-religion—keeping one's true beliefs a secret and going along with local religious rites and practices to avoid

1. CO 6:594, 610.
2. Serm. Gen. 12:5–9, February 6, 1560 (SC XI/2:612–13).

persecution. Such crypto-religion, which Calvin frames as compromise with idolatry, appears not only in a series of dedicated publications dissecting the issue between 1537 and 1564, essentially Calvin's entire career, but also less intuitively in sermons directed at Genevans and in his treatment of exile in his commentaries.[3] Just as it could show up in unexpected places, Nicodemism functioned for Calvin in surprisingly flexible ways. In fact, his approach to the subject displays how seamlessly a theology of God's provision for spiritual exiles could turn into a means of control. Calvin's ostensible concern was to challenge undecided or lukewarm French evangelicals who were content to compromise with idolatry to avoid suffering.[4] The subject concretized Calvin's theology into the practical realm of behavior: How and where one worships matters. Some historians have even posited that Calvin's loathing for Nicodemism stemmed from his own need to pretend and hide as he fled from France as a young refugee.[5] Beyond personal relevance, however, the problem of Nicodemism unveils important dimensions of Calvin's ministry to others.

It is easy to take Calvin's argument against Nicodemism at face value. He remained relentlessly on message, declaring that merely being present for idolatrous worship makes one complicit in it. Only two options exist for evangelicals facing compulsory Catholic worship: Flee, as he did, or resist at all costs.[6] But such rigid clarity obscures Calvin's more nuanced approach in practice, especially when this involved the Reformed churches in France. When strategy required it, he was quite willing for ministers and congregations to carry on in misleading ways to evade detection by French authorities.[7] In fact, Calvin's vociferous rejection of Nicodemism was well-suited to covering clandestine practices by repeatedly insisting on the opposite.[8] Does that mean that Calvin did not believe the arguments he presented against idolatry? Was

---

3. The recommended further reading at the end of this chapter includes English translations of Calvin's major anti-Nicodemite works.

4. Perez Zagorin, *Ways of Lying: Dissimulation, Persecution, and Conformity in Early Modern Europe* (Harvard University Press, 1990), 63–82; David F. Wright, "Why Was Calvin So Severe a Critic of Nicodemism?," in *Calvinus Evangelii Propugnator: Calvin, Champion of the Gospel: Papers Presented at the International Congress on Calvin Research, Seoul, 1998*, ed. David F. Wright, Anthony N. S. Lane, and Jon Balserak (Calvin Studies Society, 2006), 66–90; and Carlos Eire, *War Against the Idols: The Reformation of Worship from Erasmus to Calvin* (Cambridge University Press, 1986), 234–75.

5. Eire, *War Against the Idols*, 87–89; and Gary W. Jenkins, *Calvin's Tormentors: Understanding the Conflicts That Shaped the Reformer* (Baker Academic, 2018), 1–15.

6. Kenneth J. Woo, "Nicodemism and Libertinism," in *John Calvin in Context*, ed. R. Ward Holder (Cambridge University Press, 2020), 287–91.

7. Jon Balserak, *Geneva's Use of Lies, Deceit, and Subterfuge, 1536–1563* (Oxford University Press, 2024), 11–12, 122–65.

8. Balserak, *Subterfuge*, 11–12, 122–65.

his insistence that Nicodemites deprived themselves of the spiritual nourishment David longed for no more than an attempt to distract authorities? This is unlikely, not least because Calvin's concern for spiritual nurture through pure worship is a constant theme in his writings, appearing across all genres over his entire career. But the same argument could work in different ways.

Along with violence, martyrdom, and exile, Nicodemism defined Calvin's context as a refugee reformer. He constantly addressed it as a threat to the purity and health of his community. But was there more to Nicodemism than meets the eye? This chapter introduces Calvin's anti-Nicodemite writings, which formally address an issue that comes up repeatedly in other places, such as in his sermons or in a letter to Martin Luther. The question of religious dissimulation, hiding one's faith by pretending to be something else, arises often when Calvin presents his theology of comfort in exile. One reason for this is that Nicodemites deprive themselves of spiritual nurture. Another reason was Calvin's desire for conformity among his followers. To achieve this goal, his anti-Nicodemite argument put the same case for nurture in exile to use in multiple ways. Nicodemism threatened to dissolve Calvin's movement into a wider sea of religious options. He responded by making pure and open confession of one's faith an ongoing demand regardless of one's political situation. This argument challenged French evangelicals to forsake Roman idolatry while simultaneously rebuking tepid commitment and ingratitude in Geneva and other already-Reformed contexts.[9] Increasing dissent within francophone evangelicalism left Calvin uncertain about his theological leadership and whether his vision for the church had buy-in. His anti-Nicodemite writings effectively called for a head count. Believers had to choose sides. Calvin's vision for the church in exile could not exist simply as an idea or matter of nominal commitment. He wanted others to embody it with the fervor of Abraham and David in exile.[10]

Nicodemism was possible, perhaps even likely, anywhere during the Reformation.[11] This provoked a variety of responses. Reformed and Lutheran leaders—including Calvin, Heinrich Bullinger, Pierre Viret, Wolfgang Musculus, Peter Martyr Vermigli, and John Wigand (d. 1587)—called Protestants to choose between service to God and fear of human power.[12] These men assailed "temporizing," or shifting one's convictions to suit the demands of changing

---

9. Kenneth J. Woo, *Nicodemism and the English Calvin, 1544–1584* (Brill, 2019), 26–65; and Kenneth J. Woo, "Abraham, David, and the Problem of Exile in Calvin's Theology," *Harvard Theological Review* 118 (2025): 314–36.

10. See chap. 6, above.

11. Miriam Eliav-Feldon and Tamar Herzig, eds., *Dissimulation and Deceit in Early Modern Europe* (Palgrave-MacMillan, 2015); and Zagorin, *Ways of Lying*.

12. Woo, *Nicodemism*, 77, 104.

times.[13] Others took a more moderate stance. Luther's call for patience with reforming liturgical practices was influential among Lutherans, though Philip Melanchthon added his endorsement to a reprint of Calvin's anti-Nicodemite works.[14] Among the Reformed, Martin Bucer and Wolfgang Capito similarly urged a more gradual approach to change.[15] Several thinkers even defended dissembling. For Spiritualists like Dirck Coornhert (d. 1590), David Joris (d. 1556), and Hendrik Niclaes (d. 1570), religion was not worth dying over.[16] In Protestant England, leaders of the Catholic minority dealt with a form of Nicodemism in their ranks by railing against "church papists" accused of hiding their Catholic faith.[17] Crypto-religion did not begin with the Reformation. It was already a survival tactic for countless Jews and Muslims faced with forced conversion and expulsion from Portugal and Spain.[18] Ethnic and cultural differences meant that Muslims and Jews who wished to hide could never attain the invisibility of Christian Nicodemites, who remained indistinguishable from their neighbors.[19] It is not a stretch to call early modern Europe an "Age of Dissimulation."[20]

Calvin is perhaps the best-known adversary of Nicodemites among the reformers, credited for coining the term, which he attributes to how dissemblers described themselves. They allegedly followed Nicodemus, who waited till after dark to meet Jesus (John 3).[21] Not counting reprints of earlier material, Calvin

13. Wolfgang Musculus, *Proscaerus. Liceát ne homini Christiano, evangelicae doctrinae gnaro, papisticis superstitionibus ac falsis cultibus externa societate communicare, dialogi quatuor* (Basel, 1549).

14. Martin Luther, "Eight Sermons at Wittenberg, 1522" (*LW* 51:69–100).

15. Peter Matheson, "Martyrdom or Mission? A Protestant Debate," *Archiv für Reformationsgeschichte* 80 (1989): 154–72; Timothy R. Scheuers, *Consciences and the Reformation: Scruples over Oaths and Confessions in the Era of Calvin and His Contemporaries* (Oxford University Press, 2024), 90–101.

16. Mirjam van Veen, *"Verschooninghe van de roomsche afgoderye": De polemiek van Calvijn met nicodemieten, in het bijzonder met Coornhert* (Hes & De Graaf, 2001); and Christopher Carter, "The Family of Love and Its Enemies," *Sixteenth Century Journal* 37 (2006): 651–72.

17. Alexandra Walsham, *Church Papists: Catholicism, Conformity and Confessional Polemic in Early Modern England* (Boydell, 1999).

18. Nicholas Terpstra, *Religious Refugees in the Early Modern World: An Alternative History of the Reformation* (Cambridge University Press, 2015), 105–11.

19. John Jeffries Martin, "Marranos and Nicodemites in Sixteenth-Century Venice," *Journal of Medieval and Early Modern Studies* 41 (2011): 577–99.

20. Zagorin, *Ways of Lying*, 330.

21. *Answer to the Nicodemites* (CO 6:608); Comm. John 19:38 (*CNTC* 5:187–89; CO 47:423–24). For the broader use of Nicodemus in early modern Europe, see Federico Zuliani, "The Other Nicodemus: Nicodemus in Italian Religious Writings Previous and Contemporary to Calvin's *Excuse à Messieurs les Nicodemites* (1544)," in *Discovering the Riches of the Word: Religious Reading in Late Medieval and Early Modern Europe*, ed. Sabrina Corbellini et al. (Brill, 2015), 311–33.

published five original full-length works against religious dissimulation.[22] Intrinsically invisible, Nicodemism was never a coordinated movement. Actual practitioners were (and remain) impossible to identify accurately.[23] As a natural response to danger, crypto-religion was not only widespread but also certainly had many faces. Calvin classifies several types of Nicodemites hiding in French society, from complacent clergy and intellectuals to merchants who feared financial loss.[24] These were evangelicals who wanted to avoid hardship even though they knew that this displeased God. Thus Calvin insists that they violate their consciences while defiling pure worship.[25] When 20 percent of the Parlement of Paris dodged a compulsory reaffirmation of Catholic faith in 1562, who could blame onlookers for suspecting Nicodemism?[26] In the end, we will never know. Despite the confident claims of their enemies, successful Nicodemites left no trace.

Calvin's initial foray into the controversy, *Two Letters* (1537), accuses former friends, Nicolas Duchemin and Gérard Roussel, of selling out for prestige and power.[27] Here Calvin insists for the first time that "true devotion leads to true confession," a charge he would repeat over the next three decades.[28] Even though Calvin's strategy with French Reformed churches suggests that he accepted some forms of deception as a reasonable survival tactic, Calvin's public teaching persistently portrays Nicodemism as a lack of conviction and act of idolatry.[29] God-honoring worship is costly in the face of greed, fear, and convenience. Nicodemites simply refuse to pay.

Not everyone in Calvin's orbit agreed with this characterization. As noted earlier, Antoine Fumée, Calvin's friend in Paris, accused him of being too harsh in condemning Nicodemites from the safety of Geneva.[30] The reformist French intellectuals who once counted Calvin and Farel as allies had no

22. *Epistolae duae de rebus hoc saeculo cognitu apprime necessariis* (Basel, 1537); *Petit traicté, monstrant que c'est que doit faire un homme fidèle congnoissant la vérité de l'évangile quand il est entre les papistes: Avec une épistre du mesme argument* (Geneva, 1543); *Excuse de Iehan Calvin, à Messieurs les Nicodémites, sur la complaincte qu'ilz font de sa trop grand' rigeur* (Geneva, 1544); *Quatre sermons de M. Iehan Calvin traictans des matières fort utiles pour nostre temps, avec briefve exposition du Pseaume lxxxvii* (Geneva, 1552); and *Response à un certain Holandois, lequel sous ombre de faire les chrestiens tout spirituels, leur permet de polluer leurs corps en toutes idolatries* (Geneva, 1562).

23. There are some exceptions, such as the communities and figures examined in M. Anne Overell, *Nicodemites: Faith and Concealment between Italy and Tudor England* (Brill, 2018).

24. *Answer to the Nicodemites* (CO 6:597–602).

25. Scheuers, *Consciences*, 73–135.

26. Holt, *French Wars*, 41.

27. *Two Letters* (COR IV/4:13–15).

28. *Two Letters* (COR IV/4:10).

29. Balserak, *Subterfuge*, 10–12.

30. CO 11:646; see chap. 4, above.

problem with holding evangelical ideas alongside Catholic practice.[31] There is no evidence that they hid deeper convictions out of fear. Calvin's depiction of the Nicodemite's seared conscience does not make allowance for such examples of principled conformity to French Catholicism. Calvin's former friends Louis du Tillet and François Baudouin (d. 1573) broke with him over these very matters. They attacked Calvin's doctrinaire attitude as hypocritical. Calvin's inflexibility, not the moderation of those he criticized, constituted the real idolatry and was (in their view) the cause of schism.[32]

In the end, Calvin ceded nothing in his one-sided portrayal of Nicodemism as a lack of zeal and a knowing betrayal of God. Pure doctrine and worship were essential to defining the true church that God accompanies through spiritual exile. He could not be accused of changing his mind. Moreover, if it was meant as a cover to distract from Geneva's secret activity in France, there was no hole in this rhetorical cloth. Yet Calvin's approach to Nicodemism also carried two additional advantages. First, as an argument centered on visible conformity to God's standards in the church, it allowed Calvin to promote the characteristics of his Genevan ministry in ways that simultaneously addressed realities in France and problems concerning religious refugees in Geneva. Second, it targeted inward zeal, something notoriously difficult to measure. Beyond calling out evangelicals in Catholic worship, this could be deployed to address commitment in a church already reformed.

French Nicodemism and Calvin's Standing in Geneva

Calvin's anti-Nicodemite polemic was so consistently on message in rejecting idolatry within French Catholic contexts that its ability to address other situations is easy to miss, even for historians. It was, after all, a natural extension of his broader polemic against Rome. Moreover, all but one of his publications targeting Nicodemism appeared initially in French, signaling a more narrow audience in France. Calvin submits Rome's idolatrous Eucharist, erasure of biblical truth, and inversion of the clergy's role as teachers as evidence for his refusal to brook any middle ground with a false church and its counterfeit worship.[33] Just to be present in Roman worship is to affirm

---

31. See chap. 1, above; also Frans Pieter van Stam, "The Group of Meaux as First Target of Farel and Calvin's Anti-Nicodemism," *Bibliotheque d'humanisme et renaissance: Travaux et documents* 68, no. 2 (2006): 253–76; and Jonathan A. Reid, *King's Sister—Queen of Dissent*, 2 vols. (Brill, 2009), 553–60.

32. Jenkins, *Calvin's Tormenters*, 1–15, 93–107.

33. See chap. 7, above.

idolatry and lead others astray.³⁴ In the *Institutes*, Calvin writes that human nature is a "perpetual factory of idols."³⁵ Thus it is no wonder that a person cannot possibly remain pure inwardly. What's more, genuine faith does not disconnect inner piety from its outward expression: "True devotion leads to true confession."³⁶ Acting out in worship what one does not believe is possible only for those who turn against God and care little for others, whom they lead into sin.³⁷ Dissimulation, which abets idolatry, is strictly forbidden. Only resistance or flight remain. Calvin's ironclad insistence on this point nurtured a culture valorizing martyrdom within French Protestantism.³⁸ It was a spiritual argument with political significance. Noncommittal evangelicals threatened Calvin's hope to replace France's Catholic monarchy with a Reformed ruler.³⁹

This hope required first securing his standing in Geneva. Nicodemism was not an obvious problem in a city that had succeeded in dispelling the darkness of Roman idolatry, a sentiment minted on its coins: *post tenebras lux* (After darkness, light). Even in Calvin's own day, however, some wondered whether his strident rhetoric against Nicodemism was designed all along to influence Geneva's politics with waves of sympathetic French refugees.⁴⁰ Calvin denied the charge. Yet this very thing happened by the thousands and propelled Calvin to victory over his political opponents.⁴¹ Intended or not, his message was effective. People listened to him.

Were there other ways Calvin may have relied on Nicodemism to bring about change in Geneva? One example stands out that integrates Nicodemism, Calvin's theology of comfort in spiritual exile, and his concern to police behavior within the Genevan church. Unsurprisingly, it centers on King David's experiences in exile. But the form and timing of this message are peculiar. Calvin's book *Four Sermons* is the fourth of his five full-length works on Nicodemism, coming almost a decade after *Answer to the*

---

34. Matheson, "Martyrdom or Mission?"
35. *Inst*. I.11.8 (OS 3:96).
36. *Two Letters* (COR IV/4:10); Comm. Gen. 12:7 (CTS 1:353–56; CO 23:181).
37. Scheuers, *Consciences*, 73–103.
38. Nikki Shepardson, *Burning Zeal: The Rhetoric of Martyrdom and the Protestant Community in Reformation France, 1520–1570* (Lehigh University Press, 2007), 112–32.
39. Jon Balserak, "Revisiting John Calvin's Hostility towards French Nicodemism," in *Learning from the Past: Essays on Reception, Catholicity, and Dialogue in Honour of Anthony N. S. Lane*, ed. Jon Balserak and Richard Snoddy (Bloomsbury T&T Clark, 2015), 57–76.
40. *Four Sermons* (CO 8:419–24); Calvin to the Church of Poitiers, February 20, 1555 (Bonnet, 3:147; CO 15:443); Eugénie Droz, "Calvin et les Nicodemites," in *Chemins de l'hérésie: Textes et documents*, 4 vols. (Slatkine, 1970–76), 1:155–57.
41. William G. Naphy, *Calvin and the Consolidation of the Genevan Reformation* (Manchester University Press, 1994), 167–99.

Nicodemites (1544).⁴² His one anti-Nicodemite publication in the form of sermons, this was also the only time Calvin personally revised his preaching and saw this through to publication.⁴³ It appeared in 1552, when Calvin had local public-relations problems on his hands. Many people were still unhappy about the arrest and controversial banishment of Jerome Bolsec in the closing months of 1551 for criticizing Calvin's teaching.⁴⁴ Resentment also continued over the unpopular practice of ministers in choosing baptismal names. While there was no "radical increase in factionalism," people harbored "increasing annoyance with the ministers coupled with a distrust of their refugee compatriots."⁴⁵ Amid these local challenges, *Four Sermons* appeared, in French. Why would Calvin bother to take time, even deviating from his normal practice, to revise and publish sermons dealing with a foreign problem? Because Genevans also read French.

On the surface, the sermon collection is exactly what Calvin's preface describes: a recapitulation of his (by now) standard case against Nicodemism, for those who were slow to learn.⁴⁶ Those tempted to hide their faith must choose instead to resist or flee. However, what unfolds over four sermons is a sophisticated case for Calvin's pastoral authority in Geneva. The sequence of teaching—from Psalm 16:4; Hebrews 13:13; Psalm 27:4; and Psalm 27:8—begins with the deplorable idolatry of Nicodemism and argues that martyrdom is not too high a price to pay for resisting false religion. But the accent falls on the final two sermons and their two-part case for political exile to obtain spiritual nurture through preaching and sacraments. Believers must cherish "liberty . . . to be in a well-ordered and governed church, where the Word of God is preached and the sacraments administered as he has appointed," a "privilege" that is worth "all the trials . . . Satan might bring."⁴⁷ These final sermons contain an emotionally charged depiction of David's spiritual hunger in exile, which supplies urgency to the strongest appeal for political exile one finds in Calvin's published works.⁴⁸ Nothing should hold believers back in their pursuit of these precious gifts from their heavenly Father.

If this sounds like a message for French Nicodemites, Calvin would have been pleased. That is his declared intent. But the opening lines of the first sermon tell us that it is a warning to Genevans as well. The preacher cautions

---

42. Woo, *Nicodemism*, 26–68.
43. For the dating of the sermons to 1549, see T. H. L. Parker, *Calvin's Preaching* (T&T Clark, 1992), 60–61.
44. Naphy, *Consolidation*, 171–72.
45. Naphy, *Consolidation*, 172; see chap. 2, above.
46. *Four Sermons* (CO 8:373–74).
47. *Four Sermons* (CO 8:373–76).
48. See chap. 6, above; and also Woo, *Nicodemism*, 26–68.

the congregation not to take their "time of quiet" for granted "as something that will last forever."[49] They may yet find themselves facing the same pressures to dissimulate that afflict those in France and other locations. But there is even more to Calvin's argument here than a preemptive attempt to future-proof his church in Geneva. Everything he says about David's pining, from exile, for Jerusalem and tabernacle worship applies equally to Nicodemites in France *and* believers in Geneva. All God's people experience such hunger in the present life as wayfarers on a journey toward "God's heavenly kingdom."[50] Along the way, God accompanies pilgrims in the wilderness with special provision: "named by David as the order and polity that God has established in his church."[51] Calvin closes the third sermon with these words, then goes on to drive home the same point in the fourth, which urges believers to stop at nothing to gain this nurture.

It is not only the lukewarm evangelical in France who needs to hear this. The ungrateful Genevan also must learn from David's spiritual hunger and high regard for the ministry. Calvin's congregation comprised both those who had chosen exile to reach Geneva and those who received these refugees, with varying degrees of openness and hospitality. Calvin's preface briefly names those who "complain and murmur" about their circumstances, behaving badly after having chosen flight from idolatry.[52] The third sermon takes up this problem again: "What is the reason that we take so little fruit from sermons and the sacraments, if not that we hardly apply our attention to what is said and done there?"[53] Calvin then divides those before him into two groups. Native Genevans remain ungrateful for how God has established his church among them. Exiles among them act entitled, as if God owed them something for coming at all. The preacher says he regrets that such whiners ever set foot in the city.[54]

That unity in Geneva, rather than just honesty in France, was equally (if not more) important to Calvin when he published *Four Sermons* is obvious in other ways. A short exposition of Psalm 87 concludes the book. It reads like his biblical commentaries and repeats the lesson that the church's appearance, often weak and disappointing, does not diminish God's promises.[55] In quite literally the last words of *Four Sermons*, the appendix again invokes believers'

---

49. *Four Sermons* (CO 8:378).
50. *Four Sermons* (CO 8:409–10).
51. *Four Sermons* (CO 8:409–10).
52. *Four Sermons* (CO 8:375–76).
53. *Four Sermons* (CO 8:421).
54. *Four Sermons* (CO 8:422).
55. *Four Sermons* (CO 8:441–52).

shared identity as spiritual exiles, regardless of migration, to urge patience while an imperfect church awaits the conclusion of its sojourn.

At a moment when distrust of Calvin and his authority was a real concern, the book allowed Calvin to address criticism of his ministry indirectly, by taking up a topic of foreign concern that had immediate implications for his local ministry. Its genre, while a departure from Calvin's norm, is ideal for this purpose. As sermons reprinted to address believers in France, Calvin's rebuke of lukewarm zeal becomes multidirectional. The French Nicodemite overhears Calvin addressing native Genevans and exiles. Similarly, the Genevan reader takes Calvin's preface at face value and understands the work as one meant for a foreign controversy. Yet neither audience can be certain that Calvin is not also speaking to them. The message is clear enough: Preaching and sacraments in the true church are God's appointed means to bless God's people. Everything Calvin says about the church's ministry applies also to his own efforts as a pastor. Not insignificantly, the book presents him as preacher in Geneva, caught in the act of supplying spiritual nurture to God's elect in exile. These labors, as David recognized, should be received as nothing less than God's blessings. Calvin had reasons to make this case in 1552, and to make it as artfully as he does in *Four Sermons*. City elections the following year would result in the reorganization of the Consistory to limit the influence of the clergy, igniting new factionalism in Geneva. By contrast, 1552 was a season of mounting, if subterranean, tension. Calvin faced robust challenges to his views on predestination. Simultaneously, allies in Bern and Zurich expressed doubts about Calvin's handling of Bolsec and others charged with blasphemy.[56] In a moment of suspicion toward his teaching and motives, it behooved Calvin to take a more subtle approach to self-defense and public relations. A work ostensibly targeting hidden evangelicals in France, *Four Sermons* carried a reminder for readers in Calvin's adopted hometown—cloaked, as it were, in its attack on Nicodemism's concealed faith: The Reformed church in Geneva, along with its chief architect, is God's gift to the city.

Turning Inward: The Internal Critique of Calvin's Anti-Nicodemism

Four Sermons illustrates how Calvin's polemic against French Nicodemism could be redeployed seamlessly to argue for unity and conformity around the institutions and practices of Geneva's reform because the ingredients for this were already present. Nicodemism was both idolatry and spiritual deprivation. The answer to either problem existed in the external form of the church under

---

56. Woo, *Nicodemism*, 58–63.

Calvin's leadership. God's spiritual provision in exile, depicted in David's spiritual hunger, promised to comfort French Nicodemites and Genevans alike. In that same vein, both groups could also reject it. Access to a true ministry alone did not resolve issues like complacency, ingratitude, or conflict with Calvin and the ministers. For those without biblical preaching and sacraments, choosing to resist or flee was a move in the right direction. But the defect Calvin locates at the heart of religious dissimulation—lack of commitment and zeal for God and pure worship—can persist even among *former* Nicodemites. Thus it is unsurprising that Calvin turned his polemic inward to interrogate and prod members of his own church toward conformity with his theology. The ideal of faithfulness that his anti-Nicodemite writings set forth applies to all believers as spiritual exiles. As we have already discussed, Calvin's exegesis of both Abraham and David prominently invokes Nicodemism to hold forth aspects of their behavior as universal examples for the faithful.[57] Conspicuous zeal after Abram's altars in Canaan and spiritual longing in David's footsteps are both a summons away from idolatry and a call to daily faithfulness. It is no coincidence that Abraham and David, styled as the quintessential anti-Nicodemites, appear in these terms in Calvin's letter to Jaques de Bourgogne, lord of Falais, whose obedience to the faith of these figures was just beginning in exile.[58] Backsliding was a constant danger, even within Calvin's movement.

Were such functional Nicodemites, believers who lacked requisite commitment, present in Calvin's church? There was dissent and grumbling from groups we have already named: offended Genevans and disappointed refugees. But what about the broader waters that Calvin's ministry navigated? Factional networks had for decades been emerging within French evangelical circles in Romandy, crystallizing into Calvinist and anti-Calvinist camps.[59] Calvin's efforts to establish his standing in early-1550s Geneva addressed just part of the dissent against his teaching and leadership. His victory over local foes in 1555 came at a time when his wider influence over Reformed churches was anything but settled and sure. Calvin might have defeated the Perrinist faction in Geneva, but he lacked a firm hold on the Compté of Montbéliard and Pays de Vaud, significant and large francophone Protestant regions.[60]

What does any of this have to do with Nicodemism? Calvin's polemic was finely tuned to depict and defend the core theological commitments of his vision for comfort in exile. Predestination, ecclesiology, and worship frame the

---

57. See chaps. 4 and 6, above.
58. See chap. 6, above.
59. Michael W. Bruening, *Refusing to Kiss the Slipper: Opposition to Calvinism in the Francophone Reformation* (Oxford University Press, 2021).
60. Bruening, *Refusing to Kiss the Slipper*, 136–37.

exilic theology of pilgrimage, nurture, and homecoming that undergirded Calvin's teaching and reforms in Geneva. Precisely these areas of doctrine divided French-speaking evangelicals in Switzerland. The most sophisticated anti-Calvinist theological program belonged to Sebastian Castellio, whose wide-ranging attack on Calvin and his allies rejected Calvin's views on predestination, external worship, and church discipline.[61] In 1554 Calvin complained to his friend Simon Sulzer (d. 1585) that Castellio's views on religious toleration were gaining ground in Geneva and dividing the city's refugee community.[62] Castellio was also influential in the Vaud and other regions where Calvin's stock was falling fast. More alarmingly, such dissent could be invisible, as Michael Bruening observes: "Castellio did not really have an ecclesiology; his theology was personal, spiritual, and moral. This is one reason Calvin found him so dangerous; thousands of individuals could be 'infected' by his views while outwardly conforming to the Reformed Church. They could be Calvinists institutionally but Castellionists inwardly. They were the enemy within, a strange new type of Nicodemite within Calvin's own church."[63]

With his theology under fire, Calvin needed a way to stir commitment to the core elements of his cause. He found this in his tested messaging against Nicodemism. It seems counterintuitive to turn the critique of crypto-religion and "temporizing" against those worshiping in Reformed contexts, who ostensibly already openly confessed true faith. Yet Calvin's followers in England did exactly this. They made extensive use of Reformed and Lutheran polemic against Nicodemism to criticize fellow members of the Church of England as "Neuters" or "Neutrals," those who had all the right elements of true religion yet lacked enough zeal.[64] Was Calvin doing the same in Romandy? One would understand if he was. Caroli, Bolsec, Zebedee, and Castellio—if they are even remembered by readers today—are quickly dismissed as slanderers and heretics, bit players whose ideas were deemed deficient and quickly dispensed with despite lingering hard feelings. In reality, Castellio's ideas were an important contemporary counterweight to Calvin's. On ecclesiology, worship, and tolerance of dissent, Castellio opposed Calvin's rigid insistence on a form of external practice and discipline in writings that gained sympathetic hearing across Romandy, even into France. Calvin's concern over these developments is reflected in his shift, after 1555, from recruiting believers to Geneva toward imposing Genevan consistorial authority on churches in France. These actions,

61. Bruening, *Refusing to Kiss the Slipper*, 139–210.
62. Calvin to Sulzer, August 7, 1554 (Bonnet, 3:52–53; CO 9:83).
63. Bruening, *Refusing to Kiss the Slipper*, 156.
64. Woo, *Nicodemism,* 100–204; and Karl Gunther, *Reformation Unbound: Protestant Visions of Reform in England, 1525–1590* (Cambridge University Press, 2014), 98–129.

predictably, fueled anti-Calvinist resentment that Calvin was asserting Genevan control everywhere he could.[65]

Within this wider context, *Four Sermons* appeared at a moment of growing dissent from Calvin's views on the church and its ministry not just in Geneva, but also everywhere else (so it seemed). Calvin trained his attack against Nicodemism on the very themes disputed within the French exile movement Calvin presumed to speak for since the days of his preface to King Francis I.[66] Submission to the polity and worship of a rightly ordered church was God's means of nurturing the elect in exile. Could another readership for *Four Sermons* be potential defectors in his ranks when Calvin wanted to consolidate support in the face of vocal criticism? As early as the 1540s, Calvin depicted David and Abraham as anti-Nicodemites whose outward, zealous commitment to the principles of Calvin's ecclesiology was an example to all believers. He said as much to Falais in 1544, when neither man knew that Falais would one day depart from Calvin's fold to support Bolsec and Castellio. The theology of nurture that Calvin presents as anti-Nicodemism in *Four Sermons* was not contrived solely to combat Castellionist dissent. Its roots are deeper than the factional controversies of the 1550s, dating back to his flight from France. Yet, how could Calvin not have had such dissent in mind in 1552? As polemics-turned-internal-critique, Calvin's case against Nicodemism united the church around a common identity as spiritual exiles while subjecting that same community to further scrutiny regarding faithfulness. Abraham and David in exile model the perpetual, restless commitment Calvin wanted. Their combative zeal for purer worship and relentless hunger for the same were criteria against which all believers could be measured and found wanting. Calvin's theology of God's comfort in exile, which addressed the displaced and distressed pastorally, could also discipline the fickle toward commitment and conformity to his ideals. They needed to take worship (and their pastors) more seriously.

Conclusion

Like other reformers, Calvin engaged extensively in theological debates to clarify and defend his ideas against detractors from all sides. It would be foolish to say that his polemical concerns were unique to his situation as refugee theologian. Yet we must not neglect how exile, as both a political and a spiritual reality, influenced the way Calvin argued with opponents and the

65. Bruening, *Refusing to Kiss the Slipper*, 180–210.
66. See chap. 1, above.

content of what he said. At the heart of his theological vision was an understanding of the true church as a special object of God's concern and nurture. To this church belonged God's promises of care and homecoming after the present life of spiritual exile. In an era (like ours) of many and proliferating claims to be God's chosen people, Calvin had to identify his movement as legitimate, and he did that in part by excluding others, placing Rome and radicals on the outside, whether as reprobates, anti-Christs, Satan's agents, or all of the above. Within his own movement, Calvin used exile as a unifying and distinguishing theme to offer comfort and enforce conformity. His anti-Nicodemite works fostered identity around external forms of religion while making fervent commitment to these things the mark of spiritual pilgrims who knew their way home.

For Further Reading

In Calvin's Words

1537 *God or Baal: Two Letters on the Reformation of Worship and Pastoral Service*. Translated by David C. Noe. Reformation Heritage Books, 2020.

1537–64 *Come Out from Among Them: "Anti-Nicodemite" Writings of John Calvin*. Translated by Seth Skolnitsky. Protestant Heritage, 2001.

For Digging Deeper

Eire, Carlos. *War Against the Idols: The Reformation of Worship from Erasmus to Calvin*. Cambridge University Press, 1986.

Matheson, Peter. "Martyrdom or Mission? A Protestant Debate." *Archiv für Reformationsgeschichte* 80 (1989): 154–72.

Woo, Kenneth J. *Nicodemism and the English Calvin, 1544–1584*. Brill, 2019.

Wright, David F. "Why Was Calvin So Severe a Critic of Nicodemism?" In *Calvinus Evangelii Propugnator: Calvin, Champion of the Gospel; Papers Presented at the International Congress on Calvin Research, Seoul, 1998*, edited by David F. Wright et al., 66–90. Calvin Studies Society, 2006.

Zagorin, Perez. *Ways of Lying: Dissimulation, Persecution, and Conformity in Early Modern Europe*. Harvard University Press, 1990.

CONCLUSION

Reading a Reformer in Exile

The Catholic Calvin?

Catholic (Greek: *katholikē*) is not a word ordinarily associated with John Calvin, except with reference to his adversarial relationship to the Roman Catholic Church, which bears the same name today. The first known use of the term in Christian literature appears in the letters of Ignatius of Antioch (d. ca. 108 CE), who describes a church that is "*katholikē*" (universal), encompassing all places and peoples.[1] It is in this sense that Calvin considered himself a catholic theologian. He was convinced that his doctrine continued the teaching of Israel's prophets and Christ's apostles, which unifies God's children throughout history. Calvin's struggles against both Rome and radicals asserted the catholicity of his position against the novelty and error of theirs. Despite insisting on his theology's biblical basis over against "tradition," Calvin received historical creeds sympathetically, repeated exegetical consensus in his biblical interpretation, and cited past theologians approvingly.[2] In fact, he wrote a foreword to an unfinished anthology of homilies by the church father John Chrysostom (d. 407).[3] As discussed in chapter 7, Calvin's pursuit of ecumenical consensus with Heinrich Bullinger on the Lord's Supper

---

1. The Letter of Ignatius to the Smyrnaeans 8.2, in *The Apostolic Fathers: Greek Texts and English Translations*, 3rd ed., ed. and trans. Michael W. Holmes (Baker Academic, 2007), 254.
2. R. Ward Holder, *Calvin and the Christian Tradition: Scripture, Memory, and the Western Mind* (Cambridge University Press, 2022); and Anthony N. S. Lane, *John Calvin: Student of the Church Fathers* (Baker, 1999).
3. CO 9:831–38.

further attests to his catholic sensibilities. It also reminds us that Calvin belonged to a networked community of thinkers that belies the Reformed tradition's disproportionate association with Calvin alone.[4]

This book has shown how Calvin—as teacher, pastor, and polemicist in Geneva—portrayed his catholic theology in ways that highlight the present time as spiritual exile, specifically addressing early modern realities related to political exile. Calvin interpreted ideas already present in scripture and tradition—from exile to predestination, from providence to the church as nurturing mother—in light of the Reformation period's dynamics as an era of religious refugees. His theology cannot be separated from its concern for present comfort in contexts of violence and migration. To attempt this would be to end up with less than the Calvin who, according to Heiko Oberman, spoke deeply to spiritual exiles in his day and ever since.[5] Religious conflict meant that Reformed Christians were on the move both during and after Calvin's lifetime, resulting in interconnected communities across Europe.[6] These communities, in turn, could mobilize and support fellow Reformed exiles, such as the massive numbers (by some counts over a million) who fled Central Europe during the Thirty Years' War (1618–48).[7] For many of the scattered, Calvin's theology, formulated through his own experiences of exile, could help them make sense of lived realities in ways that united them through shared theological commitments.[8] Still, not all Calvinists in exile rallied around Calvin's theology, while others who did used it in the context of empire to justify the enslavement of fellow humans.[9] So much for a theology first pitched to assuage

---

4. Richard A. Muller, "Demoting Calvin: The Issue of Calvin and the Reformed Tradition," in *John Calvin, Myth and Reality: Images and Impact of Geneva's Reformer; Papers of the 2009 Calvin Studies Society Colloquium*, ed. Amy Nelson Burnett (Cascade Books, 2011), 3–17.

5. Heiko A. Oberman, *John Calvin and the Reformation of the Refugees* (Droz, 2009), 67; and see the introduction to this book.

6. Philip Benedict, *Christ's Churches Purely Reformed: A Social History of Calvinism* (Yale University Press, 2002), 121–291.

7. Nicholas Terpstra, *Religious Refugees in the Early Modern World: An Alternative History of the Reformation* (Cambridge University Press, 2015), 121–23; Ole Peter Grell, *Brethren in Christ: A Calvinist Network in Reformation Europe* (Cambridge University Press, 2011).

8. Ole Peter Grell, "The Creation of a Calvinist Identity in the Reformation Period," in *Religion as an Agent of Change*, ed. Per Ingesman (Brill, 2016), 149–65; Grell, *Brethren in Christ*, 1–7 et passim; and Heinz Schilling, "Peregrini und Schiffchen Gottes: Flüchtlingserfahrung und Exulantentheologie des frühneuzeitlichen Calvinismus," in *Calvinismus: Die Reformierten in Deutschland und Europa*, ed. Ansgar Riess and Sabine Witt (Sandstein, 2009), 160–68.

9. Mirjam G. K. van Veen and Jesse Spohnholz, "Calvinists vs. Libertines: A New Look at Religious Exile and the Origins of 'Dutch' Tolerance," in *Calvinism and the Making of the European Mind*, ed. Gijsbert van den Brink and Harro Höpfl (Brill, 2014), 76–99; and Charles H. Parker, *Global Calvinism: Conversion and Commerce in the Dutch Empire, 1600–1800* (Yale University Press, 2022), 102–10.

the plight of the oppressed. Yet diverse reception does not change Calvin's original situation. From his identification with David in exile to his lifelong concern for the persecuted in France, Calvin read the Bible as a refugee whose experience of exile informed his theology.

How, then, might readers in our times hold together these sides of Calvin when engaging his thought? In what sense was his both catholic theology, as it aspired to be, and refugee theology, as it was unavoidably? In an era like ours, when it is hardly obvious to most people why Calvin should be read at all, is there something about his distinctive teaching as refugee theologian that possesses a catholic, or universal, appeal? Are there ways of thinking about him that could invite new, even unlikely, readers to take him up for the first time? This book is an invitation to consider such questions. The answers will vary and, I hope, provoke more questions than can be taken up in this brief conclusion. I conclude with just three areas for consideration. Reading Calvin as refugee theologian is valuable for (1) pressing beyond traditional stereotypes, positive and negative, about the reformer and his theology; (2) providing a valuable conversation partner for Christians learning to imagine themselves in new positions within society, often in roles of reduced influence; and (3) inviting theological traditions to reassess their origin stories, which may well lead to a critical reevaluation of assumed practices and priorities, as well as to centering new voices.

An Unexpected Frenemy?

Calvin was, and continues to be, a polarizing figure. There was no love lost between his supporters and the anti-Calvinists that divided French-speaking evangelicals during his lifetime. Their mutual loathing was such that it almost did not matter what the other side said; they were always wrong. Personal relationship was frequently a more decisive factor than persuasive arguments in determining one's opinion about a range of issues, including Calvin's doctrine of predestination.[10] Consider, for example, the competing sixteenth-century biographies of the reformer compiled by friends, like Theodore Beza, and by a host of foes, from Jerome Bolsec to Jean-Papire Masson (d. 1611).[11] Hostile accounts traded on the (apparently common) sentiment among Genevans that

---

10. Michael W. Bruening, "The Predestination Debate from Jerome Bolsec to Peter Baro," in *Calvin, Exile, and Religious Refugees: Papers of the Thirteenth International Congress on Calvin Research*, ed. Arnold Huijgen and Karin Maag (Vandenhoeck & Ruprecht, 2024), 75–95.

11. Irena Backus, *Life Writing in Reformation Europe: Lives of Reformers by Friends, Disciples and Foes* (Ashgate, 2008), 125–86.

they would "rather be in hell with Beza than in heaven with Calvin," with biographers also chronicling Calvin's alleged sexual misconduct for good measure.[12] Written in 1583 but not published until after its author's death, Masson's *Life of Calvin* (1620), while critical of the reformer, is notable because it rests on evidence in ways absent from earlier attempts to paint Calvin as one-sidedly good or evil. A more methodologically rigorous, but no less divided, historiography of Calvin and Geneva would follow.[13] Indeed, the common characterization of Calvin's critics, perpetuated by history's winners, is that they were jealous and unhealthily obsessed with slandering him.[14] Even in 2009, the quincentennial of Calvin's birth, scholarly conferences continued to draw attention to this dichotomized reception of Calvin, posing again the question, "Calvin—Saint or Sinner?"[15] Indeed, I have been introduced as a guest teacher to Sunday school classes in Presbyterian churches by pastors claiming to "hate Calvin" while admitting to "never" having read him. The late historian David Steinmetz was fond of pointing out how, among Reformation scholars who should know better, certain sectors of Calvin studies were more like "Calvin falling into the hands of his friends."[16] Can this abiding polarization around Calvin, whether in academic circles or in the popular imagination, ever be remedied?

Attending to Calvin's profile as refugee theologian could offer a way through this impasse. That Calvin read the Bible as a refugee for the benefit of fellow exiles has, until relatively recently, attracted little attention despite being known by scholars. It was, after all, simply a function of responding to his environment. Yet it was never one-dimensional. The same ideas Calvin intended as encouraging were abhorred, rejected as controlling, by some contemporaries. In fact, it is hard to avoid the conclusion that Calvin employed this theology both ways, to console spiritual exiles as well as to impose conformity on the same pilgrims. This makes the refugee theologian a difficult figure, an ill fit for either the "good" or the "evil" hat that historical reception repeatedly tries to place on his head. Calvin was more sensitive to the needs of the displaced than his enemies would like to admit, and he was also calculating with his theological rhetoric in ways that embarrass those who celebrate Calvin's pastoral side. But perhaps this is just who we need—one who is neither saint nor sinner exclusively, but both. Calvin, refugee theologian, is

---

12. Backus, *Life Writing*, 160–61, 185.
13. Backus, *Life Writing*, 187–227.
14. Michael W. Bruening, *Refusing to Kiss the Slipper: Opposition to Calvinism in the Francophone Reformation* (Oxford University Press, 2021), 120.
15. See the papers presented at Putten in 2008 and collected in *Calvin—Saint or Sinner?*, ed. Herman J. Selderhuis (Mohr Siebeck, 2010); and likewise, Burnett, *John Calvin, Myth and Reality*.
16. He said this to me personally, though I know that he repeated it often in conversation.

a "frenemy" who challenges monochromatic depictions of him as friend or enemy. In the process, this perhaps gets us closer to the historical reformer. At the expense of simplistic portrayals that have persisted for centuries, recent scholarship has elevated the views of Calvin's vanquished opponents and unveils the hypocrisy latent in Calvin's sincere desire for religious reform in France.[17] This has resulted in a more complex, conflicted, and—dare we say—human, relatable, and catholic understanding of these figures. Those who claim continuity with the reformers should welcome a historically nuanced understanding of their motives and actions. They are both *more* and *less* like us than we thought.

A Familiar Voice in Unfamiliar Places

To some, the Reformed tradition's recovery of its refugee roots in a figure like Calvin is a welcome project at a time when Christianity's cultural influence appears to be waning. This latter point is debatable, insofar as the number of Christians worldwide continues to grow in Africa, Asia, and Latin America.[18] Even in the global West, comprising Europe and North America, historic strongholds of Christianity, one must be careful when correlating diminishing numbers of self-identified Christians to diminishing degrees of influence. From workday norms and annual holidays to prevailing social customs, national identity, and standards of "cultural literacy," Christianity still holds significant sway over daily life in ways that reflect its long history of privilege in the West.[19] Yet there are undeniable changes in our experiences of religion in its traditional institutional forms. In my own situation of theological education, decades of downward trends in seminary enrollment continue, and there are regular reports of theological schools closing or facing closure.[20] This reflects the decline in overall church attendance in the West, affecting both Catholics and Protestants, mainline and evangelical denominations.[21]

17. Bruening, *Refusing to Kiss the Slipper*; and Jon Balserak, *Geneva's Use of Lies, Deceit, and Subterfuge, 1536–1563* (Oxford University Press, 2024).

18. Center for the Study of Global Christianity, Gordon-Conwell Theological Seminary, "Status of Global Christianity, 2024, in the Context of 1900–2050" (2024), https://www.gordonconwell.edu/wp-content/uploads/sites/13/2024/01/Status-of-Global-Christianity-2024.pdf.

19. Khyati Y. Joshi, *White Christian Privilege: The Illusion of Religious Equality in America* (New York University Press, 2020).

20. Chris A. Meinzer, "ATS Enrollment Trend Snapshot: Fall 2023" (October 2023), https://www.ats.edu/files/galleries/ats-enrollment-trend-snapshot-fall-2023.pdf.

21. Jeffrey M. Jones, "U.S. Church Membership Falls Below Majority for First Time," Politics, *Gallup*, March 29, 2021, https://news.gallup.com/poll/341963/church-membership-falls-below-majority-first-time.aspx.

Oberman drew attention to the divorce between today's Calvinism and its refugee roots. But this began long ago. Whether New England Puritans or the Afrikaaner church of Dutch colonial South Africa, history chronicles how theology originally intended to comfort exiles and refugees turned into an apology for the establishment, even cases where the persecuted became the oppressors. In our day, Reformed churches in the West are learning to adapt to the inverse situation: loss of membership, prestige, and privileges.

In such unfamiliar circumstances, Calvin the refugee theologian could be a familiar, if unexpected, conversation partner for churches finding themselves disoriented vis-à-vis past experiences of cultural relevance and power. The Scottish pastors I taught recently in my seminary's doctor of ministry program described the challenges of ministering within a national church that traces its lineage directly to Calvin's Geneva through John Knox, another sixteenth-century religious refugee.[22] A 2023 report of the Church of Scotland reveals that the Kirk (as it is known) has lost over half its members and 60 percent of its pastors since 2000, with the average age now sixty-two in a denomination that has around forty-five hundred to five thousand buildings to maintain.[23] In the face of such drastic decline in membership and prominence over just a handful of decades, these pastors have begun revisiting Calvin with fresh questions. Among these is how the refugee roots of the Reformed tradition might resource the theological imaginations of twenty-first-century Reformed communities experiencing a sense of cultural displacement for the first time. Could their own doctrinal heritage already hold such riches?

These challenges facing the Scottish church find parallels in American denominations. While no national church exists in this context, mainline denominations such as my own Reformed Church in America and that of my seminary, the Presbyterian Church (U.S.A.), have likewise experienced sharp decline since the turn of the current century.[24] And theologically conservative evangelical churches, while generally remaining stable in size, swim in the same receding waters of Christianity's overall numbers in the West. What both groups have in common are the challenges of ministry in an increasingly divided and polarized culture that manifests its fissures and hostilities within

22. Jane Dawson, *John Knox* (Yale University Press, 2015).
23. Church of Scotland, *The Church of Scotland General Assembly 2023, Report of the Assembly Trustees*, 2.1, https://churchofscotland.org.uk/__data/assets/pdf_file/0010/107866/assembly-trustees.pdf. I am grateful to the Rev. Dr. Jamie Milliken for drawing my attention to this report.
24. Dartinia Hull, "PC(USA) 2022 Statistical Report Shows Membership Declining, New Worshiping Communities Growing," *Presbyterian Outlook*, May 3, 2023, https://pres-outlook.org/2023/05/pcusa-2022-statistical-report-shows-membership-in-decline-new-worshiping-communities-growing/.

church congregations. Alongside the many ways pastoral theology could address these realities, perhaps there is room for fresh consideration of the church as a locus of nurture for weary pilgrims. For Reformed Christians, this is an established, if overlooked, aspect of spirituality in their tradition.[25] One wonders how many ministers today intentionally cultivate a robust congregational identity as spiritual exiles, which is capable of inviting unity across substantial differences, and present the gifts of Word and sacrament as common food for hungry pilgrims. With greater awareness of how displacement functions internally and externally, including its complex psychological dimensions, our moment stands ripe for reflection on how a gospel of homecoming speaks with precision to many expressions of exile in modern life.[26] The ravages of war and disease are not the same as social alienation or cultural shift, but all these realities invite the church to meet the displaced with theological accounts of "home." Calvin the refugee theologian offers a helpful case study. Though his circumstances were different, his pastoral sensibilities, particularly in accommodating scripture's exilic themes to his situation, are worth revisiting.

Centering New Voices in a Continuing Conversation

Beyond his potential as thought partner for pastoral care of the newly disenfranchised, Calvin the refugee theologian invites previously marginalized voices to engage the Reformed tradition with a new sense of ownership. Frankly, this opportunity is something Oberman understates concerning Calvin's legacy. Failure to appreciate Calvin's concern for the exile deprives the global Reformed community of a way for all its members to embrace this rich and complex theological heritage as their own. In its worst forms, such alienation promotes the impression that the Reformed faith belongs to some, while others are invited only as guests (or treated as intruders) and thus remain perpetual foreigners. Calvin addressed tensions between refugees and the communities that received them (often not by choice) by cultivating a theological identity that included both groups as exiles, regardless of political status or social standing. Like baptism, the marginality of exilic status makes a theological claim about a community's shared origin. Pastoral theology in the Reformed tradition can

---

25. D. G. Hart, *Recovering Mother Kirk: The Case for Liturgy in the Reformed Tradition* (Baker Academic, 2003).
26. M. Jan Holton, *Longing for Home: Forced Displacement and Postures of Hospitality* (Yale University Press, 2016); Sheryl A. Kujawa-Holbrook and Karen B. Montagno, eds., *Injustice and the Care of Souls: Taking Oppression Seriously in Pastoral Care* (Fortress, 2009); and Ting-Yin Lee, "The Loss and Grief in Immigration: Pastoral Care for Immigrants," *Pastoral Psychology* 59 (2010): 159–69.

learn from Calvin's refugee vision by engaging nuanced accounts of marginality, such as those present in pan-Asian and Asian-American theology.[27]

There is also potential for better centering Reformed voices from historically marginalized groups both sympathetic and critical toward their own tradition.[28] For example, the late Taiwanese Presbyterian scholar C. S. Song (d. 2024), past president of the World Alliance of Reformed Churches, exemplified leadership in the global Reformed church that questioned Christianity's reduction to Western modes of theology.[29] Within the Anglican Communion, issues dividing churches in the West, such as human sexuality, have brought intervention from churches in Africa and other parts of the Southern Hemisphere.[30] In a North American context that witnesses society and churches riven anew by fractured political discourse and ethnic suspicion, the counterintuitive proposal of Calvinism as "refugee theology" creates opportunities for advancing dialogue. Those prone to experiencing their ecclesial tradition as outsiders might acquire a fresh agency in conversations ranging from churches to classrooms. In immigrant congregations like the one I served as pastor two decades ago, people from various nations bring preexisting political conflict and cultural difference, as well as divergent ways of relating to a new country. Such diversity and the tensions it creates easily remain invisible to the society around such communities and, it can seem, to the theology of historic Reformed confessions.

No one at that time introduced my congregation to Calvin, refugee theologian, so that we could read the reformer in exile as fellow exiles. Yet it is precisely its potential to speak to many varieties of "exilic experience" today that

27. See, e.g., Jane Naomi Iwamura, "Homage to Ancestors: Exploring the Horizons of Asian American Religious Identity," *Amerasia Journal* 22, no. 1 (1996): 161–67; Grace Ji-Sun Kim and Susan M. Shaw, eds., *Intersectional Theology: An Introductory Guide* (Fortress, 2018); Kwok Pui-Lan and Stephen Burns, *Postcolonial Practice of Ministry: Leadership, Liturgy, and Interfaith Engagement* (Lexington Books, 2016); and Jung Young Lee, *Marginality: The Key to Multicultural Theology* (Augsburg Fortress, 1995). The journals *Law & Religion* and *Political Theology* recently published a joint symposium of articles on Wong Kim Ark and James Baldwin, signaling interest in crosscurrent reflection on "belonging" as an interethnic dialogue between Asian American / Pacific Islander and Black "experience" (*Political Theology* 23, no. 5 [2022]).

28. Allan A. Boesak, *Black and Reformed: Apartheid, Liberation, and the Calvinist Tradition*, ed. Leonard Sweetman (1984; repr., Wipf & Stock, 2015); Kim Yong-Bock, "Korean Christianity as a Messianic Movement of the People," in *Minjung Theology: People as the Subject of History,* ed. Kim Yong-Bock (Orbis Books, 1983), 80–119; and Ben Bagsao Ngaya-an, *Marginality and Christian Mission in the Twentieth Century* (New Day Publishers, 2019).

29. See Song's works: *Theology from the Womb of Asia* (Orbis Books, 1986); *Jesus and the Crucified People* (Fortress, 1990); *Jesus and the Reign of God* (Fortress, 1993); and *Jesus and the Power of the Spirit* (Fortress, 1994).

30. Miranda Katherine Hassett, *Anglican Communion in Crisis: How Episcopal Dissidents and Their African Allies Are Reshaping Anglicanism* (Princeton University Press, 2007).

commends Calvin's theology to a new generation of readers. Their contexts range from the Church of Scotland to Asian-American Presbyterianism, from mainline and evangelical churches grappling with diminishing numbers to communities learning to follow leaders from historically marginalized groups.[31]

Memory and Family History

Visitors to St. Pierre Cathedral today will find a pair of monuments set into the wall at the front left of the sanctuary. One is an early memorial to Geneva's 1535 restoration of the "most holy Christian Religion" by throwing off the "tyranny of the Roman Antichrist." The engraving's 1835 restoration and installation at its current location is commemorated by another tablet set into the wall directly beneath it. This second marker attributes Geneva's reform both to God's beneficence and to the dedication of "four devout foreigners, our Great Reformers: Farel, Froment, Viret, Calvin." It is fitting that, three centuries after the Reformation, the people of Geneva recognized their history as the story of refugees.

My grandparents' experiences invite me to do the same. I will never know exactly how they made meaning of their surroundings in the midst of material loss, relational rupture, and cultural displacement. But I will always appreciate that their struggles as refugees remain part of our family's story, giving it a distinctive shape that grounds our particular stories in a shared narrative of exile. This is what Calvin, refugee theologian, believed he was doing when he read scripture's accounts of God's people in exile as a kind of family history. Doctrines like providence, predestination, and the church as a community of spiritual exiles—vividly portrayed in the stories of Abraham, David, and Israel—linked "devout foreigners" in an age of violence to a past that made sense of their present and offered hope for the future. May it be the case that our memory of this reformer, the refugee theologian, leads us to reassess our past, present, and future in creative ways that Calvin could not have imagined.

---

31. See Rubén Rosario Rodríguez, *Calvin for the World: The Enduring Relevance of His Political, Social, and Economic Theology* (Baker Academic, 2024).

APPENDIX

Questions for Continuing the Conversation

Chapter 1

1. How was Calvin's work as a theologian inseparable from his experience of exile?
2. In what ways does personal history influence your theology? Conversely, how does theology inform the way you recount past experiences?

Chapter 2

1. What surprises you most about the variety of audiences Calvin addressed? Why?
2. Does situating Calvin's ideas within specific circumstances, pressures, and ambitions that shaped them make his theology less relevant for our contexts today? Explain.
3. How would you define your religious commitments or "theological identity" in relation to others? Does this involve markers of belonging to a particular community or tradition that have changed (or stayed the same) over time?

Chapter 3

1. What does it mean to say that Calvin's *Institutes* is "incomplete" apart from his biblical commentaries? How should this influence the way one studies Calvin's theology?

2. In what ways did Calvin's doctrine of predestination offer comfort to a church comprising many religious refugees? How does this accord with your prior understanding of Calvin and predestination?

3. Do you think Calvin's characterization of the church's ministry and worship as sources of nurture, as manna in the wilderness, would have comforted his original audiences? Why or why not?

4. What would it look like for churches to adopt Calvin's view of spiritual nurture through preaching and sacraments in our day?

Chapter 4

1. In what ways does biblical exegesis, like we find in Calvin's commentaries, differ from theological works like the *Institutes*, which focus on discussing doctrinal topics? What are the strengths and limitations of each kind of writing for teaching others?

2. How is Calvin's exegesis of scripture a window into both the worlds of the Bible and Calvin's sixteenth-century situation? What lessons can we learn from studying the history of how Christian communities throughout time have interpreted biblical texts?

3. Calvin closely identified David with exile and identified himself with David. How did this influence Calvin's exegesis of the Psalms and how he applied them to believers living in his historical moment? What does this reveal about how you and others read the Bible today?

Chapter 5

1. Geneva's program for religious education involved family, church, and magistrates working in tandem. What are the strengths and weaknesses of such an approach?

2. In what ways did Reformation Geneva's new structures for religious practices also reorient the church's spirituality? How is your spirituality reflected in your practices?

3. The presence and impact of religious refugees created challenges for pastors in Geneva and influenced how they responded to these difficulties. How has the church responded to circumstances exerting pressure on pastoral ministry in your context?

Chapter 6

1. Calvin's sermons attempted to shape his listeners' theological imaginations around a shared identity as spiritual exiles. Why was this a relevant theme in his day? How might it be a relevant theme in ours?

2. What insights into the concerns of Calvin's community appear in his preaching? What don't his sermons tell us that we might be curious to know?

3. How did Calvin use Abraham and David to influence others' priorities and actions? Describe examples you have encountered of preachers today using biblical figures to address contemporary issues. What are some advantages and drawbacks of this approach to teaching?

Chapter 7

1. Calvin and other reformers loathed being thought of as innovators. Does this surprise you? Why, or why not?

2. Calvin was not alone in employing exaggeration and dehumanizing rhetoric to distance his views from others and mark certain people as outsiders to God's church. Are such practices any less prevalent today? Explain.

3. How did Calvin's polemical writings construct a distinctive identity for his community? What was at stake for Calvin's theology of the church as God's elect people in exile?

Chapter 8

1. Calvin's attack on Nicodemism was relentless but tells us little about the identities and practices of actual Nicodemites. Why is that? What does this mean for how we read Calvin's anti-Nicodemite writings?

2. Pressure to accommodate one's faith to one's surroundings can take any number of forms. Besides Nicodemism, how else might this have looked in Calvin's day? How does it look in our time?

3. Does the fact that Calvin addressed the same argument to different audiences (France, Geneva, Romandy, etc.) for multiple purposes (comfort and control) change how we should interpret his theology and its relevance for today? Explain.

INDEX

Abraham
  as example in exile, 16, 40, 123–24, 131–34, 136–38, 167, 187
  faith of, 65, 86–87, 119, 122
  and Nicodemism, 175, 177
  and predestination, 73
  and providence, 71
Adam, 59, 73–77, 82, 128–29
Against the Fantastic and Furious Sect of the Libertines Who Are Called "Spirituals," 157, 159
Amboise Conspiracy, 36
Ambrose, 129, 147
Ameaux, Pierre, 101
Anabaptism, 39, 42, 145
  Calvin's polemic against, 152–53, 157–59
Andrew of St. Victor, 77
Anglican Communion, 186
Answer to the Nicodemites, 165, 171–72
anti-Nicodemism, 25, 33, 35
  and Calvin's writings, 133, 167–74
  directed at those within Calvin's church, 174–78
  See also crypto-religion
antitrinitarianism, 23, 146, 152, 160–62
Antoine of Navarre, 37
apostasy
  and Calvin's exegesis of the prophets, 82–85
  of Rome, 148, 151–52, 162
ascension, Christ's, 52, 55, 121, 156
Augustine, 51, 55–57, 59, 61, 74–76
  Calvin's critique of, 147, 155

Badius, Conrad, 121
Balserak, Jon, 37
Baudouin, François, 170
baptism
  Calvin's theology of, 97, 112–13, 115
  and conflict in Geneva, 99–100
Basel, 3, 8–9
belonging, xx, xxxiii
  and baptism, 157
  to God, 9, 11, 16–17, 19, 22, 26, 41–42, 61, 64, 91, 123
  rhetoric of, 3–6
  and worship, 130
Bern, 10, 27, 30, 121, 174
Bernard of Clairvaux, 148
Berthelier, Philibert, 29
Beza, Theodore, 24, 36–37, 114, 127, 181–82
Blandrata, Giorgio, 160
Bolsec, Jerome, 12, 24, 101, 172, 174, 176–77, 181
Bonnet, Jules, 40
Bourse Française, 29, 32, 36, 121
Briçonnet, Guillaume, 22
A Brief Instruction for Arming All the Good Faithful Against the Errors of the Common Sect of the Anabaptists, 157–59
Bucer, Martin
  on King David, 78
  and recall of Calvin, 24
  as Reformed leader, xxix, 10–11, 38, 47, 152, 159, 161, 168
  on the Trinity, 161
Bugenhagen, Johannes, 78

193

Bullinger, Heinrich
  on the Lord's Supper, 152–53, 179
  and predestination, 61
  and banishment of Calvin, 25
  as Reformed leader, xxix, 6, 8, 37, 39, 161, 167

Cain, xxvi, 73, 77, 129–30, 132, 146
Calvin, John
  banishment from Geneva, 106
  as catholic, 179–81
  conversion of, 8–10
  embrace of in England, 38. See also *Four Sermons*
  engagement with France, 13–14
  inner circle of, 22–26
  interest in foreign affairs, 37–41
  letter to Luther, xx–xxii, xxiv
  on obedience to rulers, 32–33
  pastoral context of, 98–101
  as polarizing figure, 100–101, 181
  as preacher, 119–38
  preoccupation with reforming France, 31–37
  publication of works of, 39–40, 121–22, 133, 167–74
  relevance of reading today, xxvii–xxx, 181–87
  and sermons of nurture in exile, 119–38
  as teacher of refugees, 47–51, 82–91
  themes in preaching of, 26–27, 31, 96
  theology of baptism, 112–13, 115
  theology of the Lord's Supper, 109–12, 115
Calvinism, xxii, 38, 60, 184, 186
Canons of Dort, 60
Capito, Wolfgang, 10, 168
Caroli, Pierre, 23, 160, 176
Castellio, Sebastian, 12, 24, 56, 59, 127–28, 176–77
Charles V, Emperor, 28
Catechism of the Church of Geneva, 95, 97, 102–6, 108–9
  and spiritual exile, 104–5
Catholics, French, 6–8, 19, 22, 25, 32–33. See also polemic, Calvin's: against Roman Catholicism
Christology, 54–56, 147, 161
Chrysostom, John, 73, 147, 179
church
  exilic identity of, 123–25, 130–32
  as locus of nurture in exile, 65–69, 85–91, 105–6, 122–38
  as mother, 65, 72, 88–89, 91, 102, 105, 180
  and pastoral authority, 88–91
  as pilgrim people, 50–52, 55
  and spiritual gifts, 87–89
  true, 84. See also Sadoleto, Cardinal Jacopo
church discipline, 10, 12, 24, 28, 176
  and Adam's expulsion from the garden, 74–75
  See also Consistory, Genevan; *Ecclesiastical Ordinances*
church government, xxii, xxvi, 102, 151. See also Consistory, Genevan; *Ecclesiastical Ordinances*
Church of Scotland, 184, 187
commentaries, Calvin's
  on Ephesians, 88
  on 1–2 Timothy, 85
  on Genesis, 71, 73–77, 128, 132–34
  on Isaiah, 83
  on John, 40, 73
  on the Psalms, 8, 15, 17–18, 72, 78–81, 114
  on Romans, 11, 72, 87
  on 2 Corinthians, 71
  on the Synoptic Gospels, 40
  on Titus, 23
Company of Pastors, 12, 30, 32, 34, 36, 102, 104, 107
Concerning the Secret Providence of God (Calvin), 56.
Confession of Faith, Geneva's, 97, 102–6, 145
Consistory, Genevan, 11–12, 28, 90, 102, 105–6, 108–9, 160, 174
Constable, David, 40
Coornhert, Dirck, 168
Cop, Nicolas, 7
Crespin, Jean, 29
crypto-religion, xxi–xxii, 134, 146, 165–70, 176
Cyprian, 65, 147

David, King
  and Calvin's sermons on Job, 136–38
  and Nicodemism, 134–35, 167
  as pattern for exile, xxv, 6, 9, 13, 18, 77–82, 108, 115, 126, 134–36
Day of Prayer, 108, 116
deacons, 107
de Bure, Idelette, 11
De clementia (Seneca), 7
decree, divine. *See* predestination
de La Mare, Henri, 25
de Navarre, Marguerite, 160
de Normandie, Laurent, 36, 121
des Moulins, Bertrand, 159

Index   195

Diatribe Concerning Free Choice (Erasmus),
    144
Duchemin, Nicolas, 169
du Tillet, Louis, 170

Ecclesiastical Ordinances, 12, 26, 34, 42, 97–98,
    102, 106–10
ecclesiology
    of nurture, 85–91
    and political exile, 52, 54–55
    and Protestant division with Calvin, 42
    and spiritual exile, 68–69, 123, 175–77
    and the visible church, 64–65
    See also church
Edict of Blood, 28
Edict of Châteaubriant, 28, 34
Edward VI, King of England, 39
elders, 11, 48, 68, 106–8
election, divine, xxvi, 24, 60–64, 91, 123
    and Abraham, 132–34
    and Calvin's exegesis of the prophets, 82–85
    general, 83
    special, 83
    See also predestination
Elizabeth I, Queen of England, 37–38
Enfants de Genève, 28, 30, 100
Erasmus, 7, 80, 144
Estienne, Robert, 29
estrangement, 6–7, 12, 18, 63, 122, 128–29
Eucharist. *See* Lord's Supper
evangelicals, French
    and anti-Nicodemism, 32–34, 36
    Calvin's concern for, 16–17, 97, 160
    Calvin's conflicts with, 42, 76
    in the diaspora, 24, 84–85
    as God's elect in exile, 148–52
    and Nicodemism, 166–67, 169–71, 174
    persecution of, 4, 13, 19, 25, 28, 48, 58, 125,
        130
    view of Roman Catholics, xxi–xxii, xxvi, 77
    See also Protestants, French; Reformed,
        French
exile, xxiii–xxv
    and Abraham as model, 16, 40, 65, 71, 73,
        86–87, 99, 119, 124, 131–34, 136–38, 167,
        175
    biblical narratives of, 15–16, 19
    and Calvin's educational program in Geneva,
        102–9
    Calvin's experience of, 5–18
    and Christology, 54

church as locus of nuture in, 65–69, 85–91,
    105–6, 126–30
and homecoming, 5, 15, 35, 41, 52–53, 87, 91,
    125, 130, 152, 156–57, 176, 178, 185
King David as pattern for, xxv, 6, 9, 13, 18,
    77–82, 108, 115, 126, 134–38
political, 63, 130–32, 136
and predestination in Calvin's exegesis, 82–85
and salvation, 54–55
sustenance in, 134–38
as theological identity, 14–18, 26–27, 31,
    40–42, 72, 123–25, 130–32, 185
as universal human condition, 73–77
exile, spiritual, 41–42, 51–54, 61, 66, 72–73, 89,
    104, 111–13
and Calvin's sermons, 122–38
and predestination, 105, 128–29
present condition of, 180
exilic theology, xxv, xxvii–xxviii, xxxi, 14–18,
    24, 41, 138, 148, 176
in Calvin's preaching, 120, 122–38
as divisive, 41–42
and pastoral challenges in Geneva, 96–98
Reformation-era, 5

faith, hidden. *See* crypto-religion
Farel, Guillaume
    and *Confession of Faith*, 102–3
    and Geneva, 21–28, 102, 106, 110, 145
    as Reformed leader, 8, 41, 187
    relationship with Calvin, 10–11, 13, 169
Favre, François, 29, 90
Field, John, 60
*First Trumpet Blast Against the Monstrous
    Regiment of Women* (Knox), 38
The Form of Church Prayers and Hymns, 97,
    114–16
Four Sermons, 7, 33–36, 171–77
Francis I, King of France, 3–5, 8. See also *Institutes of the Christian Religion* (Calvin):
    preface to Francis I
Francis II, King of France, 37
Frederick III, Elector Platinate, 82
French Wars of Religion, 34
Froment, Antoine, 100, 187
Fumeé, Antoine, 90, 169

Geneva, 10–14
    Academy, 32, 39, 48
    banishment of Calvin from, 24–25, 106
    conflict in, 12–13, 27–30, 98–100

Consistory, 11–12, 28, 90, 102, 105–6, 108–9, 160, 174
  deacons in, 107
  Ecclesiastical Ordinances, 12, 26, 34, 42, 97–98, 102, 106–10
  educational program of for life in exile, 102–9
  elders in, 11, 48, 68, 106–8
  embrace of Protestantism in, 27, 30
  entanglement in Catholic practices, 98–100
  French exiles in, 29–30
  and Nicodemism, 170–77
  pastoral challenges in, 96–98
  pastoral context of, 98–101
  pattern of worship in, 109–16
  political situation of, 27–28
  preparation of Reformed pastors in, 82–83
  refugee ministry in, 26–31
  Trinitarian disputes in, 160–61
  See also Company of Pastors; Consistory, Genevan
Genevan Psalter, 35, 97, 114
Gentilis, Valentino, 160
Gilchrist, Marcus Robert, 40
Girard, Jean, 121
Gribaldi, Matteo, 160

Henry II, King of France, 28, 36, 113
Herbert of Bosham, 77
Hodge, Charles, 109–10
Hoffman, Melchior, 158
homecoming
  and Christ's exile, 54–56
  and exile, xxvi, 5, 15, 35, 41, 52–53, 87, 91, 125, 130, 152, 156–57, 176, 178, 185
Hotman, François, 21, 37
Huguenots, 4, 32, 34–35

idolatry. *See* Nicodemism
Institutes of the Christian Religion (Calvin)
  and biblical commentaries, 49–51
  1536 edition, 8, 15–17, 22, 103, 110, 160
  1539 edition, 11, 49, 52–53
  1543 edition, 151
  1559 edition, 33, 47, 52–53, 57, 60–61, 64
  1560 edition, 34
  as exilic text, 51–53
  and *Loci communes* (Melanchthon), 51–52
  On the Christian Life, 53–54
  preface to Francis I, 3–5, 8, 16, 32–33, 51, 105
Israel, 58, 83–85, 152, 187

Joris, David, 168
justification, 77–78, 86, 150, 152

Kimhi, David, 77
Knox, John, 38

La Madeleine, 107–8
Last Admonition to Joachim Westphal, 143
lectio continua, 49, 72, 121
lectures, Calvin's
  on Daniel, 83
  on Ezekiel, 83
  on Jeremiah and Lamentations, 40, 82–83
  on Minor Prophets, 83
Libertines, 28, 42, 100, 145
  Calvin's polemic against, 157, 159–60
  See also antitrinitarianism; *Enfants de Genève*
Life of Calvin (Masson), 182
Loci communes (Melanchthon), 51–52
Lord's Supper, 39, 66–67, 107, 127
  Calvin's theology of, 109–12, 115
  and consensus-seeking efforts, 152–53, 179
  and mystical presence, 109
Luther, Martin, xxix–xxx, 4, 8, 64
  letter from Calvin, xx–xxii, xxiv
  polemicism of, 143–44, 146, 148, 152–54, 161, 167–68

Maligny affair, 37
Manichaeism, 158
Marcionism, 158
Marot, Clement, 114
martyrdom, 35, 56, 63, 86, 125, 167, 171–72
Mary, Queen of England, 25, 28, 38
Masson, Jean–Papire, 181
Meaux Circle, 22, 25
Melanchthon, Philip, 161, 168
  and Calvin's letter to Lutther, xxi–xxii
  and justification, 86
  on King David, 78
  Loci communes, 51–52
  and predestination, 61
migration
  and exile, 52, 73, 81, 133
  experiences of, xx, xxii–xxiii, xxviii, 29, 41, 117, 124, 129–30, 174
  and Reformed confessional ties, 38
  and the rhetoric of belonging, 3–6
  and violence, xxiv, 56, 97, 129, 138, 162, 180
Millet, Olivier, 18
Münster. *See* Anabaptism

Münster, Sebastian, 120
Musculus, Wolfgang, 167
mystical presence, 109

"The Necessity of Reforming the Church," 143
Nevin, John Williamson, 109–10
Nicholas of Lyra, 73, 77
Niclaes, Hendrik, 168
Nicodemism, xxi–xxii, 13, 17, 22
  and Abram, 133–34
  and David, 134–35, 167
  and French Catholicism, 170–77
  and French evangelicals, 166–67
  and spiritual nurture, 167, 177
  See also anti-Nicodemism
nurture
  boundaries of within the church, 127–30
  and Calvin's sermons on spiritual exile, 122–38
  church as locus of in exile, 65–69, 85–91, 105–6
  Nicodemism as deprivation of spiritual nurture, 167, 177
  Pauline ecclesiology of, 85–91
  See also church: as locus of nurture in exile; church: as mother

Oberman, Heiko A., xix, xxiii–xxiv, xxvi–xxvii, xxxii–xxxiii, 38, 52, 180, 184–85
Olivétan, Pierre–Robert, 82
On Not Punishing Heretics (Castellio), 127
On Punishing Heretics (Beza), 127
On the Christian Life, 53–54
On the True Care of Souls (Bucer), 11

pastors
  authority of, 88–91, 126, 177
  Calvin's training of, 39, 56, 82, 84, 152
  as missionaries, 14
  office of, 10–12, 48–49
  as refugees, 28–31, 36, 96–100, 135
  roles of, 12, 67–69, 103–9
  See also Company of Pastors
Pellikan, Konrad, 120
Perceval, Claude, 159
Perrin, Ami, 28–30, 90
Perrinists, 100
persecution, religious
  bonds of, 37–38
  and Calvin's ministry, 22, 58, 64, 83, 86, 97, 123, 125
  and dedication of the *Institutes*, 3–5
  and exile, 16, 41, 51, 116
  of French Protestants, 4, 8, 25, 32–33, 152
  and Geneva as city of refuge, 13, 28–29
  and God's faithfulness, 6
  and interreligious violence, xxii–xxiii
  and Nicodemism, xxi, 133, 166
  and polemic, 145, 159, 162
  and the Reformation, xxii–xxiii
pilgrim theology, 50–51, 53
  in Calvin's sermons, 124
  and Christ's office as king, 55
Pocquet, Antoine, 159–60
polemic, Calvin's
  against anabaptism, 157–58
  against Libertines, 159–60
  and religious difference, 144–46
  against Roman Catholicism, 34, 84, 104, 146–52
  See also anti-Nicodemism; antitrinitarianism
predestination
  Calvin's distinctive formulation of, 50, 61–63
  as comfort to exiles, 10, 42, 52–56, 59–63, 105, 123, 138, 180, 187
  experiential nature of, 63–69
  and exile in Calvin's exegesis, 72–73, 82–85
  and the French Reformed, 82–85
  and Nicodemism, 174–76
  and spiritual exile, 105, 128–29
  and theological controversies, 12, 24, 39, 101, 146, 158, 181
  and vocation, 91
Presbyterian Church (U.S.A.), 184–85
Protestants, French, 5, 31–37
providence
  and exile in Calvin's exegesis, 65, 72, 76, 78–79
  as comfort to exiles, 10–11, 52–61, 63, 65, 68–70, 105, 108, 116, 123–26, 136, 180, 187
  and the French Reformed, 82–85
  and spiritual exile, 105
  and suffering, 59–60, 125, 137–38
  and vocation, 91
Psychopannychia, 14–15, 52, 65, 86–87

Raguenier, Denis, 35, 122
Rashi, 74, 77
Reformation
  contemporary evocations of, xxx–xxxii
  magisterial, xx–xxi, xxvi, xxxiii, 161
  as refugee event, xxiii–xxiv
  and religious persecution, xxii–xxiii

Reformed, French, 31–32, 34, 36, 82–85
Reformed Church in America, 184
Reformed tradition
  centering new voices in, 185–87
  as distinct from Calvinism, xxix
  refugee roots of, 183–87
refugee(s)
  Calvin's identification as, 3–6
  defined, xxiii
  French, 10–11, 29, 35, 48, 121, 171
  ministry to in Geneva, 26–31
  teaching of, 47–51, 82–91
Reply to Sadoleto, 9, 47, 148, 151, 158
Response to the Questions of Giorgio Blandrata, 160
rhetoric
  of belonging, 3–6
  prophetic, xxx
  See also polemic, Calvin's
Roussel, Gérard, 25, 169

sacraments. *See* Word and Sacrament, ministry of
Sadoleto, Cardinal Jacopo, 9, 47, 146–50
Sattler, Michael, 158
Schleitheim Confession of Faith, 158
Schreiner, Susan, 136
scripture
  authority of, 90
  Calvin's view of, 65–67, 100–101, 104, 114
  consolation of, 22, 148
  and exile, 6, 14–16, 48–50, 52, 79, 120, 122, 152–53
  historical interpretation of, 77
  as inspired, 111, 150
  private reading of, 97–98, 106
  and providence, 56–57
  and worship, 157–61
  See also Abraham; Adam; commentaries, Calvin's; David, King; sermons, Calvin's
Secret Providence (Calvin), 56
sermons, Calvin's
  on Acts, 119
  on Ephesians, 126
  on Galatians, 119, 124–25
  on Genesis, 128–30, 132–34, 165
  on Job, 136–38
  and nurture in spiritual exile, 122–38
  on Pastoral Epistles, 127
  on Psalms, 95–97, 134–38
  on 2 Samuel, 134–35, 137–38
  on 2 Timothy, 125

  on Titus, 128
  See also Calvin, John: as preacher; Calvin, John: themes in preaching of
Servetus, Michael, 127–28, 145, 160
Short Treatise on the Lord's Supper, 66–67, 96–97, 110
Simons, Menno, 158
sola scriptura, 146
Song, C. S., 186
spiritual gifts, 87–88
Steinmetz, David, 182
St. Gervais, 26, 98, 107–8, 120
St. Pierre, 26, 98, 107–8, 120, 187
Strasbourg, xxiv, 10–12, 30, 38–39, 48, 102, 121, 159
Sturm, Jean, 37
Sulzer, Simon, 176
Supplex exhortatio ad Caesarem (*Sincere Exhortation to the Emperor*), 148, 151
sustenance, 15, 68–69, 81, 89, 106, 113, 132, 134–38

Terpstra, Nicholas, xxii–xxiii, 144
Thieffry, Quintin, 159–60
Thirty Years' War, 29, 180
toleration, religious, 12, 24, 127, 146, 176
Treaty of Cateau-Cambrésis, 32
Trinity, the, 23, 145, 147–48
  theological disputes concerning, 160–61
Two Letters, 169

Vermigli, Peter Martyr, xxix, 167
Viret, Pierre, 8, 10, 21, 23–26, 35, 42, 167

Westphal, Joachim, 42, 143, 154–56, 159–60
Wigand, John, 167
Wolman, Melchior, 7
Word and Sacrament, ministry of, 68–69, 76, 97, 107–8, 134, 172–74
  and spiritual exile, 111–13, 127
  and theological conflicts in Geneva, 109–16
World Alliance of Reformed Churches, 186
worship
  Genevan pattern of, 109–16
  as sustenance for pilgrims, 89, 106
  See also baptism; Lord's Supper; Word and Sacrament, ministry of

Zell, Matthew, 10
Zurich, xxix, 8, 38, 157, 174
  Consensus, 39, 153–54
Zwingli, Ulrich, xx, xxix, 5, 8, 47, 103, 112, 129, 152–53

www.ingramcontent.com/pod-product-compliance
Lightning Source LLC
Chambersburg PA
CBHW032041150426
43194CB00006B/375